Perfect your German

Teach® Yourself

Perfect your German

Paul Coggle and
Heiner Schenke

For UK order enquiries: please contact Bookpoint Ltd,
130 Milton Park, Abingdon, Oxon, OX14 4SB.
Telephone: +44 (0) 1235 827720. *Fax:* +44 (0) 1235 400454.
Lines are open 09.00–17.00, Monday to Saturday, with a 24-hour message answering service. Details about our titles and how to order are available at www.teachyourself.com

For USA order enquiries: please contact McGraw-Hill Customer Services, PO Box 545, Blacklick, OH 43004-0545, USA.
Telephone: 1-800-722-4726. *Fax:* 1-614-755-5645.

For Canada order enquiries: please contact McGraw-Hill Ryerson Ltd, 300 Water St, Whitby, Ontario, L1N 9B6, Canada.
Telephone: 905 430 5000. Fax: 905 430 5020.

Long renowned as the authoritative source for self-guided learning – with more than 50 million copies sold worldwide – the *Teach Yourself* series includes over 500 titles in the fields of languages, crafts, hobbies, business, computing and education.

British Library Cataloguing in Publication Data: a catalogue record for this title is available from the British Library.

Library of Congress Catalog Card Number: on file.

Previously published in UK as *Teach Yourself Further German* (1994), *Teach Yourself German Extra!* (1999) and *Teach Yourself Improve your German* (2004) by Hodder Education, 338 Euston Road, London, NW1 3BH and in US by The McGraw-Hill Companies, Inc.

This edition published 2010.

Typeset by MPS Limited, a Macmillan Company.

Printed in Great Britain for Hodder Education, an Hachette UK Company, 338 Euston Road, London, NW1 3BH.

Impression number 10 9 8 7 6 5 4 3 2 1
Year 2014 2013 2012 2011 2010

Contents

Meet the authors

Do you already know some German and are you thinking of taking your German to a more advanced level? As the authors of **Perfect your German**, we would very much like to help you achieve your objectives. Both of us are enthusiastic and experienced teachers of German and we believe we have produced an excellent course that is challenging but manageable and one that has been tried, tested and recently updated.

The course includes a lot of listening and reading, as well as practice in writing and speaking, plus information on how the language works and facts about present-day German culture and society. The topics range from the world of work to the German economy and discussion of stereotypes and prejudices.

You'll also find that several of the more advanced structures are introduced in this course, such as the passive, reported speech and the use of the subjunctive.

So long as you are up for a bit of work, complete the activities and put in some practice, you will make encouraging progress.

Viel Erfolg beim Deutsch lernen!

Paul Coggle and Heiner Schenke

Only got a minute?

The aim of this course is to help you take your German further. In the first few units you will be able to consolidate and build on your previous knowledge. The course then moves on to more complex language and issues in the later units. Grammar points covered include the passive and the various uses of the subjunctive. Many of the audio recordings are based on real-life interviews with native speakers of German. The book and recordings together cover all four of the basic skills – listening and speaking, reading and writing. We will also help you build your vocabulary, increase your awareness of the many words which are borrowed from English, and learn to express your opinion on a number of topics.

German is spoken as a native language by approximately 105 million people. About a further 80 million people speak it as a second or foreign language. The standard language is called **Hochdeutsch** and this is the language taught in schools. But there are also many regional variants, especially in Southern Germany, Austria and in Switzerland. German has considerable importance within the EU because it is, along with English and French, one of the three procedural languages of the European Commission.

Towards the end of the course there are plenty of ideas and advice on how to take your German even further. **Wir wünschen viel Erfolg und viel Spaß!**

5 Only got five minutes?

What the course contains

Whether you have recently completed a beginner's German course or have studied German in the past and now want to return to it, this course will help you achieve your objective of taking your German to a higher level. The first few units are aimed at consolidating and building on your previous knowledge. The course then moves on to more complex language and issues in the later units. It is here that you will also be introduced to the more advanced points of German grammar, such as the forms and various uses of the passive and the subjunctive. Many of the audio recordings are based on real-life interviews with native speakers of German. The book and recordings together cover all four of the basic skills – listening and speaking, reading and writing. We shall also help you towards acquiring an active vocabulary of approximately 5,000 words. By the end of the course you should be able to express your opinion on a number of topics and agree or disagree with other people's opinions.

Speakers of German

German is the largest language group within the European Union with around 92 million native speakers in Germany, Austria, Luxemburg and parts of Belgium and Italy. German native speakers living outside the EU in Switzerland and other communities throughout the world bring the total to approximately 105 million. About a further 80 million people speak German as a second or foreign language. German has considerable importance within the EU not only because of the number of speakers it has, but also because it is, along with English and French, one of the three procedural languages of the European Commission.

German language and vocabulary

German belongs to the West Germanic group of languages and is related to Dutch and English and more distantly to the Scandinavian languages. German has also been influenced, particularly in vocabulary, by Latin, French and in more recent decades by English. Whilst certain German words have been borrowed into English – e.g. **Delicatessen, Doppelgänger, Kindergarten, Meister, Rucksack, Schadenfreude, Weltanschauung, Zeitgeist** – the number of English words borrowed into German is much larger and constantly growing. More recent additions have been **der Airbag, der JobCenter, crashen** (of computers), **downloaden, die E-Mail, der Laptop, shoppen**. Some of the borrowed words have taken on a different meaning in German, e.g. **das Handy** cell phone, mobile phone, **der Oldtimer** vintage car, **der Showmaster** TV host, **der Smoking** tuxedo, dinner jacket.

Recent borrowings from English are often referred to as **Denglisch** (Deutsch + Englisch). They are regarded by some German speakers as unwelcome intruders into the language and by others as a further development of the language, comparable with the importations from Latin and French in the past.

German literature

From the cultural point of view there is an enormous wealth of literature in German, much of which is available in translation, but some of which – especially poetry – must be read in the original German in order to gain the full impact of the author's use of language. Two of the best known authors born in the 18th century are Johann Wolfgang von Goethe (1749–1832) and Friedrich Schiller (1759–1805). In more recent times those best known in the English-speaking world include Franz Kafka (1883–1924), Thomas Mann (1875–1955) and Bertolt Brecht (1898–1956) as well as Erich Kästner (1899–1974), Heinrich Böll (1917–1985), Günter Grass (1927–) and Patrick Süskind (1949–).

Taking your German still further

If, after working your way through **Perfect your German**, you would like to take your German still further, then you might like to consider such activities as listening to the German news online. There is for instance a daily 100-second video news summary at www.zdf.de which would be a good starting point. You could also dip into German newspapers online, concentrating on one article at a time, trying to internalize the vocabulary as you progress.

We hope we have managed to persuade you to improve your German with us. **Wir wünschen viel Erfolg und viel Spaß!**

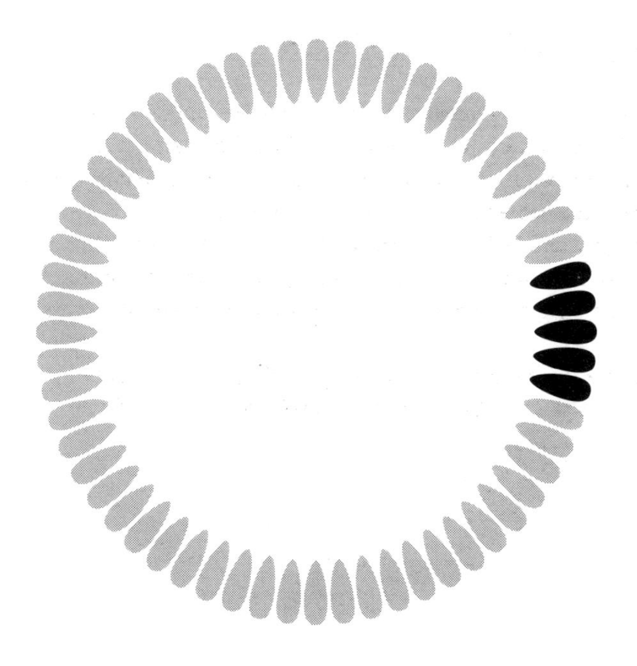

10 Only got ten minutes?

Improving your German

Whether you have recently completed a beginner's German course or have studied German in the past and now want to return to it, this course will help you achieve your objective of taking your German to a higher level. The first few units are aimed at consolidating and building on your previous knowledge. The course then moves on to more complex language and issues in the later units. It is here that you will also be introduced to the more advanced points of German grammar, such as the forms and various uses of the subjunctive. Many of the audio recordings are based on real-life interviews with native speakers of German. The book and recordings together cover all four of the basic skills – listening and speaking, reading and writing. We shall also help you towards acquiring an active vocabulary of approximately 5,000 words. By the end of the course you should be able to express your opinion on a number of topics and agree or disagree with other people's opinions.

Where German is spoken

German is spoken as a native language by approximately 105 million people. About a further 80 million people speak it as a second or foreign language. German is the official language or one of the official languages in Germany, Austria, Luxemburg, Liechtenstein, Switzerland and the Südtirol area of Italy.

There are communities of German native speakers in Russia (approx. 2.9 million), Canada (over 438,000), the Südtirol (Alto Adige) region of Italy (over 290,000), the USA (around 100,000), the Walloon Region of Belgium (73,000) and Romania (45,000).

The remaining German speakers in the United States are quite often members of religious groups, such as the Amish and Mennonites. It was, you may recall, an Amish family that featured in the 1985 film 'Witness'. The Amish, based in former times mainly in German-speaking Switzerland, began migrating to Pennsylvania in the 18th century as part of a larger migration from the Palatinate region of Germany. They were driven to migrate by religious conflicts, poverty, and religious persecution. Their language came to be referred to as Pennsylvania Dutch (where 'Dutch' is really 'Deutsch'). Nowadays it is primarily the Old Order Amish and Old Order Mennonites who continue to speak Pennsylvania Dutch.

German language and vocabulary

German belongs to the West Germanic group of languages and is related to Dutch and English and more distantly to the Scandinavian languages. German has also been influenced, particularly in vocabulary, by Latin, French and in more recent decades by English.

Many words in both languages have their origins in their shared Germanic past, for example **Apfel** *apple*, **backen** *to bake*, **Bad** *bath*, **danken** *to thank* and **Garten** *garden*. You may not always spot the link between two words straight away, as with **Zaun** *fence*. This is in fact the same word in origin as the English town. Early settlements often had fences around them to keep out wild animals, etc. The huntsmen returning to the settlement would go back to the fenced area or to what historical linguists think was called the **tuna.**

Both English and German have borrowed words from Latin. The similarities are sometimes obvious, sometimes less so, for example tegula **Ziegel** *tile*, pirum **Birne** *pear*, caseus **Käse** *cheese*, planta **Pflanze** *plant*. While the Norman invasion of England brought many Norman French words into English, German too was influenced, although to a much lesser extent, by French, e.g. **Visage** *face*, **ordinär** *uncouth*, **frivol** *frivolous*, **Affäre** *affair*, **Restaurant** *restaurant*.

Whilst certain German words have been borrowed into English – e.g. **Delicatessen, Doppelgänger, Kindergarten, Meister, Rucksack, Schadenfreude, Weltanschauung, Zeitgeist** – the number of English words borrowed into German is much larger and constantly growing. More recent additions have been **der Airbag, der JobCenter, crashen** (of computers), **downloaden, die E-Mail, der Laptop, shoppen**. Some of the borrowed words have taken on a different meaning in German, e.g. **das Handy** *cell phone*, *mobile phone*, **der Oldtimer** *vintage car*, **der Showmaster** *TV host*, **der Smoking** *tuxedo*, *dinner jacket*.

Recent borrowings from English are often referred to as **Denglisch** (Deutsch + Englisch). They are regarded by some German speakers as unwelcome intruders into the language and by others as a further development of the language, comparable with the importations from Latin and French in the past.

Spelling reforms

German spelling is much more consistent than English. Most words are pronounced as they are spelt. German spelling was not fully standardized till 1901 when the **Reichsamt des Innern** *Reich Ministry of the Interior* convened the 2nd Berlin Orthography Conference. In 1902 the rulings of this conference became legally binding and were subsequently laid down in Konrad Duden's dictionary **Vollständiges Orthographisches Wörterbuch der deutschen Sprache** *Complete orthographical dictionary of the German language*.

In 1994 representatives of the Ministries of Culture and of the Interior in Austria, Switzerland and the Federal Republic of Germany agreed on a common draft for a spelling reform.

After a further 13 years of discussion and resistance to the reforms, the new spelling rules became legally binding in schools in 2007.

German news agencies now write their material according to the recommendations of **Duden** (http://www.duden.de) and **Wahrig** (http://www.wahrig.de).

In Switzerland a few words continue to be spelt differently, e.g. Swiss German **Müesli,** German **Müsli,** but on the whole spelling is now standardized across the German-speaking regions.

The alphabet

The German alphabet uses the same 26 letters as the English alphabet, but with an additional four letters. Three of these are formed by adding an Umlaut above the letters **a, o** and **u: ä, ö, ü.** They are used in words such as **Bäcker** *baker*, **schön** *beautiful, nice* and **Übung** *exercise*. German speakers are strict about using the Umlaut and do not omit it. For writing e-mails or blogs it is acceptable to add an 'e' after the vowel instead of using the **Umlaut**: e.g. **Bäcker Baecker, schön schoen.**

The fourth extra letter is **ß** which is called **scharfes s** or **eszett.** This is used after a long vowel in words such as **Straße** *street* and **Fußball** *football*. After a short vowel **ss** is used: **Pass** *passport*, **Kuss** *kiss*.

In Switzerland the **ß** is not in normal usage; **ss** is used instead, e.g. **Massstab** *standard, benchmark*.

Word stress

All words of more than one syllable have what is called word stress. This means that at least one of the syllables is longer and louder than the other syllables. Word stress in German often falls on the first syllable, as in **Deutschland** *Germany* and **Mittagessen** *lunch*. But the word stress can appear on other syllables as well, e.g. **erlauben** *to allow*, **telefonieren** *to telephone*, **Metzgerei**

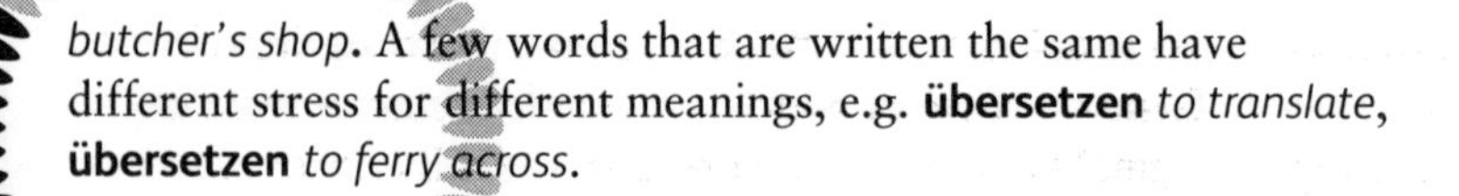

butcher's shop. A few words that are written the same have different stress for different meanings, e.g. **übersetzen** *to translate*, **übersetzen** *to ferry across*.

Capital letters

You will no doubt already know that all nouns are written with a capital letter in German: **Bank** *bank*, **Haus** *house*. There have been moves to abandon this practice, but so far they have not succeeded. Some people use lower case initials in informal writing, such as e-mails.

Some adjectives which are written with a capital letter in English are written with lower case letters in German, e.g. adjectives describing nationality: **mein deutscher Freund** *my German (boy-) friend*, **ein englisches Buch** *an English book*. Similarly, words denoting political and religious groups have lower case initials, e.g. **eine sozialistische Regierung** *a Socialist government*, **ein katholisches Land** *a Catholic country*.

German literature

One of your aims in taking your German further may be to attempt to read literature in the original German. In order to be able to read and understand well, you will need to increase your vocabulary considerably, since literature by its very nature is linguistically extremely rich. One way of approaching this task is to start off by using parallel text versions where the German is printed on the left-hand page and the English version on the right. In this way you will grow in confidence as your vocabulary increases. You can then move on to tackle literary works on your own, even if you do still need to look up certain key words in a dictionary.

From the cultural point of view there is an enormous wealth of literature in German, some of which – especially poetry – must be read in the original German in order to gain the full impact of the author's use of language. Two of the best known authors born in the 18th century are Johann Wolfgang von Goethe (1749–1832) and Friedrich Schiller (1759–1805). In more recent times those best known in the English-speaking world include Franz Kafka (1883–1924), Thomas Mann (1875–1955) and Bertolt Brecht (1898–1956) as well as Erich Kästner (1899–1974), Heinrich Böll (1917–85), Günter Grass (1927–) and Patrick Süskind (1949–).

Taking your German still further

If, after working your way through **Perfect your German**, you would like to take your German still further, then you might like to consider such activities as listening to the German news online. There is, for instance, a daily 100-second video news summary at www.zdf.de which would be a good starting point. You could also dip into German newspapers online, concentrating on one short article at a time, trying to internalize the vocabulary as you progress.

We hope we have managed to persuade you to improve your German with us. **Wir wünschen viel Erfolg und viel Spaß!**

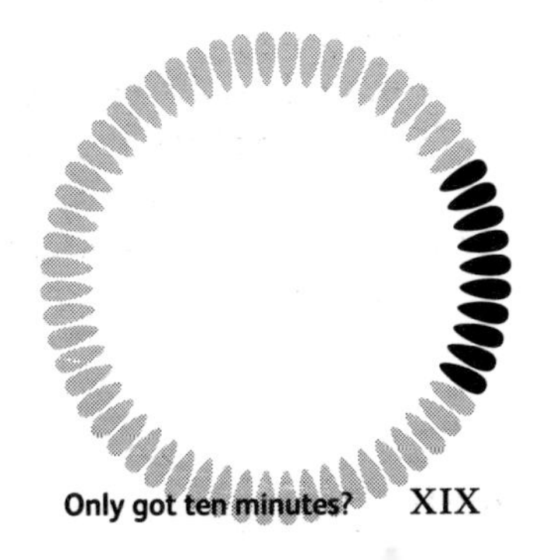

Introduction

Welcome to **Perfect your German**

Is this the right course for you?
Perfect your German is designed for a number of different kinds of learner.

- *Are you an adult learner who has completed a beginner's course such as Complete German?*
- *Perhaps you are taking up German again after a break from it?*
- *Are you looking for a course that will help you to achieve an advanced standard in German?*
- *Do you want to study on your own?*
- *Are you intending to learn with the support of a class?*
- *Are you preparing for an examination at an advanced level and do you want a thorough revision course?*

If so, you will find this course very well suited to your purposes.

Developing your skills

The language introduced in this course is centred around realistic everyday situations ranging from talking about daily routines, interests and hobbies to expressing opinions or talking about health issues or the media.

The first units are designed to consolidate and build on your previous knowledge, focusing on some of the essential language functions and grammatical points. You will then progress to dealing with more complex language and issues in the subsequent units.

The course covers all four of the basic skills – listening and speaking, reading and writing. If you are working on your own, the audio recordings will be all the more important, as they will provide you with the essential opportunity to listen to German and to speak it within a controlled framework.

The structure of this course

The *Perfect your German* course consists of two components:

a the course book containing 10 course units and a reference section
b the recordings which are available on CD.

In order to obtain maximum benefit from the course you should have both the course book and the recording.

The course units

The course units can be roughly divided into the following categories, although there is obviously a certain amount of overlap from one category to another.

Statement of aims

At the beginning of each unit you will be told what you can expect to learn, in terms of:

- *what you will be able to do in German by the end of the unit and*
- *the language points that are being introduced.*

Presentation of new language

This is usually in the form of spoken language which has been recorded 🔊 and which is supported by transcriptions either in the body of the units or in the back of the book. Some assistance with vocabulary is also given.

Practice of the new language

Practice is organized in such a way that you first demonstrate your understanding. You then progress to exercises which require you to utilize the language forms.

Description of language forms and grammar

Information on the forms of the language is presented in two ways:

- *in digestible 'bites' entitled* ***Sprachinfos*** *at various points within the course units*
- *in the grammar section, or* ***Grammatik****, towards the end of each course unit.*

Learning the forms of the language will enable you to construct your own sentences correctly.

Pronunciation and intonation

You can do quite a lot to improve your pronunciation and intonation by working on your own, listening to and imitating native speakers of German. But you will probably also benefit from a few pointers as you progress through the course. For this reason we include specific advice on the recordings.

Insight boxes

Here you will find more details on certain grammar points, tips on how to learn the language and information on various aspects of life in German-speaking countries – on such topics as the German system of education and training and the health-care system. These are in German, to give you more practice reading and understanding German language texts.

Vocabulary

In addition to the vocabulary given in each unit, there are German–English and English–German reference glossaries at the back of the book.

Monitoring your progress

There is a **Testen Sie sich!** section and a checklist at the end of each unit. Answers to the tests are provided in the Key towards the end of the book. This enables you to check your answers and decide whether you have made sufficient progress to move on to the next unit.

The reference section

This contains:

- *transcripts of the listening comprehension recordings*
- *a key to the activities and exercises*
- *Taking it further*
- *a list of German irregular verbs*
- *a glossary of grammatical terms*
- *a German–English glossary*
- *an English–German glossary*
- *an index of grammar points*

How to use this course

Make sure at the beginning of each course unit that you are clear about what you can expect to learn.

Much of the language in the course is presented in spoken form. It is therefore important to obtain the recording. Most units contain three recorded dialogues or monologues – the first and the last are also presented in written form in the body of the unit. The transcripts of the second recording in each unit can be found at the back of the book.

Start by listening to the first recording. Try to get a feel for what is being said before you look at the printed text in the book. After this first hearing, refer to the printed text and the vocabulary in order to study the material in more detail. Listen to the recording several times until you feel familiar with it. Don't forget that even when you *recognize* what you hear and read, you will probably still have some way to go before you can *produce* the language correctly and fluently.

Some of the recordings are intended to be listen-only exercises. The main point of listening exercises is to improve your listening skills, so don't be tempted to go straight to the transcriptions at the back of the book in order to read what you are meant to hear. The transcriptions are really only there to help you if you get stuck.

As you move through the unit, read the information about language points, so that you understand how a given feature of the language works. We have tried to make the grammar explanations as user-friendly as possible, and to present these in relatively small chunks. Of course it is up to you how much time you wish to spend on studying and sorting out the grammar points. Some people find that they can do better by getting an ear for what sounds right; others need to know in detail how the language is put together.

In case you are unfamiliar with some of the terminology used, there is a Glossary of grammatical terms at the back of the book. If you need to find out where a particular point of grammar is introduced or explained, refer to the Grammar index.

The exercises are strategically interspersed throughout the unit. When you have completed an exercise, check your answers carefully at the back of the book. If you have a 'study buddy' it's a good idea to check each other's answers. Most of the exercises have fixed answers, but some are a bit more open-ended. In such cases we usually give just one possible set of answers. In some cases you can use the recording and/or transcripts to check your answers. The recording will also help you check the pronunciation of new vocabulary.

In most units there is a simple interpreting exercise. This is your chance to produce spoken German within a controlled framework. Model responses are provided on the recording.

It is a good idea to make your own list of new words and phrases for each unit. Nouns should be listed together with their gender and plural, e.g. **das Dach** (-¨**er**) *roof*.

Before you move on to a new unit you can then monitor your progress in vocabulary learning. Try covering up the English side of your list and producing the English equivalents of the German. If you find that relatively easy, go on to cover up the German side and produce the German equivalents of the English. Trying to recall the context in which words and phrases were used may help you to learn them better.

To enjoy success in learning a language, you need to work at it regularly. Don't try to do too much at once. For most people 20 minutes a day is more productive than two hours in a block once a week.

1

Leute, Leute

In this unit you will learn how to

- ***talk about personal details***
- ***ask other people about themselves***
- ***ask different types of questions***
- ***use prepositions***
- ***identify gender, and form the plural of nouns***

Aufnahme 1

Ein Interview mit Frau Peters

Hören Sie, was Frau Peters über sich erzählt, und machen Sie dann Übungen 1 und 2.

Listen to what Frau Peters says about herself and then do **Übungen** 1 and 2.

CD1, TR 1, 01:51

Reporter	Frau Peters, können Sie ein bisschen über sich erzählen?
Frau Peters	Ja, natürlich. Mein Name ist Ulrike Peters. Ich bin 1962 in Berlin geboren, bin dort auch aufgewachsen und lebe jetzt seit 12 Jahren hier in Köln.
Reporter	Und sind Sie berufstätig?
Frau Peters	Ja, ich arbeite halbtags als Fremdsprachen-Sekretärin bei einer Versicherungsfirma. Normalerweise arbeite ich am Vormittag, von halb neun bis ein Uhr, und die Arbeit macht mir sehr viel Spaß.
Reporter	Und welche Sprachen sprechen Sie?
Frau Peters	Ich spreche fließend Französisch und Englisch. Ich habe vier Jahre in Bristol gelebt und dort an der Universität studiert. Außerdem kann ich ein bisschen Spanisch und Italienisch.
Reporter	Sind Sie denn verheiratet?
Frau Peters	Ja, ich bin seit fast 10 Jahren mit meinem Mann verheiratet und wir haben zwei Kinder.
Reporter	Was macht denn Ihr Mann?
Frau Peters	Mein Mann ist selbstständig. Er ist Architekt und hat ein kleines Architektenbüro hier in Köln.
Reporter	Und haben Sie ein Hobby?
Frau Peters	Im Moment habe ich leider nicht viel Zeit. Ich interessiere mich aber sehr für Sprachen und gehe einmal in der Woche zu einem Englischkurs für Fortgeschrittene. Die Klasse macht mir sehr viel Spaß.

Übung 1 Richtig oder falsch?

Korrigieren Sie die falschen Aussagen.

Decide whether the following statements are true or false and correct the false statements. As with all exercises, you can check your answers in the Key at the back of the book.

Beispiele: Frau Peters ist in Köln geboren. ***Falsch. Sie ist in Berlin geboren.*** →
Sie arbeitet halbtags bei einer Versicherungsfirma. ***Richtig.***

a Die Arbeit gefällt ihr nicht.
b Sie hat vier Jahre in Schottland gelebt.
c Sie ist seit über 10 Jahren verheiratet.
d Ihr Mann ist Angestellter in einem Architektenbüro.
e Sie geht zu einem Anfängerkurs in Englisch.

QUICK VOCAB

auf/wachsen *to grow up*
berufstätig sein *to be working, to work*
die Versicherungsfirma (-firmen) *insurance company*
fließend *fluent(ly)*
selbstständig *self-employed*
für Fortgeschrittene *for advanced learners*
der Anfängerkurs (-e) *beginner's course*

Insight: Es macht mir Spaß

Haben Sie gemerkt, was Frau Peters sagt, wenn ihr ihre Arbeit oder ihre Englischklasse gefällt? **Die Arbeit macht mir sehr viel Spaß** and **Die Klasse macht mir sehr viel Spaß.**

Spaß bedeutet nicht nur *fun* im Deutschen, sondern kann auch *joy/enjoyment* ausdrücken.

Übung 2 Welches Wort fehlt?

Fill the gaps with the appropriate word from the box.

fließend Spaß verheiratet halbtags interessiert selbstständig berufstätig

Beispiel: Frau Peters arbeitet. → ***Sie ist berufstätig.***

a Sie arbeitet Teilzeit. → Sie arbeitet ______.
b Ihre Arbeit gefällt ihr. → Ihre Arbeit macht ihr ______.
c Frau Peters hat einen Ehemann. → Sie ist ______.
d Ihr Mann hat eine eigene Firma. → Er ist ______.
e Sie spricht sehr gut Französisch. → Sie spricht ______ Französisch.
f Ein Hobby von ihr sind Sprachen. → Sie ______ sich für Sprachen.

Sprachinfo

Präpositionen *Prepositions*

To say where you're from, where you work or study, etc. you need certain prepositions.

Here are a few important prepositions for this purpose:

to come **from**	Ich komme **aus** Berlin.
to work **as**	Er arbeitet **als** Architekt.
to work **for** a company	Ich arbeite **bei** einer Versicherungsfirma.
to work **in** an office	Sie arbeitet **in** einem Büro.
for twelve years	Sie wohnt **seit** 12 Jahren in Köln.

Can you work out from the dialogue how you would say to ***study at*** *and* ***to be married*** *to in German? Remember that you can check all your answers in the Key.*

Übung 3 Wie heißen die Präpositionen?

Darren wrote a short biographical note about himself in German but wasn't sure about which prepositions to use. Can you help him?

Ich bin am 3. Dezember 1989 (a) Manchester geboren. Meine Mutter kommt auch (b) Manchester, aber mein Vater kommt (c) Dublin. Im Moment studiere ich (d) der Universität hier. Nebenbei jobbe ich (e) Kellner (f) einem Hotel. Ich bin nicht verheiratet, aber ich habe (g) vier Jahren eine Freundin, Tracy. Sie kommt (h) Bath und ist Therapeutin (i) einem Krankenhaus. Später möchte ich gern (j) Informatiker arbeiten.

Sprachinfo

Fragen *Questions*

In German there are two main types of question. The first starts with a question word, such as **woher?**, **wie?**, **was?**, etc.:

Woher kommen Sie?
Was macht Ihr Mann beruflich?

Here the question word is usually in the first position and followed by a verb.

The second type of question is often called a 'yes/no question' (**ja/nein** question), because it requires an answer in the affirmative or the negative. Here the verb appears in the first position:

Kommen Sie aus Deutschland?
Ist Ihr Mann berufstätig?

*Now read through the dialogue again. How many **ja/nein** and w-questions can you find?*

Übung 4 Was passt zusammen?

Find the right answer for each question.

a Wie heißen Sie, bitte?
b Kommen Sie denn aus Kanada?
c Und wo sind Sie geboren?
d Sind Sie verheiratet?
e Haben Sie Kinder?
f Und sind Sie berufstätig?
g Wie lange lernen Sie Deutsch?

i Ja, seit sieben Jahren.
ii Ich arbeite bei der Royal Bank of Scotland.
iii Ich lerne es seit fünf Jahren.
iv Mein Name ist John Harrison.
v In der Nähe von Glasgow.
vi Nein, aus Schottland.
vii Ja, zwei Töchter und zwei Söhne.

Und was antworten Sie? Now go through the questions a–g and answer them for yourself.

Aufnahme 2

CD1, TR 1, 3:45

Drei Kandidaten stellen sich vor

Übung 5

In einer Fernsehshow stellen sich drei Personen vor. Hören Sie sich die Aufnahme an und finden Sie die fehlenden Informationen.

Three candidates introduce themselves on a German TV show. Listen to the recording and fill in the missing information in the grid on the next page.

Remember that the transcripts of the recordings which don't appear in the units are printed in the back of the book. Here is a reminder of the words you might need for the marital status column: **single/ledig** *single*, **geschieden** *divorced* and **verwitwet** *widowed*.

	Alter	*Familienstand*	*Wohnort*	*Beruf*	*Hobbys*
Martin			*Apolda, in Thüringen*		
Petra				*Hotelfachfrau*	
Max					

You can check your answers in the transcript or in the Key.

QUICK VOCAB

vor/stellen *to introduce*
die Ausgabe (-n) *here: edition*
in der Nähe von *close to, near*
das Bockbierfest (-e) *bock beer festival*
ein zeitraubender Job *a time-consuming job*
die Hotelfachfrau *hotel manageress*
die Pension (-en) *guesthouse*
führen *(here) to run*
gefährlich *dangerous*

Übung 6 Welche Frage passt?

Which of the three questions prompts each answer?

1 Ja, ich bin der Martin.
- **a** Wie heißen Sie denn?
- **b** Können Sie sich bitte vorstellen?
- **c** Und wie ist Ihr Nachname?

2 Nicht so viel. Aber ich gehe gern ins Kino.
- **a** Bleibt Ihnen denn Zeit für ein Hobby?
- **b** Und was machen Sie gern in Ihrer Freizeit?
- **c** Gehen Sie gern ins Kino?

3 Ich bin Hotelfachfrau.
- **a** Was machen Sie in Ihrer Freizeit?
- **b** Was sind Sie von Beruf?
- **c** Was sind Ihre Hobbys?

4 Nein. Ich bin single und noch zu haben.

a Und sind Sie single?
b Und sind Sie ledig?
c Und sind Sie verheiratet?

5 Ich liebe es gefährlich und mache Bungeespringen.

a Was machen Sie denn nicht gern?
b Was für Hobbys haben Sie?
c Was machen Sie beruflich, Max?

Insight: Wo man Deutsch spricht

Deutsch spricht man nicht nur in Deutschland, sondern auch in Österreich, in der Schweiz, in Südtirol (Italien) und in Luxemburg. Insgesamt gibt es etwa 105 Millionen Menschen, die Deutsch als Muttersprache sprechen. Das Standarddeutsch heißt Hochdeutsch, aber es gibt auch sehr viele Dialekte, vor allem in Süddeutschland, in Österreich und der Schweiz (das sogenante *Schwyzerdütsch*).

Zwischen Deutschland, Österreich und der Schweiz gibt es natürlich viele politische, soziale und kulturelle Verbindungen. So ist es zum Beispiel üblich, dass Menschen aus diesen drei Ländern zusammen in TV-Sendungen oder Radioprogrammen auftreten. Deshalb wird man in einer deutschsprachigen Radio- oder TV-Sendung sehr oft verschiedene Akzente und Dialekte hören.

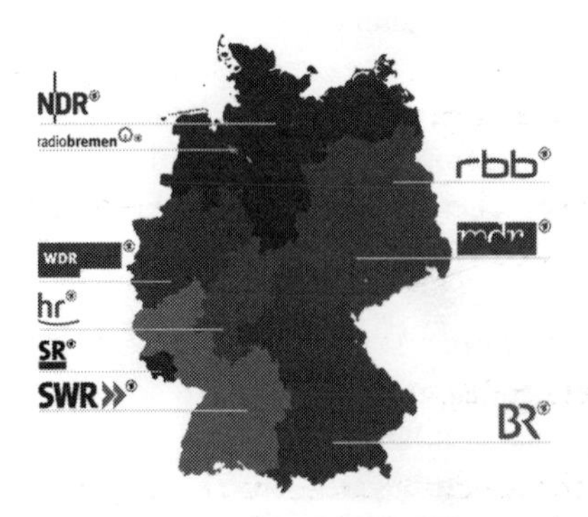

The ARD is one of the main public broadcasting organizations in Germany.
*Mitglieder der ARD**

Übung 7 Sagen Sie's auf Deutsch!

CD1, TR 1, 6:29

Which phrases in **Aufnahme 2** were used to express the following? If you are not sure, look at the transcript at the back of the book. You can check your answers on the recording and also remind yourself of the correct pronunciation.

a Can you please introduce yourself briefly.
b What do you do for a living? (lit. What are you by profession?)
c What do you do in your spare time?
d What sort of hobbies do you have?
e I like going to the cinema.
f In the holidays I go surfing.

Sprachinfo

Geschlecht *Gender*

Here are a few guidelines which might help you work out the genders of certain nouns based on the endings.

Masculine nouns	-ig, -ismus, -ist, -ling, -or
Feminine nouns	-a, -e, -ei, -enz, -heit, -ie, -ik, -ion, -keit, -schaft, -tät, -ung, -ur
Neuter nouns	-chen, -(i)um, -lein, -ment, -tel, -tum

Note that there are some exceptions to these general guidelines such as **das Genie** or **der Moment.**

The vast majority of nouns ending in **-e** are feminine (**die Frage, die Kneipe** etc.), but watch out for a few exceptions such as **der Name.**

Übung 8 Wie heißen die Artikel?

Do you know the gender of the following nouns? Try to do the exercise first and then check the endings against the guidelines in the **Sprachinfo.**

a die Bundesrepublik
b ___ Nation
c ___ Wirtschaft
d ___ Dokument
e ___ Kapitalismus
f ___ Impressionismus
g ___ Museum
h ___ Gymnasium
i ___ Klasse

Aufnahme 3

Im Inter-City-Express nach Berlin

Susanne und Marcus lernen sich im ICE auf der Fahrt nach Berlin kennen. Hören Sie sich den Dialog an und beantworten Sie die Fragen.

Übung 9

a Fährt Susanne das erste Mal nach Berlin?
b Warum fährt Marcus nach Berlin?
c Wo wohnt Marcus?
d Was macht die Freundin von Marcus in Berlin?
e Was studiert Susanne und was möchte sie werden?
f Was möchte eine Schulfreundin Susanne in Berlin zeigen?
g Wie findet Marcus die meisten Leute in Berlin?

CD1, TR 1, 7:39

Marcus Fährst du das erste Mal nach Berlin?
Susanne Ja. Ich wollte Berlin schon seit langem besuchen, aber hatte nie genug Zeit. Und du? Warst du schon mal in Berlin?
Marcus Ja, schon öfters. Meine Freundin wohnt dort und darum fahre ich fast jedes zweite Wochenende dorthin.
Susanne Und woher kommst du?
Marcus Ich wohne in Hannover.
Susanne Na, das ist ja nicht so weit.

Marcus	Nicht so weit? Tja, aber auf Dauer ist diese Fahrerei ganz schön kostspielig.
Susanne	Und was macht deine Freundin in Berlin?
Marcus	Sie studiert Film an der HdK, der Hochschule der Künste. Sie ist natürlich sehr glücklich, dass sie dort einen Studienplatz bekommen hat. Und was machst du? Studierst du auch?
Susanne	Ja, ich studiere Medizin in Göttingen. Ich möchte gern Kinderärztin werden.
Marcus	Und was willst du in Berlin machen?
Susanne	Ich besuche eine alte Schulfreundin von mir, die seit einem Jahr in Berlin wohnt und in einer Kneipe arbeitet. Sie will mich ihren Freunden vorstellen und mir natürlich das Berliner Nachtleben zeigen. Darauf freue ich mich schon.
Marcus	Mir gefällt Berlin sehr gut. Ich finde, dass die meisten Leute sehr offen sind. Überhaupt kann man hier Menschen aus der ganzen Welt treffen. Das macht die Stadt sehr lebendig. Dir wird es bestimmt sehr gut gefallen.

QUICK VOCAB

auf Dauer *in the long term*
die Fahrerei *travelling (+ negative connotations)*
kostspielig *expensive*
der Studienplatz (-¨e) *university place*
der Kinderarzt (-¨e)/die Kinderärztin (-nen) *paediatrician*
darauf freue ich mich *I am looking forward to that*
lebendig *lively*

Insight: ich freue mich

Haben Sie gemerkt, was Susanne sagte, als sie über das Nachtleben in Berlin sprach: **Darauf freue ich mich schon.** *I'm looking forward to that (already).*

Den Ausdruck (**ich freue mich auf**) benutzt man in sehr oft im Deutschen. Man kann zum Beispiel sagen:

Ich freue mich auf das Wochenende.	*I am looking forward to the weekend.*
Ich freue mich auf die Ferien.	*I am looking forward to the holidays.*

Übung 10 Ergänzen Sie

Study the dialogue once more and complete these phrases with the missing information.

a Susanne wollte Berlin ...
b Marcus kommt ...
c Die Fahrerei ist auf Dauer ...
d Seine Freundin ist glücklich, dass ...
e Susanne möchte gern ...
f Sie besucht eine ...
g Marcus sagt, in Berlin kann man ...
h Das macht die Stadt ...

Grammatik

1 Präpositionen *Prepositions*

As you saw in a **Sprachinfo** earlier, the prepositions used in German are often different from those which English-speakers might expect. Here are a few guidelines to help you decide which preposition to use in a given context. The list is not comprehensive, but it does give you the most commonly found usages.

a Origins/details

to live **in** –	Claudia wohnt **in** Dresden.
to come **from** –	Ich komme **aus** Berlin.
to be married **to** –	Sie ist **mit** Michael verheiratet.

b Work

to work **in** an office –	Sie arbeitet **in** einem Büro.
to work **as** –	Er arbeitet **als** Architekt.
to work **for** a company –	Ich arbeite **bei** einer Versicherungsfirma.

c Time

20 years **ago** –	**Vor** 20 Jahren ...
For 20 years –	**Seit** 20 Jahren ...

d Study/leisure time

to go **to** school/to attend school –	Die Kinder gehen **in** die Schule/ Die Kinder gehen **zur** Schule.
to study **at**–	Er studiert **an** der Humboldt-Universität.
to go **to** a course/to attend a course –	Sie geht **zu** einem Englischkurs.

Don't forget that a preposition + definite article is frequently combined to form one word:

an + dem	Er ist **am** 3. Dezember geboren.
in + das	Jörg geht **ins** Büro.
zu + dem	Frau Heinze muss **zum** Arzt.
zu + der	Er geht **zur** Arbeit.

For information on Präpositione, see Unit 5 and Unit 7.

2 Geschlecht *Gender*

In a **Sprachinfo** earlier you saw that there are guidelines to help you work out and remember the gender of nouns in German. Here are a few more pointers that you may find helpful.

Männlich *Masculine*
Days of the week, months and the four seasons: der Dienstag, der April, der Sommer.

Makes of car: der BMW, der Toyota, der Mercedes.
Alcoholic drinks: der Wein, der Schnaps, der Gin (exception: das Bier).

Weiblich *Feminine*
Names of motorbikes and ships: die Honda, die Titanic.
Names of many flowers: die Rose, die Butterblume.

Sächlich *Neuter*
Most metals: das Eisen, das Gold, das Silber.
Names of hotels, restaurants and cinemas: das Ritz, das Abaton.
Infinitives used as nouns: das Tanzen, das Bungeespringen.

3 Pluralformen der Nomen *Plural of nouns*

Like knowing the genders, forming the plural is often seen as quite difficult in German. Here is an overview of the most common forms which might make it easier for you:

1 Most masculine nouns add an **-e** in the plural and very often an umlaut:

der Tisch → die Tisch**e**; der Ball → die B**ä**ll**e**

But there are important exceptions, where no umlaut is added, e.g.:

der Tag → die Tag**e**; der Schuh → die Schuh**e**

2 Most feminine nouns add **-n** or **-en**:

die Tasche → die Tasche**n**; die Frau → die Frau**en**

There are also a number of common feminine nouns which add an **-e** + umlaut:

die Hand → die H**ä**nd**e**; die Stadt → die St**ä**dt**e**

3 Neuter nouns often add **-e**, but no umlaut:

das Bier → die Bier**e**; das Haar → die Haar**e**

Another commonly found ending is **-er** + an umlaut where possible:

das Kind → die Kind**er**; das Buch → die B**ü**ch**er**

Note: 'Imported' nouns Some nouns imported from English and French simply add -s in the plural:

der Chef → die Chefs; das Team → die Teams.

TESTEN SIE SICH!

A) MEHR ÜBUNGEN

When you have completed sections A and B, mark your answers to the written tests by checking them in the Key. In the case of the *Und jetzt Sie*! test, compare your answers with those given on the recording or look them up in the Key.

We recommend that you continue to work on this unit until you can answer over three-quarters of the questions correctly.

1 Wie heißen die Artikel?

Using the guidelines in the **Sprachinfo** on noun endings and the notes in the grammar section, can you find the right article for each of the following nouns? Group the nouns in the appropriate column of the box.

Woche
Mittwoch
Sonntag
Natur
Landschaft
Region
Passion
Rose
Silber
Gold
Temperatur
Sommer
Winter
Dezember
Sprache
Pension
Fußballmanschaft
Freundschaft
Schnaps
Wein
Ferrari
Audi
Gymnasium
Mädchen
Märchen
Tanzen
Schwimmen
Nationalität
Identität
Intelligenz

der	*die*	*das*
Mittwoch	Woche	

2 Give the plural form of these nouns:

- **a** der Beruf → die Berufe
- **b** der Kurs → die ______
- **c** der Gast → die ______
- **d** der Schnaps → die ______
- **e** der Zug → die ______
- **f** die Kneipe → die ______
- **g** die Stadt → die ______
- **h** das Haus → die ______
- **i** das Restaurant → die ______
- **j** das Büro → die ______

3 Stellen Sie Fragen

Philipp Häfner was interviewed for a magazine in Berlin. Here are his answers. Can you work out what the questions were?

Beispiel: Mein Name ist Philipp Häfner. →
Wie ist Ihr Name, bitte?/Wie heißen Sie?

- **a** Nein, ich komme nicht aus Berlin, aber ich wohne jetzt in Berlin.
- **b** Aufgewachsen bin ich in Salzburg.
- **c** Ich spreche fließend Englisch, Französisch und Italienisch.
- **d** Ich bin DJ in einigen Clubs in Berlin.
- **e** Nein, ich bin single.
- **f** Nein, ich habe keine Kinder.
- **g** Ich gehe gern in Konzerte und fotografiere gern.

4 Und jetzt Sie!

Herr Brandt is a guest on a TV show. Take on his role, using the English prompts to guide you.

Tip: Pause the recording while you think of your German responses.

CD1, TR 1, 9:07

Moderator	Herr Brandt, können Sie ein bisschen über sich erzählen?
Sie	*Say yes, of course. Say that your name is Matthias Brandt and that you were born in 1955 in Hanover, but that for 20 years you have lived in Berlin.*
Moderator	Und sind Sie berufstätig?
Sie	*Say yes, you are self-employed. Say that you are an architect.*
Moderator	Und sind Sie verheiratet?
Sie	*Say yes and that you have one daughter, Steffi. Explain that your daughter is a student and studies at the university of Heidelberg.*
Moderator	Und haben Sie ein Hobby?
Sie	*Say that you like going to the cinema and that you like reading. Say that you are also interested in languages.*
Moderator	Leben Sie gern in Berlin?
Sie	*Say yes. Say that the people in Berlin are friendly and Berlin is really interesting.*

Und was sagen Sie? This time answer the questions for yourself and change Berlin into your home town.

B) LESETEXT

Leute, Leute

1 Lesen Sie den Text und beantworten Sie die Fragen:

- **a** Wie alt ist Chris?
- **b** Seit wann hat er seinen Führerschein?
- **c** Sitzt er in seiner Freizeit gern am Computer?
- **d** Seit wann hat er ein eigenes Auto?
- **e** Was ist das Problem mit seinem Auto?
- **f** Als was möchte er später arbeiten?

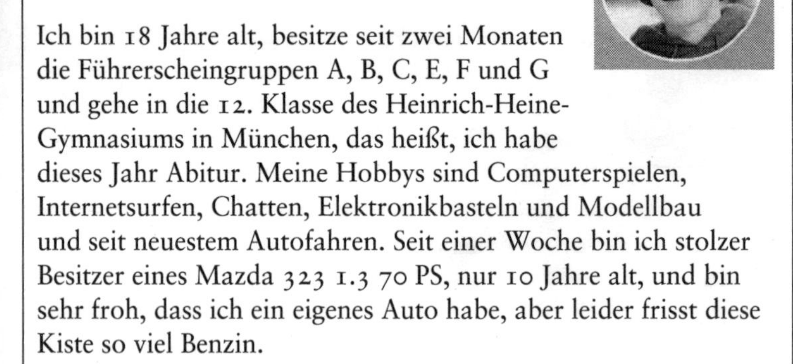

Chris's Page

Über mich:

Ich bin 18 Jahre alt, besitze seit zwei Monaten die Führerscheingruppen A, B, C, E, F und G und gehe in die 12. Klasse des Heinrich-Heine-Gymnasiums in München, das heißt, ich habe dieses Jahr Abitur. Meine Hobbys sind Computerspielen, Internetsurfen, Chatten, Elektronikbasteln und Modellbau und seit neuestem Autofahren. Seit einer Woche bin ich stolzer Besitzer eines Mazda 323 1.3 70 PS, nur 10 Jahre alt, und bin sehr froh, dass ich ein eigenes Auto habe, aber leider frisst diese Kiste so viel Benzin.

Immerhin habe ich schon ein paar Touren zum Starnberger See und nach Nürnberg gemacht. In den Ferien möchte ich gern mit dem Mazda bis nach Italien fahren.

Was ich nach dem Studium machen will, weiß ich noch nicht genau. Ich denke, dass ich in München bleiben werde. Später würde ich gern mal als Programmierer arbeiten, vielleicht bei Siemens. Aber erst mal muss ich das Abitur machen.

QUICK VOCAB

der Führerschein (-e) *driving licence*
das Abitur *German school-leaving exam taken at age 18+*
das Elektronikbasteln *hobby electronics*
der Modellbau *model building*
die Kiste (-n) *(here) old banger (car)*
das Benzin *petrol*
fressen *(usually) to eat (of animals); (here) to guzzle*
der Starnberger See *a large lake about 25 km from Munich*

CHECKLISTE

Now that you have completed Unit 1, can you

1. give details about yourself? ☐
2. ask other people for their personal details? ☐
3. form 'yes/no' and 'wh-' questions correctly? ☐
4. name four typical masculine, six typical feminine and four typical neuter endings for nouns? ☐
5. use prepositions correctly when giving personal details? ☐
6. name typical plural endings for masculine, feminine and neuter nouns? ☐
7. understand a basic homepage written in German? ☐

2

Mein Tagesablauf

In this unit you will learn how to
- ***talk about daily routines, including work and home life***
- ***express frequency of events***
- ***use verbs in the present tense***
- ***arrange word order***
- ***identify separable and inseparable verbs***

Aufnahme 1

CD1, TR 2, 0:23

Lorenz Müller ist 26 Jahre alt und Lehrer an der Friedrich-Schiller-Universität Jena. Er erzählt, wie sein Tagesablauf an Wochentagen und am Wochenende aussieht.

Hören Sie sich die Aufnahme an und beantworten Sie dann die Fragen in Übung 1.

Mein Tagesablauf beginnt morgens gegen halb acht, wenn ich aufstehe und anschließend frühstücke. Zum Frühstück esse ich normalerweise Brötchen mit Marmelade oder mit Nutella und trinke eine Tasse Kaffee, türkisch.

Meine Seminare beginnen meistens erst am frühen Nachmittag oder sogar erst am frühen Abend. Mittagspause habe ich zwischen zwölf und zwei. Ich esse dann in der Mensa. Wenn ich keine Seminare habe, komme ich dann am frühen Nachmittag nach Hause, gehe einkaufen oder erledige, was sonst an Arbeit in der Wohnung anfällt. Am Abend lese ich ausgiebig die Zeitung, schaue Nachrichten im Fernsehen, manchmal dann noch einen Film. Gewöhnlich lese ich aber etwas, beziehungsweise höre Radio oder eine Schallplatte.

Meistens gehe ich aber dann erst mittags in die Stadt, in die Universität, weil meine Seminare erst später stattfinden. So habe ich also Zeit, am Vormittag zu Hause am Schreibtisch zu arbeiten, Seminare vorzubereiten, beziehungsweise zu lesen. Zur Arbeit fahre ich meistens mit dem Bus, aber manchmal laufe ich auch in die Stadt – es sind nur zehn Minuten zu Fuß.

Am Wochenende besuchen wir öfters Freunde, gehen essen, besuchen die Schwiegereltern oder gehen ein wenig spazieren. Aber es muss auch all die Arbeit getan werden, die während der Woche liegen geblieben ist. Es wird gewaschen, sauber gemacht, aufgeräumt.

Hobbys habe ich insofern keine, da glücklicherweise mein Beruf mein Hobby geworden ist. Ich beschäftige mich ausgiebig mit der Literatur und schreibe auch selbst.

Übung 1 Richtig oder falsch?

Korrigieren Sie die falschen Aussagen.

a Lorenz Müller steht normalerweise um 8.30 Uhr auf.
b Am Vormittag arbeitet er meistens zu Hause.
c Bis zur Universität ist es weit.
d Normalerweise isst er zu Hause.
e Seine Seminare gibt er meistens am Nachmittag.
f Abends geht er oft in die Kneipe.

QUICK VOCAB

laufen *to walk (coll.), to run*
wie sein Tagesablauf aussieht *what his daily routine looks like*
gegen *(here) around (time)*
statt/finden *to take place*
beziehungsweise *or, alternatively*
die Mensa *refectory, university dining hall*
was sonst an Arbeit anfällt *whatever jobs need doing*
ausgiebig *thoroughly*
die Schwiegereltern *parents-in-law*
insofern *(here) as such*
sich beschäftigen mit *to concern oneself with*

Insight: Das Passiv

Haben Sie die verschiedenen Passiv-Konstruktionen im Text bemerkt?

es wird gewaschen	*washing is done; (here) we do the washing*
es wird sauber gemacht	*cleaning is done; (here) we do the cleaning*
es wird aufgeräumt	*clearing-up is done; (here) we do the clearing-up*

Mehr über das Passiv in Einheit 9.

Übung 2 Wie heißt das auf Deutsch?

Finden Sie im Text die deutschen Wörter für:

a to get up
b to have breakfast
c to take place
d to walk/to run
e to go shopping
f to start
g to visit

Insight: Normalerweise, meistens usw.

Hier sind einige Wörter, die man oft im Deutschen benutzt, wenn man über seinen Tageslauf spricht:
meistens (*mostly*), normalerweise (*normally*), öfters (*often*), gewöhnlich (*usually*), manchmal (*sometimes*), gelegentlich (*occasionally*), selten (*seldom*, *rarely*), nie (*never*)

Welche von diesen Wörtern benutzt Herr Lorenz Müller? Hören Sie sich die Aufnahme noch einmal an und unterstreichen Sie die benutzten Wörter in der Box oben.

Words used to relate a sequence of events:

zuerst *(at) first*	Zuerst haben wir etwas gegessen.
dann *then*	Dann haben wir uns unterhalten.
danach *after that, then*	Danach haben wir Zeitung gelesen.
als Nächstes *next*	Als Nächstes haben wir Kaffee getrunken.
anschließend *afterwards*	Wir sind dann anschließend ins Theater gegangen.
später *later*	Später haben wir noch einen alten Freund besucht.
zum Schluss *finally*	Zum Schluss habe ich ihn wieder in sein Hotel gebracht.

Sprachinfo

Wortstellung *Word order*

You might remember that in German the verb is usually the second element in the sentence. So, if you start the sentence with a word or phrase other than the subject, the subject has to go straight after the verb. This is called 'subject–verb inversion':

1	2	3	
	VERB	SUBJECT	
Zum Frühstück	trinkt	Lorenz	eine Tasse Kaffee.
Am Wochenende	besuchen	sie	öfters Freunde.

Übung 3

Start these sentences with the italicized phrase and make any other changes to the sentence that are necessary.

Beispiel: Ich stehe *um 7.30 Uhr auf.* →
Um 7.30 Uhr stehe ich auf.

a Ich mache *zuerst* 15 Minuten Yoga.
b Ich trinke Orangensaft *zum Frühstück* und esse ein Croissant mit Marmelade.
c Ich gehe *normalerweise* gegen acht Uhr aus dem Haus.
d Wir arbeiten *meistens* bis 18.00 Uhr.
e Wir besuchen *am Wochenende* öfters Freunde oder gehen essen.
f Mein Freund and ich fahren am Wochenende *manchmal* zum Windsurfen an den Starnberger See.

Übung 4 Was macht Herr Müller normalerweise?

Do you remember what Lorenz Müller usually does on a typical day? Put the following phrases in the right order.

( ) frühstückt
( ) liest und hört Musik
(*1*) steht gegen halb acht auf

( ) gibt Seminare an der Universität
( ) fährt oder geht zur Arbeit
( ) arbeitet zu Hause am Schreibtisch
( ) isst in der Mensa

Now re-tell his daily routine in complete sentences.

Beispiel: 1 ***Normalerweise steht Herr Müller gegen halb acht auf.***

1 Normalerweise ...
2 Dann ...
3 Danach ...
4 Anschließend ...
5 Mittags ...
6 Später ...
7 Abends ...

What about your daily routine? Write down what you usually do. Use the previous two exercises as a guide.

Aufnahme 2

CD1, TR 2, 2:47

Was macht Frau Wolfram?

Corinna Wolfram ist 22 Jahre alt und arbeitet als Kellnerin in München. Sie ist vor zwei Jahren von Würzburg nach München gezogen. Hören Sie, was sie erzählt, und unterstreichen Sie die richtige Antwort.

You are not expected to understand all the details of the recorded conversations on a first hearing. Just try to get the main information. You will probably understand more on a second hearing, especially if you have a look at the vocabulary box first. Then, if you find you are still having difficulties, you can look at the transcripts of the recordings at the back of the book.

Übung 5 Welche Antwort stimmt?

a Ihre Gaststätte ist bis um Mitternacht/bis nach Mitternacht geöffnet.
b Sie kommt oft vor eins/um eins/gegen eins/halb zwei nach Hause.
c Dann liest sie/hört sie Musik/geht sie ins Bett.
d Sie steht um neun/um halb neun/halb zehn/um halb zehn Uhr auf.
e Zum Frühstück trinkt sie Orangensaft/Grapefruitsaft/Tomatensaft.
f Ihre Arbeit fängt um vier Uhr nachmittags/um vier Uhr morgens an.
g Zweimal in der Woche hat sie Spanischstunden/Englischstunden.
h Ihre Eltern sieht sie dreimal/viermal/fünfmal im Jahr.

QUICK VOCAB

Es kommt darauf an, ob ... *It (all) depends whether ...*
jemandem zur Verfügung stehen *to be at someone's disposal*
Ich stelle mich unter die Dusche. *I take a shower. (lit. I put myself under the shower)*
die Scheibe (-n) *(here) slice*
in Anspruch nehmen *to take up, make demands on*
auf/frischen *to freshen up, polish up*
höchstens *at (the) most*
zu Weihnachten *at Christmas*
bei Geburtstagen *on birthdays*

Übung 6 Welche Antwort passt?

Decide which of the three answers best fits the question.

1 Corinna, seit wann wohnst du in München?
- **a** Ich bin jetzt 22 Jahre alt.
- **b** Ich bin vor zwei Jahren hierher gezogen.
- **c** Höchstens viermal im Jahr.

2 Was machst du, wenn du nach der Spätschicht nach Hause kommst?
- **a** Es kommt darauf an, ob ich Frühschicht oder Spätschicht mache.

- **b** Bis 4 Uhr nachmittags kann ich machen, was ich will.
- **c** Ich stelle mich unter die Dusche und gehe sofort ins Bett.

3 Warum willst du eigentlich dein Englisch auffrischen?
- **a** Weil wir in der Gaststätte so viele Ausländer haben.
- **b** Weil ich so gut Englisch spreche.
- **c** Weil das nicht allzu viel Zeit in Anspruch nimmt.

4 Treibst du Sport?
- **a** Ja, einmal in der Woche bringe ich meine Wäsche zum Waschsalon.
- **b** Ab und zu räume ich mein Zimmer auf.
- **c** Ja, ich gehe ziemlich oft windsurfen.

5 Gehst du oft deine Eltern besuchen?
- **a** Ja, sie besuchen mich oft.
- **b** Leider nicht öfter als viermal im Jahr.
- **c** Nein, sie wohnen in der nächsten Straße.

Insight: Präpositionen und Festtage (*festivals*)

In der Aufnahme fragt Martina: „Und wie oft siehst du deine Eltern?"

Corinna antwortet: „Höchstens viermal im Jahr *zu* Weihnachten und *bei* Geburtstagen."

Der Gebrauch der Präposition in Verbindung mit Festtagen ist regional verschieden: *zu Weihnachten* sagt man vor allem in Süddeutschland, während *an Weihnachten* in Norddeutschland gebräuchlich ist.

Je nach Region kann man auch *zu Geburtstagen*, *an Geburtstagen* oder sogar *bei Geburtstagen* sagen.

Es gibt hier kein „richtig" oder „falsch" – der Gebrauch hängt von der Region ab.

Übung 7 Sagen Sie's auf Deutsch!

CD1, TR 2, 5:21

Which phrases in the recording with Corinna were used to express the following? To check, you can find them in the previous exercises or at the back of the book.

a It (all) depends ...
b around one (o'clock)
c I'll take a quick shower.
d a slice of toast
e now and again
f four times a year at most
g at Christmas
h on birthdays

Sprachinfo

Trennbare verben *Separable verbs*

In this unit you came across a number of verbs like **aufstehen** or **fernsehen**, so-called separable verbs:

aus/sehen	*to look*
auf/räumen	*to clear up*
fern/sehen	*to watch television*
statt/finden	*to take place*
vor/bereiten	*to prepare*

Remember that the prefix, the first part of these verbs (**auf-**, **vor-**, etc.), often has to separate from the verb stem (**-räumen**, **-bereiten**, etc.): Heute **räume** ich mein Zimmer **auf**.

Note that with modal verbs, such as **können**, **müssen**, etc., the separable verb does not split up: Ich **muss** mein Zimmer **aufräumen**.

Übung 8 Trennbare Verben

Form at least ten separable verbs by adddding a prefix from the left circle to a main verb from the right circle. For some verbs there is more than one possibility. Make sure you understand the meaning of the verbs.

Beispiel: ***anfangen** = to start* (also: **anmachen** = *to switch on*)

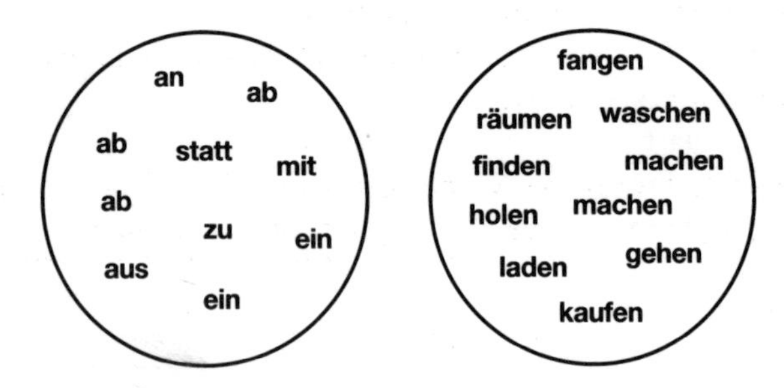

Übung 9 Welche Verben passen?

Fill in the gaps in these sentences using separable verbs from the box below.

einladen	fernsehen	abwaschen
vorbereiten	stattfinden	abräumen
auffrischen	anfangen	

Beispiel: a *fangen … an*

a Die Seminare ______ erst am Nachmittag ______.
b Am Vormittag ______ er sich auf den Unterricht ______.
c Die Geschirrspülmaschine ist kaputt. Herr und Frau Müller ______ selber ______.
d Nach dem Essen ______ Frau Wolfram das Geschirr ______.
e Das Konzert ______ am Samstag in der Konzerthalle ______.
f Viele Kinder ______ mehr als drei Stunden pro Tag ______.

g Er ______ sehr gern Gäste zu sich nach Hause ______.
h Ich muss mein Deutsch ______.

Insight: Mehr über trennbare Verben

Vorsicht! Obwohl die Bedeutung eines trennbaren Verbs oft leicht zu erraten ist – z. B. **ausgehen** *to go out* – gibt es auch viele Verben, bei denen man die Bedeutung lernen muss. Das sehen Sie hier am Beispiel des Präfixes *ein*:
einholen *to catch up with*, **einladen** *to invite*, **einmachen** *to preserve*, **einrichten** *to furnish*

Wenn man aber solche Verben ein paarmal im Kontext hört oder liest, lernt man ziemlich schnell was sie bedeuten.

Aufnahme 3

Frau Beitz, 78, ist Rentnerin und Witwe. Sie erzählt über ihren Alltag.

Übung 10

Hören Sie sich die Höraufnahme an und entscheiden Sie, ob die folgenden Aussagen richtig oder falsch sind.

a Sie steht um 7 Uhr auf.
b Zum Frühstück isst sie Croissants.
c Nach dem Frühstück liest sie Zeitung.
d Sie besucht gerne eine ihrer Freundinnen.
e Meistens isst sie in einem Restaurant zu Mittag.
f Sie strickt einen Pullover für ihren Sohn.
g Sie sieht nicht gern Unterhaltungssendungen.
h Sie geht gegen 22 Uhr ins Bett.

Lesen Sie dann den Dialog und überprüfen Sie Ihre Antworten.

🔊 CD1, TR 2, 6:31

Paul	Frau Beitz, Sie sind Rentnerin und wohnen hier allein. Wird Ihnen nicht manchmal langweilig?
Frau Beitz	Aber nein! Mir wird nie langweilig. Es gibt ja allerhand zu tun. Meistens stehe ich schon um 7 Uhr auf. Ich hole dann ein paar Brötchen von der Bäckerei und koche Kaffee. Ich frühstücke ganz gemächlich – im Sommer sitze ich in der Morgensonne auf meinem Balkon. Anschließend lese ich die Zeitung. Ich interessiere mich nämlich sehr für Politik.
Paul	Sehen Sie auch fern?
Frau Beitz	Ja, aber erst abends und dann nur selten. Während des Tages gehe ich lieber eine von meinen Freundinnen besuchen oder wir gehen zusammen im Stadtpark spazieren. Gelegentlich esse ich in einem Restaurant zu Mittag.
Paul	Haben Sie Familie?
Frau Beitz	Ja, mein Sohn Helmut kommt mich fast immer am Wochenende besuchen. Er wohnt mit seiner Frau in Hamburg, also gar nicht weit weg. Wir machen dann samstags oder sonntags schöne Ausflüge in die Umgebung – mal die Ostseeküste entlang nach Wismar oder Rostock, mal in nördlicher Richtung nach Kiel oder Flensburg.
Paul	Haben Sie irgendwelche Hobbys?
Frau Beitz	Ich stricke gern. Ich bin gerade dabei, einen Pullover für meine Urenkelin zu stricken. Sie ist erst drei Jahre alt und wohnt in Osnabrück. Im März war ich eine Woche dort bei meiner Enkelin und ihrem Mann zu Besuch.
Paul	Und was für Fernsehprogramme schauen Sie sich gerne an?
Frau Beitz	Vor allem Nachrichtensendungen, Podiumsdiskussionen und Dokumentarfilme. An Ratesendungen und Unterhaltungsserien habe ich gar kein Interesse.
Paul	Und wann gehen Sie ins Bett?
Frau Beitz	Normalerweise erst gegen Mitternacht. In meinem Alter braucht man ja nicht mehr so viel Schlaf!

QUICK VOCAB

Wird Ihnen nicht langweilig? *Don't you get bored?*
gemächlich *leisurely*
der Ausflug (-¨e) *excursion, day trip*
die Umgebung (-en) *surrounding area*
der/die Urenkel/in (-) *great-grandson/great-granddaughter*

stricken *to knit*
ich bin gerade dabei, ... *I'm just (in the process of) ...*
sich etwas an/schauen *to watch something (e.g. on TV)*
die Nachrichtensendung (-en) *news (broadcast)*
die Podiumsdiskussion (-en) *panel discussion*
der Dokumentarfilm (-e) *documentary (film)*
die Ratesendung (-en) *panel game*
die Unterhaltungsserie (-n) *light entertainment programme*

Übung 11 Complete the sentences

Study the dialogue once more and then complete these phrases with the missing information.

a Wird Ihnen nicht manchmal ...?
b Meistens stehe ich schon ...
c Im Sommer sitze ich in der Morgensonne ...
d Ich interessiere mich sehr ...
e Gelegentlich esse ich in einem Restaurant ...
f Wir machen samstags oder sonntags Ausflüge ...
g Ich bin gerade dabei, einen Pullover für meine Urenkelin ...
h An Ratesendungen und Unterhaltungsserien habe ich ...

Grammatik

1 Verbendungen im Präsens *Verb endings in the present tense*

Remember that the form of a verb you find in a dictionary is called the **infinitive** (hören – *to hear*, wandern – *to hike*). By cutting off the **-en** or **-n** of the infinitive form you get what is called the stem.

Here is a short summary of the verb endings for regular verbs in the present:

ich spiel**e**	wir spiel**en**
du spiel**st**	ihr spiel**t**

Sie spiel**en**	Sie spiel**en**
er/sie/es spiel**t**	sie spiel**en**

Note that there are a number of verbs whose stem-s end in **-d** or **-t**. These need an extra **-e-** for the 2nd person singular and plural and the 3rd person singular:

arbeiten ich arbeite du arbeitest er/sie/es arbeitet ihr arbeitet

2 *Verben mit Vokalwechseln* *Verbs with vowel changes*

There are also a number of verbs which require a vowel change for the 2nd and 3rd person singular.

Note that verbs whose stem vowel is **e** often change to **i** or **ie** and verbs with an **a** or **au** in their stem need an umlaut:

essen	ich esse	du **i**sst	er/sie/es **i**sst
lesen	ich lese	du l**ie**st	er/sie/es l**ie**st
fahren	ich fahre	du f**ä**hrst	er/sie/es f**ä**hrt
laufen	ich laufe	du l**ä**ufst	er/sie/es l**ä**uft

3 Trennbare und untrennbare Verben *Separable and inseparable verbs*

a The following prefixes are always **inseparable**:
be-, ge-, ent-, emp-, er-, ver-, zer-.

b The following prefixes can be **separable** or **inseparable**:
durch-, hinter-, über-, um-, unter-, unter-, voll-, wider-, wieder-.

Verbs with these prefixes tend to be **separable** when the meaning is more concrete, and **inseparable** when they carry a more abstract meaning, e.g.:

übersetzen *to ferry over* (separable)	**übersetzen** *to translate* (inseparable)

Er setzte das Boot an das andere Ufer über.	**Sie übersetzte den Text ins Deutsche.**
He ferried the boat over to the other bank.	*She translated the text into German.*

c Nearly all other prefixes are separable:
ab-, an-, auf-, aus-, ein-, mit-, um-, statt-, zu-, etc.

Insight: Betonung (*stress*) bei trennbaren und untrennbaren Verben

1 Bei trennbaren Verben liegt die Betonung auf dem Präfix.
aufstehen, **ein**kaufen, **aus**gehen, **um**steigen, **statt**finden

2 Bei untrennbaren Verben liegt die Betonung auf dem Verbstamm:
be**such**en, em**pfeh**len, er**zäh**len, ver**steh**en

3 Bei Verben, die trennbar und untrennbar sein können:

(trennbar) um**fahren:** Er fährt den Polizisten **um**!	*He is running the policeman over!*
(untrennbar) umfahren: Sie um**fährt** den Erdball.	*She is circumnavigating the globe.*

4 Wortstellung *Word order*

Although German word order is relatively flexible, there are some basic rules.

a Earlier in this unit you were reminded of **subject–verb inversion** when the sentence starts with a phrase other than the subject, so that the verb is the second idea:

1	2	3
Abends	sehe	ich meistens fern.

b Another rule of thumb is TIME (when?) – MANNER (how?) – PLACE (where/where to?):

	TIME	*MANNER*	*PLACE*
Ich fahre	morgen	mit dem Wagen	nach Berlin.
Er geht	vor der Arbeit	noch schnell	ins Fitnessscenter.

Of course, not all these elements have to be present at once:

Ich fahre	morgen	–	nach Berlin.
Er geht	–	noch schnell	ins Fitnesscenter.

Sometimes all three elements are present, but one of them comes in first position, so **subject–verb** inversion becomes necessary:

TIME	*verb*	*subject*	*MANNER*	*PLACE*
Morgen	fahre	ich	mit dem Wagen	nach Berlin.

TESTEN SIE SICH!

A) MEHR ÜBUNGEN

Bear in mind that you should carry on working on this unit until you can answer over three-quarters of the questions correctly for all sections of the test.

1 Welches Verb passt am besten?

Find the most suitable verb. The first one has been done for you.

laufen auffrischen stellen machen besuchen aufräumen
abwaschen treiben stricken arbeiten geben übersetzen

a Freunde: ***besuchen***
b sich unter die Dusche: ______
c das Geschirr: ______
d zum Bus: ______
e Sport ______
f ein Seminar: ______
g das Zimmer: ______
h einen Pullover: ______
i in einer Gaststätte: ______
j einen Text: ______
k einen Ausflug: ______
l die Deutschkenntnisse: ______

Can you identify which of the verbs have a vowel change or add an umlaut in the present tense and which verbs are separable?

2 Wortstellung

Put the phrase in brackets into the appropriate position in the main sentence.

Beispiel: Frau Peters frühstückt im Café. (fast jeden Morgen) →

Frau Peters frühstückt fast jeden Morgen im Café.

- **a** Claudia fährt im Winter mit der U-Bahn. (zur Universität)
- **b** Kommst du mit ins Kino? (heute Abend)
- **c** Theo und Anke gehen in der Mittagspause ins Restaurant. (zu Fuß)
- **d** Manfred fährt nachmittags zu seinem Freund ins Krankenhaus. (mit seinem Auto)
- **e** Hans Martinek geht oft ins Fitnesscenter. (nach der Arbeit).
- **f** Frau Tiedke kauft abends noch schnell ein. (im Supermarkt)
- **g** Die Fuhrmanns wollen nächstes Wochenende eine Radtour machen. (an die Ostsee)

3 Marianne redet mit ihrer Freundin über ihren Tagesablauf

Setzen Sie die Sätze in die richtige Reihenfolge.

Reconstruct the following dialogue between Marianne (M) and her friend Barbara (B). Start with sentence (f).

- **a** (B) Ja, ich esse meistens in einem Restaurant eine warme Mahlzeit.
- **b** (B) Es kommt darauf an, ob ich arbeite oder ob ich frei habe.
- **c** (M) Und was machst du abends nach der Arbeit?
- **d** (B) Doch. Ich gehe gern windsurfen. Aber das mache ich am Wochenende oder in den Ferien.
- **e** (B) Meistens erledige ich, was an Arbeit in der Wohnung anfällt. Manchmal schaue ich auch fern oder stricke.
- **f** (M) Wie sieht eigentlich dein Tagesablauf aus?
- **g** (B) Wenn ich arbeite, stehe ich um 7 Uhr auf, wasche mich, frühstücke und fahre mit dem Bus ins Büro.
- **h** (M) Wie ist es, wenn du arbeitest?
- **i** (M) Hast du sonst keine Hobbys?
- **j** (M) Isst du in der Stadt zu Mittag?

1	2	3	4	5	6	7	8	9	10
f									

4 Und jetzt Sie!

Übernehmen Sie die folgende Rolle und sprechen Sie mit Hilfe der englischen Hinweise über Ihren Tagesablauf. Benutzen Sie die Vokabeln, die in dieser Lektion vorgekommen sind. Die Antworten hören Sie auf der Audioaufnahme.

Take on the following role and, with the help of the English prompts, talk about your daily routine. Use the vocabulary that you have met in this unit. The answers can be heard on the recording.

Remember to pause the recording while you think of your German response.

CD1, TR 2, 8:20

Bekannte	Wann stehst du eigentlich morgens auf?
Sie	*Tell her that during the week you usually get up at around seven, at weekends mostly at around half past nine.*
Bekannte	Was frühstückst du normalerweise?
Sie	*Say that you normally get rolls from the bakery. Say that you then make coffee and eat rolls with jam and butter, and drink a glass of juice. Say that you also usually read the paper.*
Bekannte	Und wie fährst du zur Arbeit?
Sie	*Say that you mostly go by car, and only seldom by bus.*
Bekannte	Hast du denn auch eine Mittagspause?
Sie	*Tell her that you usually have a lunch break between 12.30 and 13.15. Say that you mostly eat in your company and only occasionally have lunch in a restaurant.*
Bekannte	Und was machst du am Abend, nach der Arbeit?
Sie	*Tell her that you usually watch the news on TV, read a book or listen to the radio.*

Bekannte Sie	Und was machst du gerne am Wochenende? *Answer that you sometimes visit friends or your parents, go for a walk occasionally, or do the work that has been left during the week. Say that on Sundays you sometimes make day trips in the surrounding area.*

Und was machen Sie selber?

Go through the questions again and this time answer for yourself.

B) LESETEXT

Lesen Sie den folgenden Text und beantorten Sie dann die Fragen a – e.

Der Weg zur Arbeit

Die meisten nehmen das Auto

Rund vier Prozent der Deutschen können den Arbeitstag stressfrei beginnen, da sie direkt an ihrem Arbeitsplatz wohnen. Das bedeutet, dass sie nach dem Frühstück schon im Büro, im Laden oder in der Werkstatt stehen.

Das sind aber die Ausnahmen. Die anderen müssen sich dagegen jeden Morgen auf den Weg zur Arbeit machen. Die meisten – etwa 60 Prozent – fahren mit dem Auto. Einige finden es bequemer mit dem Auto, andere wohnen so weit außerhalb, dass es für sie keine andere Möglichkeit gibt, als den eigenen

Wagen zu benutzen. Mit öffentlichen Verkehrsmitteln – Bahn oder Bus – fahren etwa 13 Prozent zur Arbeit.

Nur neun Prozent gehen zu Fuß zur Arbeit und noch weniger (etwa acht Prozent) fahren mit dem Fahrrad. Diese Leute haben aber das schöne Gefühl, dass sie etwas für die Umwelt tun.

Der Weg zur Arbeit ist für viele Menschen weiter geworden. Vor 10 Jahren betrug die Entfernung von der Wohnung bis zum Arbeitsplatz für 52 Prozent weniger als 10 km – heute wohnen nur noch 45 Prozent weniger als 10 km von der Arbeitsstelle entfernt. Jeder Sechste (16,2 Prozent) muss sogar mehr als 25 km bis zum Arbeitsplatz fahren.

QUICK VOCAB

der Laden (-¨) *shop*
die Werkstatt (¨-en) *workshop*
die Ausnahme (-n) *exception*
außerhalb *here: out of town*
die öffentlichen Verkehrsmittel (pl.) *public transport*
das Gefühl (-e) *feeling*
die Umwelt *environment*

a What does the figure of 4% represent?
b How do most Germans get to work and why do they choose this method?
c How do about 13% travel to work?
d What sort of feeling do people get who walk to work or go by bicycle?
e What is said about one in six Germans?

CHECKLISTE

Now that you have completed Unit 2, can you

1 talk about your daily routine, during the week and at weekends? ☐

2 talk about your work or studies? ☐

3 say how often events occur? ☐

4 use the correct verb endings in the present tense? ☐

5 check that you are using the correct word order in German? ☐

6 be sure which verbs are separable and which are inseparable and give three examples of each kind? ☐

7 understand a short text on how people travel to work? ☐

3

Ausbildung oder Studium?

In this unit you will learn how to

- ***talk about education and training***
- ***talk and write about past events***
- ***discuss plans for the future***
- ***use the present perfect and simple past tenses***
- ***form the future tense***
- ***use irregular verbs***

Aufnahme 1

Lehre oder Studium?

In der folgenden Höraufnahme spricht Birgit mit ihrem Onkel über ihre Arbeit in Deutschland und warum sie nicht studieren wollte.

Hören Sie sich den Dialog an und beantworten Sie die Fragen in Übung 1.

QUICK VOCAB

die Banklehre *banking apprenticeship*
die Zweigstelle (-n) *branch*
der Akademiker (-) *graduate*
das Abitur *school-leaving examination taken at 18+*
das Hochschulstudium *study at an institution of higher education*

CD1, TR 3, 0:39

Heinz Deine Mutter hat mir gesagt, dass du bei der Deutschen Bank eine Lehre machst. Hast du denn nicht studieren wollen?

Birgit Eigentlich doch. Aber ich musste auch einsehen, dass gerade hier in Deutschland für Akademiker Schwierigkeiten bestehen, Arbeit zu finden. Und ich wollte auf keinen Fall arbeitslos werden. Ich habe mich deshalb um eine Banklehre beworben.

Heinz Kennst du denn Leute, die studiert haben und nachher keine Stellung gefunden haben?

Birgit Oh, ja! Sehr viele sogar. Bei uns gibt es eben zu viele Studenten. Es hat ja jeder, der Abitur gemacht hat, das Recht auf ein Hochschulstudium, und die Universitäten sind deswegen überfüllt. In Berlin studieren zum Beispiel etwa 146 000 Menschen. In ganz Deutschland sind es ungefähr 1,8 Millionen. Die Wirtschaft kann so viele akademisch qualifizierte Leute einfach nicht aufnehmen.

Heinz Als ich aber vor drei Jahren hier war, hast du dich – wenn ich mich recht erinnere – für die englische Sprache besonders interessiert. Hast du das denn aufgeben müssen?

Birgit	Aber gar nicht! Jeden Tag mache ich von meinen Englischkenntnissen Gebrauch. Und im Augenblick lerne ich intensiv Italienisch, da ich im Oktober für ein ganzes Jahr zu unserer Zweigstelle in Florenz geschickt werde.
Heinz	Und du bedauerst es wirklich nicht, dass du nicht studiert hast?
Birgit	Doch, ein bisschen! Aber ich bin ehrlich gesagt mit meinem Beruf sehr zufrieden.

Übung 1

a Bei welcher Bank macht Birgit eine Lehre?
b Was ist auch für Akademiker schwierig?
c Wie viele Menschen studieren in Deutschland?
d Welche Sprache, außer Deutsch, benutzt Birgit jeden Tag?
e Wohin geht Birgit im Oktober für ein Jahr?

QUICK VOCAB

ein | sehen *to recognize, acknowledge*
bestehen *to exist*
überfüllt *overcrowded*
sich bewerben um *to apply for*
sogar *even*
auf | nehmen *to accept, absorb*
Gebrauch machen von *to make use of*

Deutsche Bank 

Übung 2 Wie heißt das im Text?

Finden Sie für die Wörter in kursiv die Ausdrücke im Text mit den gleichen Bedeutungen.

Beispiel: ich musste *verstehen* → ich musste ***einsehen***

a es gibt Schwierigkeiten –
b eine Arbeit bekommen –
c die Universitäten sind zu voll –
d die Wirtschaft kann so viele Leute nicht beschäftigen –
e ich nutze meine Englischkenntnisse –

Übung 3 Richtig oder falsch?

Lesen Sie den Dialog noch einmal und korrigieren Sie die falschen Aussagen.

a Für Akademiker in Deutschland gibt es keine Probleme, eine Arbeit zu finden.
b Birgit kennt nur wenige Leute, die studiert haben und jetzt arbeitslos sind.
c Ein Problem ist, dass die deutschen Universitäten zu voll sind.
d Die deutsche Wirtschaft kann so viele Akademiker nicht beschäftigen.
e Birgit hat in ihrem Beruf leider keine Möglichkeit, ihre Englischkenntnisse zu nutzen.

Sprachinfo
Über die Vergangenheit sprechen *Talking about the past*

If you want to talk about the past in German, for instance about your education, remember to use the *present perfect tense*, which is generally used in spoken German.

However, there are a number of exceptions. If you look back to **Aufnahme 1**, you'll find a couple of examples:

> Aber ich *musste* auch einsehen, dass …
> Und ich *wollte* auf keinen Fall arbeitslos werden.

These are modal verbs, which are more frequently used in the simple past tense, even in the spoken language.

Other exceptions include verbs like **sein, haben** and **geben:**

Ich war letzte Woche krank.
Ich hatte eine Erkältung.
Es gab nichts zu essen.

Note that these rules are not rigidly adhered to. There is, for instance, an example of the present perfect tense being used for a modal verb early on in ***Aufnahme*** *1. Can you find it?*

Übung 4 Wie heißen die Partizipien?

Do you remember how the so-called *past participles* (the verb form used in the present perfect tense) go? If you would like to refresh your memory, see the grammar section at the end of this unit.

a arbeiten → ***gearbeitet***
b studieren → ______
c bewerben → ______
d passieren → ______
e verbringen → ______
f gehen → ______
g werden → ______
h fahren → ______
i besuchen → ______
j verkaufen → ______

Which four of these verbs take **sein** in the present perfect tense?

Übung 5 Was hat Martin gemacht?

How would Martin Klostermann talk about his education and training? Put the following sentences in the appropriate tense, keeping in mind the points made in the **Sprachinfo**.

Beispiel: *Ich/in Karlsruhe/aufwachsen.* →
Ich bin in Karlsruhe aufgewachsen.

a Dort/ich/auch die Schule/besuchen.
b Mit 19 Jahren/ich/das Abitur/bestehen.
c Danach/ich/eine Lehre/anfangen.
d Ich/mich/bei der Dresdner Bank/bewerben.
e Es/geben/viele Bewerber,/aber/ich/haben/Glück.
f Ich/dürfen/auch drei Monate/in einer Zweigstelle in New York/ arbeiten.
g Dort/ich/sehr viel/lernen/und/können/auch mein Englisch/ verbessern.
h Vor einem halben Jahr/ich/meine Banklehre/abschließen.

Sprachinfo

Über die Vergangenheit schreiben *Writing about the past*

Just as the present perfect tense is mostly used for talking about the past, so the Präteritum or 'simple past' is the tense mostly used in the written language. You will find this tense in newspaper articles, novels or, of course, in fairy tales, which usually start with the sentence **Es war einmal ...**

If you want to remind yourself of how to form the simple past, have a look at the grammar section.

Übung 6

This time imagine that Martin Klostermann wants to write about his experiences. Put the sentences from **Übung 5** in the simple past tense.

Beispiel: Ich/in Karlsruhe/aufwachsen. →
Ich wuchs in Karlsruhe auf.

Lesetext

Lesen Sie den Text und machen Sie dann Übung 7.

Das deutsche Bildungs- und Ausbildungssystem

In Deutschland, wie in anderen Ländern, gehen viele Kinder in ihren ersten Jahren in einen Kindergarten. Das ist aber nicht obligatorisch. Erst mit sechs Jahren muss man zur Schule gehen. Diese erste Schule, die man vier Jahre lang besucht, heißt Grundschule. Nach der Grundschule wird meistens entschieden, in welchen Schultyp ein Kind anschließend geht.

Da die Bildung in Deutschland Sache der verschiedenen Bundesländer ist, gibt es unterschiedliche Bildungssysteme. Aber in der Regel gibt es nach der Grundschule ein dreigliedriges System – die Hauptschule, die Realschule und das Gymnasium. Die Hauptschule führt mit 15 oder 16 Jahren zum Hauptschulabschluss und ist beruflich orientiert. Die Realschule führt mit 16 Jahren zur mittleren Reife und ist oft der Beginn einer mittleren Karriere in der Wirtschaft oder im öffentlichen Dienst. Das Gymnasium bietet eine akademische

Bildung und führt mit 18 oder 19 Jahren zum Abitur, das man traditionellerweise braucht, wenn man studieren möchte.

In einigen Bundesländern findet man alle drei Bildungsmöglichkeiten unter einem Dach in der so genannten Gesamtschule.

In Deutschland muss man 12 Jahre lang, also bis zum 18. Lebensjahr, zur Schule gehen. Nach neun Jahren (in manchen Ländern 10 Jahren) darf man die Vollzeitschule verlassen. Man beginnt dann meistens eine Lehre im Handwerk oder in der Industrie, die dann zu einem bestimmten Beruf, wie z.B. Kraftfahrzeugmechaniker/in, Schreiner/in, Friseur/in oder Industriekaufmann/-kauffrau führt. Neben der Lehre muss man auch die Berufsschule besuchen.

Mit dem Abitur hat man theoretisch das Recht, an einer Universität oder Hochschule zu studieren. In der Praxis gibt es heutzutage für viele Fächer ein Quotensystem. Das Studienjahr hat zwei Semester – das Wintersemester und das Sommersemester.

Wer zum Beispiel Lehrer werden möchte, muss meistens vier bis fünf Jahre studieren und legt am Ende das Staatsexamen ab.

Fast alle Universitäten bieten heutzutage auch Bachelor- und Masterkurse an. Wie auch in anderen Ländern dauert das Bachelorstudium meistens drei Jahre und das Masterstudium noch ein oder zwei Jahre. Mit dem Bachelor und Master hofft man in Europa vergleichbare Abschlüsse zu schaffen.

QUICK VOCAB

das Semester (-) *term, semester*
das Staatsexamen (-) *state examination (a degree that is also a teaching qualification)*
ab/legen *to sit, take (an exam)*
der Abschluss (-¨e) *leaving examination*
der/die Schreiner (-)/in (-nen) *carpenter*
vergleichbar *comparable*

Übung 7 Welches Wort passt zu welcher Definition?

Kindergarten	**Staatsexamen**	**Hauptschule**	**Realschule**
Gymnasium	**das Abitur**	**Berufsschule**	**Grundschule**

a können Kinder besuchen, bevor sie in die Schule gehen: ______
b dorthin müssen alle Kinder gehen: ______
c führt oft zu einer Lehre im Handwerk oder in der Industrie: ______
d der Abschluss dort heißt mittlere Reife: ______
e dort macht man das Abitur: ______
f muss man besuchen, wenn man eine Lehre macht: ______
g braucht man, wenn man studieren möchte: ______
h ein Abschluss, den man an der Universität macht: ______

FRIEDRICH-SCHILLER-UNIVERSITÄT JENA

Semestertermine

	Sommersemester	Wintersemester
Semesterdauer	01. April – 30. September	01. Oktober – 31. März
Vorlesungszeit	12. April – 17. Juli	11. Oktober – 05. Februar

Sprachinfo

Und die Zukunft? *And the future?*

Now that you have revised the past tenses in this unit, it is time to look at ways of talking about the future in German, e.g. career plans.

The future tense in German is formed by using **werden** together with the infinitive form of the relevant verb:

Wirst du im Sommer nach England **fahren**? *Will you go to England in the summer?*
Ich werde dich anrufen. *I will call you.*

However, it is quite common to use the present tense to refer to the future, especially if this is indicated by an expression of time:

Fährst du im Sommer nach England? *Are you going to England this summer?*
Ich **bin** bald fertig. *I'll be ready soon.*

Note that **werden** on its own means *to become*:

Was möchtest du **werden**? *What do you want to be (i.e. become)?*

For more information about the future tense, see the Grammar section later in this unit.

Insight: werden/wollen

1 Wenn man „I will" auf Deutsch sagen möchte, benutzt man **werden**: Ich werde morgen meinen Freund besuchen. *I will visit my friend tomorrow.*

2 Wenn man auf Deutsch sagt: **Ich will** ... bedeutet das *I want to/I plan to*: Ich will morgen meinen Freund besuchen. *I plan to visit my friend tomorrow.*

Mehr über das Modalverb **wollen** und seine verschiedenen Formen finden Sie in Einheit 8.

Übung 8 Was werden Sie machen?

Beantworten Sie die Fragen, indem Sie **werden** benutzen. *Remember the rules on word order that you learned in Unit 2.*

Beispiel: Wann macht Andrea ihr Examen? (im Juni) →
Sie wird im Juni ihr Examen machen.

a Wann kommt Peter in die Schule? (nächsten Sommer)
b Um wie viel Uhr fängt das Seminar an? (um 16.00 Uhr)

c Wer hält die Vorlesung? (Frau Dr. Martini)
d Bei welcher Firma macht Susanne ihre Lehre? (bei der Telekom)
e Wo machen Sie Ihren Sprachkurs? (in Madrid)
f Wann fangen Sie Ihren neuen Job an? (in zwei Wochen)

Aufnahme 2

Studium – und was dann?

Sie haben schon in Aufnahme 1 gehört, dass es auch für Studenten nicht leicht ist, eine Arbeit zu finden.

Im folgenden Dialog diskutieren zwei Studentinnen, was sie nach ihrem Studium machen wollen.

Hören Sie sich den Dialog an und machen Sie dann die nächsten Übungen.

CD1, TR 3, 3:09

Ilona Ist hier noch frei?
Vera Ja, bitte schön. Ich studiere Anglistik im vierten Semester. Was studierst du?
Ilona Chemie im neunten Semester. Isst du jeden Tag hier in der Mensa zu Mittag?
Vera Nein. Es kommt darauf an, ob ich zu einem Seminar oder zu einer Vorlesung muss. Womöglich arbeite ich zu Hause und esse dann auch da zu Mittag.
Ilona Du hast aber Glück! Wir Chemiestudenten müssen jeden Tag ins Labor. Versuche durchführen kann man eigentlich nur im Labor. Bald bin ich aber mit dem Studium fertig. Ende nächsten Semesters will ich das Staatsexamen ablegen.
Vera Und was möchtest du dann werden?
Ilona Ich werde mich um eine Stellung beim Umweltministerium bewerben. Die Konkurrenz ist zwar ziemlich stark, aber vielleicht schaffe ich es trotzdem. Und du, was hast du vor?

Vera Ich möchte Gymnasiallehrerin für Englisch werden. Bis ich mit dem Studium fertig bin, wird hoffentlich wieder Nachfrage nach Lehrern bestehen.

Ilona Hast du auch in England studiert?

Vera Ja, ich habe vor zwei Jahren ein Jahr in Canterbury studiert. Es hat ungeheuer viel Spaß gemacht.

QUICK VOCAB

die Anglistik *English language and literature*
der Versuch (-e) *experiment*
durch | führen *to conduct, carry out*
die Stellung (-en) *position*
das Umweltministerium *Ministry of the Environment*
die Konkurrenz *competition*
schaffen *to manage (coll.)*
die Nachfrage *demand*
ungeheuer *huge(ly); immense(ly)*

Übung 9 Richtig oder falsch?

Korrigieren Sie die falschen Aussagen.

a Vera studiert Anglistik im ersten Semester.
b Chemie-Studenten müssen meistens im Labor arbeiten.
c Ilona will in einem Jahr das Staatsexamen ablegen.
d Sie wird sich beim Finanzministerium bewerben.
e Vera möchte Englischlehrerin werden.
f Sie hofft, dass die Situation für Lehrer besser sein wird.

Übung 10

Lesen Sie noch einmal Aufnahme 2. Wie viele Beispiele für das Futur mit **werden** können Sie finden? Welche sind sie?

Insight: Hochschulen in Deutschland

Die älteste Universität ist Heidelberg. Sie wurde 1386 gegründet. Bekannt sind auch die Universitäten von Jena und Tübingen, wo zum Beispiel der Astronom Johannes Kepler studiert hat.

Johannes Kepler (1571–1630)

Die meisten Universitäten werden vom Staat finanziert. Es gibt aber auch einige Privathochschulen wie die Universität Witten-Herdecke oder die European Business School in Schloss Reichartshausen.

Mehr als 37% eines Jahrgangs gehen heutzutage an eine Hochschule.

Übung 11 Sagen Sie's auf Deutsch!

Can you say the following in German? Listen to **Aufnahme 2** for help. You will have to make changes in most instances.

a Is this seat free?
b I have been studying English literature and linguistics for one and half years.
c Aren't you lucky!
d At the end of the next semester I intend to take my final exam.
e And what would you like to be?
f And what are your plans?
g I would like to teach English in a grammar school.
h It was great fun.

Grammatik

1 Vergangenheitsformen im Deutschen *Past tenses in German*

Present perfect tense

To form the present perfect tense use the appropriate form of **haben** or **sein** together with the past participle of the required verb.

REGULAR VERBS

Past participles of regular verbs are normally formed by putting **ge-** in front of the stem and **-t** at the end:

hör-en   ich habe **ge**hör**t**   spiel-en   ich habe **ge**spiel**t**

IRREGULAR VERBS

The past participles of most irregular verbs have **ge-** in front and **-en** at the end. The stem also changes in many cases:

ess-en → ich habe gegessen
sing-en → wir haben gesungen

IMPORTANT POINTS

a Haben or **sein?**

Although most verbs need **haben** in the present perfect tense, there are quite a few important verbs which form their present perfect tense with **sein**. Here are some hints on how to spot them:

- verbs indicating motion from one place to another: **gehen, fliegen, laufen,** etc.:
  Ich bin ins Kino gegangen.
- verbs indicating a change of state (**aufwachen, wachsen, werden, sterben**):
  Die Bevölkerung von L.A. ist gewachsen.
- important exceptions: **bleiben** *to stay,* **sein** *to be*

b Separable verbs
The past participles of separable verbs, whether regular or irregular, have the **-ge-** in between the separable particle and the verb:

abholen → ab-ge-holt   abfahren → ab-ge-fahren

c Past participles with no **ge-** in front

The past participles of inseparable verbs (see Unit 2) do not take **ge-**:

bezahlen → bezahlt   verstehen → verstanden

Verbs ending in **-ieren** also fall into this category:

telefonieren → telefoniert   passieren → passiert

Simple past tense

REGULAR VERBS

To form the simple past tense of regular verbs, take the stem and add the appropriate endings:

spiel-en → spielten	
ich spiel**te**	wir spiel**ten**
du spiel**test**	ihr spiel**tet**
Sie spiel**ten**	Sie spiel**ten**
er/sie/es spiel**te**	sie spiel**ten**

IRREGULAR VERBS

Irregular verbs usually have a change in the stem vowel and add the following endings. Note that there are no endings for **ich** and **er/sie/es**:

fahr-en → fuhren	
ich fuhr	wir fuhr**en**
du fuhr**st**	ihr fuhr**t**
Sie fuhr**en**	Sie fuhr**en**
er/sie/es fuhr**en**	sie fuhr**en**

MIXED VERBS

There are a number of verbs (e.g. **bringen, denken, wissen, kennen**), often referred to as mixed verbs, which have a change in the vowel but take the endings of the regular verbs, both in the present perfect tense and in the simple past:

Example: **denken**: Ich habe oft an Sie gedacht. →
Er dachte viel an seine Familie.

Note that some verbs need an extra -e- between certain consonants, such as **t-(s)t, n-(s)t** and **d-(s)t**:

Regular verbs: **antworten → antwortete → geantwortet**
regnen → regnete → geregnet

Irregular verbs: **finden → du fandest**
halten → du hieltest

Insight: Lerntipp – Vokalwechsel

Oft folgen irreguläre Verben im Perfekt und Präteritum einem bestimmten Schema.

Die folgenden Vokalwechsel gibt es sehr oft:

1	ei - i - i	schn**ei**den - schn**i**tt - geschn**i**tten
		r**ei**ten - r**i**tt - ger**i**tten
2	i - a - u	f**i**nden - f**a**nd - gef**u**nden
		tr**i**nken - tr**a**nk - getr**u**nken
3	ei - ie - ie	bl**ei**ben - bl**ie**b - gebl**ie**ben
		schr**ei**ben - schr**ie**b - geschr**ie**ben
4	ie - o - o	fl**ie**gen - fl**o**g - gefl**o**gen
		z**ie**hen - z**o**g - gez**o**gen
5	e - a - o	st**e**rben - st**a**rb - gest**o**rben
		spr**e**chen - spr**a**ch - gespr**o**chen

2 Das Futur *The future tense*

The future tense in German is formed with the present tense of **werden** together with the infinitive of the verb in question:

ich werde spielen	wir werden spielen
du wirst spielen	ihr werdet spielen
Sie werden spielen	Sie werden spielen
er/sie/es wird spielen	sie werden spielen

The future tense has rather limited use in German and the present tense is used more widely in German than it is in English to refer to future time:

Morgen um diese Zeit sind wir in Berlin.	*We'll be in Berlin this time tomorrow.*
Wann sagst du mir, ob du kommst?	*When will you tell me whether you'll be coming?*

It is certainly possible to use the future tense in most instances where future time is being referred to, and this also applies to the example sentences above:

Morgen um diese Zeit werden wir in Berlin sein.
Wann wirst du mir sagen, ob du kommen wirst?

Nevertheless, the present tense is usually preferred so long as the context makes the time reference clear.

The future tense tends to be used for:

predictions

Heute wird es nicht mehr regnen.	*It won't rain any more today.*
Das wirst du bereuen!	*You'll regret that!*

promises

Ich werde dir morgen im Geschäft helfen.	*I'll help you in the shop tomorrow.*
Ich werde nicht zu spät kommen.	*I won't be late.*

firm intentions

Ich werde im Sommer in Italien arbeiten.	*I'll work in Italy in the summer.*
Ich werde heute Abend mitkommen.	*I'll come along this evening.*

supposition

Du wirst heute wohl nichts essen wollen.	*You'll no doubt not want to eat anything today.*
Du wirst wohl müde sein.	*You'll probably be tired.*

probability

Er wird wohl heute Abend ankommen.	*He'll probably arrive this evening.*
Anna wird wohl krank sein.	*Anna must be ill.*

Note that the modal particle **wohl** is often used with the future tense to express supposition or probability.

TESTEN SIE SICH!

A) MEHR ÜBUNGEN

Bear in mind that you should carry on working on this unit until you can answer well over three-quarters of the questions correctly in all sections of the tests.

1 Welches Verb passt am besten?

studieren bewerben machen feiern besuchen ablegen schreiben treffen diskutieren lesen durchführen unterrichten

a eine Ausbildung machen
b sich bei einer Firma: ______
c an einer Universität: ______
d Versuche: ______
e sich mit Freunden: ______
f in der Bibliothek: ______
g ein Seminar: ______
h vor einer Klasse: ______
i über ein Thema: ______
j eine Examensarbeit: ______
k ein Staatsexamen: ______
l eine große Party: ______

2 Verben ohne ge- im Partizip Perfekt

Look at the verbs in **Übung** 1 again. Several of them do not form their past participles with **ge-**. Which are they?

🔊 **CD1, TR 3, 6:09**

3 Hilda und Werner erzählen ihren Freunden von ihren Plänen für die kommenden Wochen.

Setzen Sie die folgenden Sätze in die Gegenwartsform. Überprüfen Sie dann Ihre Antworten auf der Höraufnahme.

Beispiel: Nächste Woche werde ich einen Sommerferienjob suchen.
→ ***Nächste Woche suche ich einen Sommerferienjob.***

a Morgen werden wir unsere Eltern besuchen.
b Am Dienstag werde ich im Garten arbeiten.
c Demnächst werden wir das Haus renovieren lassen.
d Ich werde bald mit meinem Englischkurs anfangen.
e Im Oktober werden wir nach England fahren.
f Im September wird Martin in die Schule kommen.
g In zwei Wochen werde ich meinen Job als Bedienung anfangen.
h Übermorgen werde ich zum Friseur gehen.
i Am Wochenende werden wir zum Windsurfen gehen.
j Übrigens, das Abendessen wird gleich fertig sein!

4 Und jetzt Sie!

You talk to a friend about your career plans after doing the **Abitur**. Complete the dialogue with the help of the English prompts. Note that the German word for carpentry apprenticeship is **die Schreinerlehre**.

🔊 **CD1, TR 3, 8:00**

Freund	Was hast du denn jetzt nach dem Abitur vor?
Sie	*Tell him that you actually wanted to study, but that you absolutely didn't want to be unemployed, that's why you intend to do an apprenticeship.*
Freund	Was für eine Lehre möchtest du denn machen?
Sie	*Tell him that you really want to do a carpentry apprenticeship, but that the people who have done* **Hauptschulabschluss** *or* **mittlere Reife** *have better chances at that.*

Freund	Warum bewirbst du dich denn nicht um eine Stelle als Industriekaufmann?
Sie	*Tell him that you know that more and more people with* **Abitur are** *applying for these places, but that you would prefer to work creatively rather than do an office job.*
Freund	Und was willst du machen, wenn es mit der Schreinerlehre nicht klappt?
Sie	*Tell him that then you would like to study biology and become a teacher, and hopefully, there will be a demand for teachers once again when you have done your final exam.*

B) LESETEXT

Wie kann Antonio seinen Beruf mit seinem Hobby kombinieren? Im Internet sucht er Ideen im *Musikforum*.

Lesen Sie die Texte und beantworten Sie die Fragen. Zur Hilfe finden Sie auch einige Vokabeln am Ende der Texte.

i Antonios Text

Antonio Dabei seit: 1.2.2010 Ort: Köln	Ich bin 21 Jahre alt und würde sehr gerne etwas mit Musik studieren oder eine Ausbildung in diesem Bereich machen. Ich habe schon eine Lehre in der Elektrobranche hinter mir. Ich spiele seit etwa 10 Jahren Saxofon. Nebenbei spiele ich auch Klavier – aber nur einfache Sachen. Ich nehme auch Gesangsunterricht und singe ehrenamtlich in einem Chor. Hat jemand vielleicht einen Tipp, wo und wie ich meinen Beruf mit meinem Hobby verbinden kann? Ich wohne in der Nähe von Köln. Ein Musikstudium als Lehrer will ich mir nicht antun, weil ich gehört habe, dass es sehr schwer ist, damit später sein Geld zu verdienen. Wäre super, wenn jemand mir helfen kann.

Richtig oder falsch? Korrigieren Sie die falschen Aussagen.

- **a** Antonio möchte eine Ausbildung im Musikbereich machen oder studieren.
- **b** Im Moment macht er eine Lehre in der Elektrobranche.
- **c** Er spielt Saxofon und auch sehr gut Klavier.
- **d** Antonio glaubt, dass es kein Problem ist, als Musiklehrer sein Geld zu verdienen.

ii Carsten T und Queen Mona antworten.

Carsten T Dabei seit: 9.3.2008 Ort: Düsseldorf	Hallo Antonio, manchmal ist es nicht ganz einfach die richtige Entscheidung zu treffen. Warum willst du eigentlich nicht Lehrer werden? Musik kannst du auch auf Lehramt studieren. Lehrer an einem Gymnasium verdienen übrigens sehr gut. Aufstiegsmöglichkeiten gibt es auch und die vielen Ferien sind auch nicht schlecht. Du hast eine handwerkliche Ausbildung in der Elektrobranche. Es gibt einen Studiengang, zum Beispiel in Berlin, dessen Abschluss der „Toningenieur" ist. Da könntest du von deiner Ausbildung profitieren. Carsten

a Apart from good career prospects, what two other features of music teaching does Carsten recommend?

b Why does Carsten suggest studying to be a sound engineer?

Queen Mona Dabei seit: 18.8.2009 Ort: Dortmund	Hi Antonio, ich glaube, in Detmold kann man auch Tontechnik studieren. Du spielst doch auch Saxofon und Klavier. Glaubst du, du könntest dein Wissen weitergeben? Mit Musikunterricht kann man nämlich als Student relativ viel Geld machen. Ich verlange beispielsweise 20 Euro pro Klavierstunde (45 Min). Nehmen wir an, du hast fünf, sechs Schüler, dann sind das schon mal fast 500 Euro im Monat, das ist schon gute Kohle. Auf jeden Fall musst du etwas machen, was dich wirklich interessiert. Queen Mona

c What question does Queen Mona ask Antonio?
d Why does she recommend teaching music to Antonio?
e What is her final piece of advice to Antonio?

der Bereich (-e) *area, field*
die Elektrobranche (-n) *electronics sector*
der Unterricht *lesson(s)*
ehrenamtlich *in an honorary capacity (i.e. unpaid)*
sich etwas antun *(here) to subject oneself to something*
auf Lehramt studieren *to study for a teacher training qualification*
die Aufstiegsmöglichkeiten (pl) *career opportunities/prospects*
die Tontechnik *acoustic engineering*
weiter I geben *pass on*
die Kohle (-n) *(here) dough (coll. for money); coal*

QUICK VOCAB

CHECKLISTE

Now that you have completed Unit 3, can you

1 talk about education and training in Germany and in your country? ☐

2 talk and write about past events, for instance about your education? ☐

3 use regular and irregular verbs correctly? ☐

4 use the present perfect and simple past tenses appropriately? ☐

5 talk about plans for the future? ☐

6 form the future tense with **werden** + infinitive? ☐

7 understand a discussion about study options? ☐

4

Aus der Arbeitswelt

In this unit you will learn how to
- ***talk about jobs***
- ***discuss conditions of work***
- ***use co-ordinating and subordinating conjunctions***
- ***apply punctuation***

Aufnahme 1

Was sind Sie von Beruf?

In der folgenden Höraufnahme unterhalten sich Herr Krause und Frau Kubig auf einem Flug von Stuttgart über ihre Reiseziele und ihre Berufe.

Hören Sie sich den Dialog an und beantworten Sie dann die Fragen in Übung 1.

CD1, TR 4, 0:24

Herr Krause	Wohin fliegen Sie? Nach Budapest?
Frau Kubig	Nein, nach Wien. Und Sie?
Herr Krause	Ich fliege nach Budapest. Ich habe dort geschäftlich zu tun. Machen Sie Urlaub in Wien?
Frau Kubig	Nein. Ich gehe zu einem Ingenieurkongress. Ich bin nämlich Bauingenieurin.

Herr Krause	Was?! Da muss ich aber staunen! Bauingenieur habe ich mir immer als Männerberuf vorgestellt.
Frau Kubig	Ach, nein. Wir bilden zwar immer noch nur eine kleine Minderheit, aber Frauen gibt es schon seit mehreren Jahren in diesem Beruf.
Herr Krause	Ja, wenn man so ein bisschen genauer hinschaut, findet man heutzutage Frauen in fast jedem Beruf.
Frau Kubig	Und was sind Sie von Beruf, wenn ich fragen darf?
Herr Krause	Ich bin leitender Angestellter bei einer Firma, die Werkzeugmaschinen herstellt. Ich fliege nach Budapest, um Verhandlungen mit einer ungarischen Firma zu führen.
Frau Kubig	Und wie gefällt Ihnen Ihr Beruf?
Herr Krause	Eigentlich habe ich nur selten genügend Zeit, mir diese Frage zu stellen! Ich bin jetzt seit sieben Jahren bei der Firma Pfauter beschäftigt und bin im Allgemeinen sehr zufrieden. Bloß möchte ich etwas mehr Zeit haben für meine Frau und meine Kinder.
Frau Kubig	Zeitmangel ist ja eines der größten Probleme, wenn man berufstätig ist. Und Geschäftsreisen nehmen natürlich viel Zeit in Anspruch.
Herr Krause	Sicher, aber für mich ist das Reisen einer der attraktivsten Aspekte meiner Arbeit.
Frau Kubig	Für mich auch.

QUICK VOCAB

der Bauingenieur (-e)/-in (-nen) *civil engineer*
der leitende Angestellte (-n) *executive manager*
die Werkzeugmaschine (-n) *machine tool*
Ich habe dort geschäftlich zu tun. *I've got business to do there.*
die Minderheit (-en) *minority*
genau(er) hinschauen *to take a close(r) look*
staunen über *to be amazed at*
sich etwas vorstellen *to imagine something*
her | stellen *to produce*
die Verhandlung (-en) *negotiation*
die Geschäftsreise (-n) *business trip*
der Zeitmangel *lack of time*

Übung 1 Beantworten Sie die Fragen.

a Was macht Frau Kubig in Wien?
b Gibt es viele Bauingenieurinnen?
c Wie lange arbeitet Herr Krause schon bei seiner Firma?
d Was stellt die Firma her?
e Warum fliegt er nach Budapest?
f Was wünscht er sich?
g Was macht beiden an ihren Berufen Spaß?

Übung 2 Wie heißt das im Text?

Finden Sie für die Wörter in *kursiv* die Ausdrücke im Text mit den gleichen Bedeutungen.

Beispiel: Machen Sie Ferien? → Machen Sie ***Urlaub***?

a eine Minderheit *sein* –
b etwas *produzieren* –
c bei einer Firma *angestellt* -
d *im Großen und Ganzen* -
e *glücklich* –

Sprachinfo

Wie man Sätze verbindet *Linking sentences*

It is important to know how to link sentences in German. Here are some useful words:

aber *but*	**sondern** *but*
denn *for, since, because*	**und** *and*
oder *or*	

These words, called conjunctions, are usually used to join sentences which could also stand on their own:

Er heißt Peter. Er arbeitet in Bonn. → Er heißt Peter **und** er arbeitet in Bonn.

Petra kommt aus Köln. Sie lebt in L.A. → Petra kommt aus Köln, **aber** sie lebt in L.A.

Note when using these conjunctions the word order doesn't change, i.e. the verb in the second clause remains the second item in the clause.

As you might know, there is also another group of conjunctions in German which send the verb to the end of the clause. They include:

dass *that* **weil** *because*
obwohl *although* **wenn** *when, whenever, if*

Here are three examples:

Ich denke, dass Wien eine interessante Stadt ist.
Ich lerne Deutsch, weil ich geschäftlich oft nach Berlin fahre.
Mir macht mein Job Spaß, obwohl ich oft lange arbeiten muss.

As you can see from the last example above, when there is more than one verb in a clause of this type (for instance a modal verb + infinitive), the modal verb is in the final position.

*What about **wenn**? There are three examples in **Aufnahme** 1. Can you find them?*

Übung 3 Bilden Sie lange Sätze.

Join the following sentences together by using **und**, **aber**, **oder**, **denn** or **sondern**.

a Frau Kubig kommt aus Stuttgart. Sie ist Bauingenieurin.
b Sie fährt nach Wien. Sie möchte einen Kongress besuchen.
c Herr Krause ist kein Ingenieur. Er ist leitender Angestellter.
d Seine Arbeit gefällt ihm. Er lernt viele neue Dinge.
e Er reist viel. Geschäftsreisen nehmen viel Zeit in Anspruch.
f Trinken Sie noch Kaffee? Brauchen Sie jetzt einen Schnaps?

g Machen Sie jetzt die nächste Übung? Möchten Sie eine Pause machen?

Übung 4 Herr Johnson lernt Deutsch. Warum eigentlich?

Schreiben Sie, warum Herr Johnson Deutsch lernt. Benutzen Sie **weil**.

Beispiel: Er braucht es für seinen Beruf. →
Herr Johnson lernt Deutsch, weil er es für seinen Beruf braucht.

a Er ist geschäftlich oft in München.
b Er muss Verhandlungen auf Deutsch führen.
c Er möchte die Süddeutsche Zeitung lesen.
d Er trinkt gern Weine aus Rheinhessen.
e Seine Freundin kommt aus Berlin.

Und Sie? Warum lernen Sie Deutsch? Finden auch Sie sechs Gründe und schreiben Sie sie auf.

Aufnahme 2

CD1, TR 4, 3:52

Was machst du jetzt für eine Arbeit?

Im folgenden Dialog begegnen sich Gerd und Heiko zum ersten Mal nach ihrer Studienzeit. Hören Sie sich den Dialog an und unterstreichen Sie die richtigen Antworten.

Übung 5

a Heiko unterrichtet im Moment Spanisch/Deutsch/Französisch als Fremdsprache.
b Seine Arbeit gefällt ihm im Allgemeinen gut/sehr gut/nicht.
c Das Einzige, was ihm nicht gefällt, ist die Bezahlung/Arbeitszeit/Arbeitsatmosphäre.

d Eigentlich möchte er Hauptschullehrer/Realschullehrer/ Gymnasiallehrer werden.
e Gerd macht gerade seinen Zivildienst/seinen Militärdienst/eine Ausbildung.
f Seine Arbeit ist aufregend/anstrengend/langweilig.
g Er möchte als Soziologe/Sozialarbeiter/im Sozialamt arbeiten.

Insight: denn/weil

Die Präpositionen **denn** und **weil** bedeuten beide *because*. Aber Vorsicht: bei **denn** bleibt das Verb an Position 2, aber bei **weil** geht es ans Ende:

Ich lerne gern Deutsch, **denn** ich **finde** es ist eine schöne Sprache.
Ich lerne gern Deutsch, **weil** ich es eine schöne Sprache **finde**.

QUICK VOCAB

was für ein(e/n) *what kind of (coll.)*
unterrichten *to teach, instruct*
die Fremdsprache (-n) *foreign language*
fleißig *hard-working*
etwas nötig haben *to need something*
die Bezahlung (-en) *pay*
der/die Anwärter/-in (-/-nen) *candidate (for a job)*
der Zivildienst *community service*
körperlich/geistig behindert *physically/mentally handicapped*
der Sozialarbeiter (-)/die Sozialarbeiterin (-nen) *social worker*
der Sozialpädagoge (-n)/die Sozialpädagogin (-nen) *person with a degree in social education*

Übung 6 Welche Antwort passt?

1 Lange nicht gesehen! Wie geht's dir?
- **a** Ihm geht's nicht so gut.
- **b** Ich unterrichte Deutsch.
- **c** Gut, danke.

2 Und wie gefällt dir deine Arbeit?
  a Sie macht ihr viel Spaß.
  b Im Allgemeinen sehr gut.
  c Da sie es nötig haben, so schnell wie möglich die deutsche Sprache zu erlernen.

3 Und was machst du eigentlich zur Zeit?
  a Ich werde wohl ein bis zwei Jahre warten müssen.
  b Ich möchte Gymnasiallehrer für Deutsch und Englisch werden.
  c Ich mache gerade meinen Zivildienst.

4 Und was hast du danach vor?
  a Ich komme mir jedenfalls nützlicher vor.
  b Ich möchte Sozialarbeiter werden.
  c Ich wünsche dir viel Glück dabei.

Insight: Der Arbeitsmarkt in Deutschland

Im Vergleich zu Großbritannien ist das produzierende Gewerbe (*manufacturing industry*) in Deutschland immer noch sehr wichtig. Aber auch andere Sektoren wie der Gesundheitsbereich (*health care*) oder das Erziehungswesen (*education*) spielen eine wichtige Rolle. In den letzten Jahren sind zudem im Dienstleistungsbereich (*service sector*) und bei den neuen Technologien viele neue Arbeitsplätze entstanden.

Wie auch in anderen Industrieländern ist vielen Deutschen bewusst, dass es den „Job fürs Leben“ kaum noch gibt. Die Arbeitslosigkeit ist immer noch ein Problem in Deutschland, vor allem in den östlichen Bundesländern.

Insight: Die populärsten Berufe

	Jungen	*Mädchen*
1	Kraftfahrzeugmechatroniker*	Bürokauffrau
2	Industriechemiker	Kauffrau im Einzelhandel
3	Kaufmann im Einzelhandel	Medizinische Fachangestellte
4	Anlagenmechaniker für Sanitär-, Heizungs- und Klimatechnik	Friseurin
5	Koch	Zahnmedizinische Fachangestellte
6	Elektroniker für Energie- und Gebäudetechnik	Industriekauffrau
7	Metalbauer	Fachverkäuferin im Lebensmittelhandwerk
8	Kaufmann im Groß- und Außenhandel	Kauffrau für Bürokommunikation
9	Maler und Lackierer	Verkäuferin
10	Mechatroniker*	Hotelfachfrau

*Mechaniker + Elektroniker = Mechatroniker

Statistisches Bundesamt, Datenreport.

Übung 7 Sagen Sie's auf Deutsch!

CD1, TR 4, 5:30

Which German phrases were used in **Aufnahme 2** to say the following? Check your answers on the recording or in the Key.

a Long time – no see!
b What kind of work are you doing at the moment?
c in general
d They need to ...
e if that is the case

Sprachinfo

Berufstitel *Job titles*

It is now common in German to give job titles in both the male and the female forms and not simply to subsume females under male job titles. Here are some examples:

> **Arzt – Ärztin** *doctor*; **Busfahrer – Busfahrerin** *bus driver*; **Manager – Managerin** *manager*; **Rechtsanwalt – Rechtsanwältin** *solicitor*.

As you can see, **-in** is usually added for the female form and some words also require an umlaut.

There are only a few exceptions to this pattern. The most common are:

> **Krankenpfleger – Krankenschwester, Kaufmann – Kauffrau.**

The words for civil servants and employees don't follow the usual pattern:

> **Beamter – Beamtin, Angestellter – Angestellte.**

When a group of people is being referred to that contains both males and females, it is also common to use the feminine plural, but with a capital 'I', e.g. **StudentInnen, KollegInnen**.

Wir suchen ab sofort für unseren Spezialtiefbau einen/eine

Diplom-Bauingenieur/in

als Bauleiter/in.

Sollten Sie an einer vielseitigen, interessanten und auch anspruchsvollen Tätigkeit interessiert sein, richten Sie bitte Ihre schriftlichen und aussagefähigen Bewerbungsunterlagen an nachfolgende Adresse:

Spezial - Tiefbau - Systeme GmbH
Dürkheimer Straße 32 D - 65934 Frankfurt
http://www.stsffm.de

Aufnahme 3

CD1, TR 4, 6:27

Frau Andresen erzählt von ihrem Beruf

Frau Andresen ist Grafikdesignerin und berichtet über ihren Beruf. Hören Sie, was sie sagt, und beantworten Sie die Fragen.

Übung 8

a Wie ist ihre normale Arbeitszeit?
b Wie ist die Arbeitsatmosphäre?
c Was gefällt ihr an ihrem Job?
d Was mag sie nicht?

e Wie viel verdient sie?
f Was möchte sie in ein paar Jahren machen?

Lesen Sie dann den Text und überprüfen Sie Ihre Antworten.

Mein Name ist Claudia Andresen und ich arbeite als Grafikdesignerin bei einer PR-Firma. Ich fange morgens meistens so gegen neun Uhr an und mache dann um halb fünf, fünf Feierabend. Wenn wir wichtige Aufträge haben, dann arbeite ich natürlich auch mal länger, wenn es sein muss auch mal am Wochenende, aber im Allgemeinen ist das eigentlich selten.

Die Arbeitsatmosphäre ist generell sehr gut. Wir sind insgesamt fünf Grafikdesigner und -designerinnen und arbeiten sehr eng in einem Team zusammen. Da wir über viele Dinge ähnlich denken und alle Sinn für Humor haben, verstehen wir uns ganz gut.

Mir gefällt an meinem Job, dass ich sehr kreativ sein kann. Es ist eigentlich nie langweilig oder Routine, da wir immer an neuen Projekten arbeiten. Außerdem mag ich die Arbeit im Team sehr gern, das heißt, dass wir uns austauschen und über Ideen sprechen. Was mir nicht gefällt ist der Termindruck, unter dem wir oft arbeiten müssen. Wenn wir wichtige Deadlines haben – und die haben wir sehr oft – dann ist es schon sehr stressig.

Mit der Bezahlung bin ich sehr zufrieden. Ich verdiene etwa 3000,– Euro brutto im Monat. Bevor ich hier in der Firma angefangen habe, habe ich einige Jahre als Teilzeitkraft gearbeitet, ohne richtiges Urlaubsgeld, Weihnachtsgeld und ohne Kranken- und Rentenversicherung. Als Vollzeitkraft bekommt man das natürlich alles.

Mein Traum für die Zukunft ist es, mich in ein paar Jahren selbstständig zu machen und meine eigene Firma zu gründen. Dann habe ich noch mehr Verantwortung und vielleicht auch mehr Stress – aber das wäre eine gute Herausforderung für mich.

Übung 9 Wie heißt das auf Deutsch?

In the text are lots of useful words for talking about work and working conditions. Find German expressions and words for the following:

a (pressure of meeting) deadlines
b salary/pay
c part-time worker
d full-time worker
e holiday pay
f extra month's salary (at Christmas)
g pension scheme
h self-employed
i responsibility
j challenge

Übung 10

Lesen Sie den Text noch einmal und ergänzen Sie.

a Claudia Andresen arbeitet in ...
b Die Arbeitsatmosphäre ...
c Ihre Kollegen haben alle Sinn ...
d Ihr Beruf ist nie ...
e Mit ihrer Bezahlung ist sie ...
f Was ihr nicht gefällt ist, wenn sie unter ...
g In der Zukunft möchte sie sich ...
h Das ist für sie eine ...

Grammatik

1 Konjunktionen *Conjunctions*

In the **Sprachinfo** you saw that there are two main groups of conjunctions, one that does not affect the word order (including

und and **aber**) and the other which sends the verb to the end of the clause.

Those in the first group are called **co-ordinating conjunctions** and those in the second group are called **subordinating conjunctions.**

If two sentences are joined together with a subordinating conjunction (such as *because* or *although*), one clause becomes the main clause (**Hauptsatz**) and the other the subordinate clause (**Nebensatz**):

Sentence 1: Er blieb zu Hause.
Sentence 2: Er war krank.
Er blieb zu Hause, weil er krank war.
Main clause *Subordinate clause*

As you saw earlier, subordinating conjunctions have the effect of sending the finite verb to the end of the subordinate clause:

Main clause	*Subordinate clause*
Ich musste um 6 Uhr aufstehen,	**obwohl** ich sehr müde **war.**
Wir werden zu Hause bleiben,	**weil** es stark **regnet.**
Er ist immer allein,	**wenn** ich ihn **sehe.**

It is quite common for the subordinate clause to come before the main clause. When this happens, the finite verb has to come at the beginning of the main clause:

Subordinate clause	*Main clause*
Obwohl ich sehr müde war,	**musste** ich um 6 Uhr aufstehen.
Weil es stark regnet,	**werden** wir zu Hause bleiben.
Wenn ich ihn sehe,	**ist** er immer allein.

Here is a list of subordinating conjunctions which appear quite frequently in German:

als	*when (with past tense)*	**ob**	*whether*
bis	*until*	**obwohl**	*although*

damit	*so that*	**während**	*while*
dass	*that*	**wenn**	*when/if*
nachdem	*after*		

Note that there is always a comma between the main clause and the subordinate clause.

You may notice a tendency in colloquial German not always to put the finite verb at the end of the sentence or clause when using **weil**:

Ich konnte nicht kommen, weil ich arbeitete bis spät.

2 Zeichensetzung: Kommas *Punctuation: commas*

Commas are important in written German.

They are used to separate a main clause and a subordinate clause, as you can see in the following examples:

Obwohl wir sehr müde waren, mussten wir früh aufstehen.
Ich werde heute zu Hause bleiben, weil ich viel zu tun habe.

But avoid overusing commas. There is a temptation to put a comma after the introductory phrase in such sentences as:

Heute um 10 Uhr ist er nach München gefahren.

No comma is needed here, as there is no subordinate clause.

As a result of the spelling reform in Germany the use of a comma before **und** and **oder** is now less common. There should be no comma, even if **und** combines two main clauses:

Sie arbeitet als Designerin und ihre Firma liegt im Stadtzentrum.

TESTEN SIE SICH!

A) MEHR ÜBUNGEN

The Arbeitsagentur acts as a job centre and also deals with claims for employment-related benefits.

1 Berufe

i In this unit you met a number of German job titles. Can you still remember the German words for *civil engineer*, *executive*, *employee* and *civil servant*?

ii Do you know what the following job titles are in English? If you are not sure, check in a dictionary.

Aktienhändler
Apotheker
Architekt
Arzt
Bäcker
Bauarbeiter
Buchhändler
Dolmetscher
Elektriker
Friseur
Goldschmied
Informatiker
Journalist
Juwelier
Klempner
Kellner
Koch
Krankenpfleger
Künstler
Landwirt
Lehrer
Makler
Metzger
Modedesigner
Rechtsanwalt
Reiseleiter
Richter
Schauspieler
Schriftsteller
Sozialarbeiter
Tierarzt
Übersetzer
Verkäufer
Werbetexter
Wirt
Zahnarzt

You have probably realized that all job titles here are given in the masculine form. For the feminine form most simply add **-in**, but there are:

a five words where an umlaut is also needed,
b and one which is different.

Can you find them?

2 Und wer macht was?

Finden Sie die passenden Berufe.

Beispiel: sie schreibt Computerprogramme → ***Informatikerin***

(**a**) Sie schneidet Haare: ______; (**b**) sie behandelt Patienten: ______; (**c**) er repariert zum Beispiel Toiletten: ______; (**d**) sie unterrichtet Kinder: ______; (**e**) er bedient in einem Restaurant: ______; (**f**) sie verkauft zum Beispiel Aspirin: ______; (**g**) er übersetzt Texte: ______; (**h**) er arbeitet auf einem Bauernhof: ______; (**i**) sie berät Leute mit psychischen Problemen: ______; (**j**) sie handelt an der Börse: ______; (**k**) sie entwirft die Pläne für ein Gebäude:______.

3 Was passt besser: Weil oder obwohl?

i Join the two sentences together by using **weil** or **obwohl**. Make any necessary changes to the word order.

Beispiel: Frau Kubig mag ihren Beruf. Sie kann viel reisen. →
Frau Kubig mag ihren Beruf, weil sie viel reisen kann.

a Herr Krause fliegt oft nach Budapest. Er hat dort geschäftlich zu tun.
b Claudia gefällt ihr Beruf. Sie muss oft unter Termindruck arbeiten.
c Sie arbeitet gern im Team. Ihre Kollegen haben alle Sinn für Humor.

d Sie möchte sich selbstständig machen. Das bedeutet mehr Stress.
e Claudia möchte eine eigene Firma gründen. Dies ist eine Herausforderung.

ii And now rewrite the sentences, by starting with the **weil** or **obwohl** clause.
Beispiel: ***Weil** sie viel reisen kann, mag Frau Kubig ihren Beruf.*

4 Und jetzt *Sie!*

You (Anna) meet an old friend, Anke, in town and exchange information about work. Complete the dialogue with the help of the English prompts.

CD1, TR 4, 8:29

Anke Hallo, Anna. Lange nicht gesehen! Sag mal, was bist du jetzt von Beruf?
Sie Tell her that you are a building engineer (civil engineer), that you are generally satisfied with your occupation, that you especially like the travelling, but that one of the biggest problems is the lack of free time. Ask her what she is doing now.
Anke Ich war fünf Jahre lang leitende Angestellte bei einer Kleiderfabrik, die aber leider nicht mehr konkurrenzfähig war. Deshalb bin ich im Moment arbeitslos.
Sie You say that you imagine that to be very difficult. Ask her how she is coping, and what she intends to do.
Anke Beim jetzigen Wirtschaftsklima ist es schwer, eine Stellung zu finden. Ich möchte deshalb einen Computerkurs machen, und hoffe, dass ich dann bessere Chancen habe.
Sie You say that this is a good idea, and that currently a lot of jobs are offered which require knowledge in that field. Wish her good luck.
Anke Vielen Dank!

B) LESETEXT

Ein Lebenslauf

1 Below is an example of a German CV.

Can you work out what the terms **Persönliche Daten, Schulausbildung, Hochschulausbildung, Praktika, Berufspraxis, besondere Kenntnisse, EDV** would be in an English CV?

2 **Richtig oder falsch?** Study the CV in more detail and answer the questions:

- **a** Wo verbrachte Maria ihre Kindheit?
- **b** Wann machte sie ihr Abitur?
- **c** Wie lange studierte sie?
- **d** Wo arbeitete sie nach ihrem Studienabschluss?
- **e** In was für einer Position arbeitet sie im Moment?

QUICK VOCAB

Stellvertretende Referentin der Personalabteilung	*(here) female deputy head of an HR department*
die Fortbildung (-en)	*continuing education, here: staff development*

Lebenslauf

Persönliche Daten:	Schrader, MariaBerndstr. 724310 Hamburg Tel.: 030/4567352 Geb. am 1.04.1980 in München Verheiratet, 1 Kind

Schulausbildung:	
1986–1990	Grundschule München
1990–1999	Schiller-Gymnasium München Abschluss: Abitur (2,1)
Hochschulausbildung:	
10/1999–6/2005	Universität Hamburg Studium der Psychologie Schwerpunkt: Angewandte Psychologie Abschluss als Dipl.-Psychologin Gesamtnote: 1 Thema der Diplomarbeit: Die Bewältigung interpersoneller Stresssituationen am Arbeitsplatz
Praktika:	
2001	Personalabteilung Springer Jacoby, München
2003	Marketingabteilung Otto-Versand, Hamburg
Berufspraxis:	
9/05 – 7/07	Personalberaterin bei Unilever, Hamburg
7/07 – 6/09	Stellvertretende Referentin der Personalabteilung bei Unilever, Hamburg
seit 7/09	Referentin für Personalfortbildung bei Hapag-Lloyd, Hamburg
Besondere Kenntnisse:	
EDV	Textverarbeitung (MS Word) Tabellenkalkulation (Excel) PowerPoint
Fremdsprachen	Englisch–sehr gut Französisch–sehr gut Japanisch–Anfängerkenntnisse

Hamburg,
17.1. 2010

CHECKLISTE

Now that you have completed Unit 4, can you:

1 talk about occupations and name eight in both the masculine and the feminine forms? ☐

2 talk about good and bad aspects of work? ☐

3 say why you do or don't like certain things? ☐

4 use coordinating and subordinating conjunctions correctly and name three of each? ☐

5 place commas correctly? ☐

6 understand a typical CV in German? ☐

5

Interessieren Sie sich für Kultur?

In this unit you will learn how to
- ***talk about your interests, likes and dislikes***
- ***discuss different ways of spending your free time***
- ***apply verbs + prepositions***
- ***form infinitive clauses***

Aufnahme 1

Marion, der Kulturmensch

Marion und Cornelia unterhalten sich darüber, was sie in ihrer Freizeit machen und was ihre Interessen und Hobbys sind.

Hören Sie sich den Dialog an und beantworten Sie dann die Fragen in Übung 1.

CD1, TR 5, 0:26

Marion Übrigens, Cornelia, ich habe zwei Karten für die Oper am Samstagabend. Hast du nicht Lust mitzukommen?

Cornelia Das ist ja sehr nett von dir, Marion, aber ehrlich gesagt interessiert mich die Oper nicht besonders. Ich bin zwar schon kulturinteressiert, aber im Allgemeinen ziehe ich sportliche Aktivitäten vor.

Marion	Ach, komm, du musst doch auch mal was anderes sehen als immer nur den Sportplatz! Ich meine, ich habe natürlich Verständnis dafür, wenn jemand Sport machen will, aber ich persönlich kann mich dafür gar nicht begeistern. Sport hat mich eigentlich schon immer gelangweilt.
Cornelia	Und was sind deine Vorlieben?
Marion	Nun ja, ich interessiere mich eben für alles, was mit Kultur zu tun hat – in einer Großstadt wie München gibt es da ja alle Möglichkeiten. Ich bin gerne auf dem Laufenden, was die neuesten Filme, Theaterproduktionen und so weiter angeht. Was ich auch ganz toll finde ist, dass hier so viele Filme in der Originalsprache mit Untertiteln gegeben werden. Da kann ich wenigstens auch meine Sprachkenntnisse aufpolieren!
Cornelia	Und magst du nur moderne Theaterstücke?
Marion	Selbstverständlich schätze ich auch die Klassiker wie Goethe und Schiller. Abgesehen davon besuche ich auch regelmäßig Ausstellungen – letzten Sonntag war ich in der großen Impressionisten-Ausstellung, einfach fantastisch. Hier wird ja so viel Interessantes und Aufregendes geboten!
Cornelia	Interessierst du dich auch für Musik?
Marion	Sicherlich! Ich mag sowohl klassische als auch moderne Musik. Letzten Monat war ich erst wieder auf einem Konzert von Herbert Grönemeyer.

Übung 1 Richtig oder falsch?

Korrigieren Sie die falschen Aussagen.

a Marion möchte mit Cornelia in die Oper gehen.
b Cornelia ist kulturinteressiert, treibt aber lieber Sport.
c Marion interessiert sich auch für Sport.
d Sie sagt, dass man in München nicht viel machen kann.

e Sie sieht gern Filme in der Originalsprache.
f Marion interessiert sich für Theater, aber besucht selten Ausstellungen.

QUICK VOCAB

sich begeistern für *to be enthusiastic about*
die Vorliebe (-n) *preference*
auf dem Laufenden sein *to be informed, up to date*
an | gehen *to concern*
der Untertitel (-) *subtitle*
auf | polieren *to brush up*
schätzen *(here) to appreciate*

Insight: Sport – machen/treiben

Man kann sagen: Ich *mache* Sport oder Ich *treibe* Sport.

Beides ist korrekt. Das Verb **treiben** ist formeller.

Insight: Ein Rocksänger

Herbert Grönemeyer ist ein bekannter deutscher Rocksänger und Komponist, der viele Preise gewonnen hat. Mehr unter: http://www.groenemeyer.de

Übung 2 Vorlieben und Abneigungen

In **Aufnahme 1** there are a number of commonly used expressions of *preferences* and *dislikes*. Read through the text again and find the German expressions for:

a I am interested in everything that …
b What I find great is …
c I appreciate the classics like …
d In general I prefer …
e That doesn't interest me.
f Sport has always bored me.

Sprachinfo

Verben und Präpositionen *Verbs and prepositions*

Many German verbs, like English verbs, are followed by a preposition. It is important to learn these verbs together with their preposition, as the German and English are often different:

*I wait **for** the bus.* → Ich warte **auf** den Bus.
*I am interested **in** music.* → Ich interessiere mich **für** Musik.

Here are some useful examples:

sich ärgern über	*to be annoyed about*
sich erinnern an	*to remember*
sich freuen auf	*to look forward to*
sich freuen über	*to be pleased about*
glauben an	*to believe in*
träumen von	*to dream of*

You might have noticed that many of the verbs are reflexive, i.e. they include the *reflexive pronouns* **sich**, **mich**, **uns**, etc. For example, if you want to say *I am looking forward to the holiday*:

Ich freue **mich** auf den Urlaub.

Note that prepositions such as **auf**, **an** and **über**, which can be followed either by the accusative or dative case, usually require the accusative in verb + preposition constructions. Prepositions which normally take the dative case do so in this instance, too:

Wir unterhielten uns lange *mit der* Sängerin.
Ich habe heute Nacht *von dem* Konzert geträumt.

Note that in a negative statement **nicht** comes after the verb and the reflexive pronoun (if there is one), and before the preposition:

Sie glaubt **nicht** an Ufos.
Er interessiert sich **nicht** für moderne Musik.

For more details see the grammar section of this unit.

Übung 3 Welche Satzteile passen zusammen?

a	Frau Beitz interessiert sich sehr	**i**	mit ihren Kollegen.
b	Birgit bewirbt sich	**ii**	an das letzte Gespräch.
c	Er erinnerte sich	**iii**	von einer eigenen Firma.
d	Herr Krause freut sich	**iv**	über ihre Reiseziele.
e	Er und Frau Kubig unterhalten sich	**v**	auf seine Familie.
f	Claudia Andresen versteht sich gut	**vi**	für Politik.
g	Sie spricht mit ihnen	**vii**	um eine Banklehre.
h	Claudia träumt	**viii**	über ihr neues Projekt.

Übung 4 Welche Verben brauchen welche Präpositionen?

a sich interessieren: *für*
b sich erinnern: ___
c denken: ___
d sich bewerben: ___
e sich unterhalten: ___ / ___
f sich verstehen: ___
g sprechen: ___ / ___
h träumen: ___
i warten: ___

Note that **sich unterhalten** and **sprechen** can have two prepositions: **mit** when you speak directly to a person and **über** when you speak about someone or something.

Insight: denken/nachdenken

1 denken an – *to think of, to think about* (often: to remember or imagine sth.)

Er denkt an seine Kindheit.	*He thinks of/about his childhood.*
Denk doch an deine Gesundheit!	*Think of/about your health!*

2 nachdenken über – *to think about sth. or sbd. thoroughly, to reflect on*

Sie denkt über das Gespräch nach.	*She thinks about/reflects on the conversation.*
Denken Sie noch einmal darüber nach!	*Think about it again!*
Ich muss darüber noch einmal nachdenken.	*I'll have to think about that again.*

Übung 5 Wie heißen die Fragen?

When asked her opinion on various matters, this is what Frau Andresen said. But what were the questions? Find an appropriate question for each answer.

Beispiel: Nein, ich interessiere mich nicht für Fußball. Fußball finde ich langweilig. → ***Interessieren Sie sich für Fußball?***

a Ja, ich ärgere mich über das Wetter. Das ist schrecklich.
b Ja, ich verstehe mich gut mit meinen Kollegen. Sie sind alle sehr nett.
c Ufos? Nein, ich glaube nicht an Ufos. Das ist doch Quatsch.
d Ja, ich interessiere mich sehr für Kunst, besonders schätze ich abstrakte Malerei.
e Nein, für Techno-Musik kann ich mich nicht begeistern. Sie ist viel zu laut.
f Ja, ich freue mich auf die Ferien. Da fahre ich nach Mallorca.

After you have found the questions, go through them and this time answer them for yourself. Give a reason for your opinion.

Aufnahme 2

CD1, TR 5, 2:13

Pläne für den Sommer

Sebastian und Jochen unterhalten sich darüber, was sie in den Sommerferien machen wollen. Hören Sie sich den Dialog an und unterstreichen Sie die richtigen Antworten.

Übung 6

a Sebastian will einen Flugschein/Führerschein/Waffenschein machen.
b Jochen möchte seinen zweiten/dritten/vierten Tanzkurs machen.

c Danach möchte er auf Turnieren/Wettkämpfen/Tanzabenden tanzen.
d Außer Tanzen singt/segelt/schwimmt er noch in seiner Freizeit.
e Er sagt, es ist eine gute Gelegenheit, neue Menschen/Leute/Personen kennen zu lernen.
f Sebastian meint, es würde ihm nicht gefallen, so eingebunden/gebunden zu sein.
g Er zieht es vor, seine Freizeit individuell/frei/flexibel zu gestalten.

der Führerschein (-e) *driving licence*
die Fahrschule (-n) *driving school*
an | melden *to register, enrol*
der Deckel (-) *(here coll. for) driving licence*
die Hochzeit (-en) *wedding*
eingebunden *tied*
etwas vor | ziehen *to prefer something*

QUICK VOCAB

Übung 7 Welche Antwort passt?

1 Also, was hast du eigentlich so geplant?
- **a** Sie werden im Sommer nach Griechenland fahren.
- **b** Ich werde meinen Führerschein anfangen.
- **c** Das ist übrigens dem Peter passiert.

2 Wie viele Stunden brauchst du denn?
- **a** Heute Abend um 7 Uhr.
- **b** Es fängt am Sonntag an.
- **c** Na ja, 20 ist so der Durchschnitt.

3 Hast du denn eine Partnerin für den Kurs?
- **a** Ja, du kennst doch die Sybille, oder?
- **b** Vielleicht den Marco.
- **c** Ja, den Kurs mache ich alleine.

4 Da muss man doch ziemlich oft trainieren, oder?
- **a** Nein! Das glaube ich dir nicht.
- **b** Ach, aber außer dem Tanzen mache ich eigentlich nichts weiter.
- **c** Aber das wäre mir ehrlich gesagt zu viel.

Sprachinfo

Infinitiv mit zu *Infinitive with* **zu**

In German there are a number of expressions, often useful when talking about hobbies, leisure time etc., which require **zu** + *infinitive*:

Ist es teuer, in die Oper zu gehen?	*Is it expensive to go to the opera?*
Er hat keine Zeit zu kommen.	*He doesn't have the time to come.*

As you can see, **zu** + *infinitive* go to the end of the sentence or clause. The second part of this sentence also needs to be separated from the main clause by a comma, unless it consists only of **zu** + infinitive, as in the second example.

Verbs that often need **zu** + *infinitive* are: **aufhören** to stop, **hoffen** to hope, **vorziehen** to prefer, **versuchen** to try.

Many expressions which consist of a verb + adjective are often followed by an *infinitive* + **zu**:

Es ist möglich, ...	*It is possible ...*
Es ist wichtig, ...	*It is important ...*

The same applies to expressions which consist of a **verb** + **noun**:

Ich habe (keine) Lust ...	*I (don't) fancy ...*
Es macht Spaß...	*It is fun ...*

There are four examples of infinitives + **zu** in **Übung 6** and **Übung 7**. Can you find them?

For more information, see also the grammar section.

Übung 8

Complete the answers to the following questions by using a **zu** + infinitive construction.

Beispiel: Fährst du im Sommer nach Griechenland? →
Ja, ich hoffe, im Sommer nach Griechenland zu fahren.

a Geht ihr heute Abend tanzen? Nein, wir haben keine Lust, ...
b Willst du eigentlich bald deinen Führerschein machen? Ja, ich habe vor, ...
c Kann man dort auch ein Bier trinken? Nein, dort ist es nicht möglich, ...
d Geht ihr nachher noch ins Restaurant? Ja, wir haben Lust, ...
e Bekommt man noch Karten für das Konzert? Nein, es ist unmöglich, ...
f Möchtest du lieber deine Freizeit selbst gestalten? Ja, ich ziehe es vor, ...

Aufnahme 3

Helga and Peter Schneider unterhalten sich mit Birgit über ihre Hobbys und was man in der Freizeit machen kann. Hören Sie sich den Dialog an und entscheiden Sie, ob die folgenden Aussagen richtig oder falsch sind.

Hier sind einige Schlüsselwörter:

QUICK VOCAB

der Kegelclub (-s) *bowling club*
etwas aus | fallen lassen *to skip something, give something a miss*
sich aus | schließen *to exclude oneself, not to take part in something*
gesellig *sociable*

Übung 9

	R	F
a Birgit und Alex geben in zwei Wochen eine große Party.	☐	☐
b Helga und Birgit bekommen Besuch von Keglern aus England.	☐	☐
c Weil sie in einem Club sind, können sie sich nicht ausschließen.	☐	☐
d Helga gefällt es besonders, dass man beim Kegeln die gleichen Leute trifft.	☐	☐
e Birgit sagt, sie braucht Zeit für sich selber.	☐	☐
f Helga und Peter haben noch nie eine Städtereise mit dem Club unternommen.	☐	☐

Lesen Sie dann den Text und überprüfen Sie Ihre Antworten.

CD1, TR 5, 5:58

Birgit Hallo, ihr beiden. Habt ihr nächstes Wochenende schon was vor? Alex und ich geben eine große Party.

Helga Toll, da kommen wir gern, nicht wahr, Peter?

Peter Vielen Dank für die Einladung, Birgit, aber nächstes Wochenende sind Helga und ich mit dem Kegelclub in England, in unserer Partnerstadt. Hast du das etwa vergessen, Helga?

Birgit Könnt ihr das denn nicht mal ausfallen lassen? Wir haben doch so lange schon nicht mehr zusammen gefeiert.

Helga Ich weiß, Birgit. So ein Pech! Es tut uns ja auch wirklich leid, aber das ist schon seit Wochen geplant. Und du weißt ja, wie das ist in so einem Club – da kann man sich schlecht ausschließen, wenn solche Veranstaltungen organisiert werden. Das sagt uns auch nicht immer zu.

Birgit Habt ihr denn nie daran gedacht auszutreten? Also, ich hätte davon schon längst genug. Da kann man sich ja gar nichts anderes mehr vornehmen außer Kegeln.

Peter Das ist eigentlich das Einzige, was uns beiden nicht so gut gefällt. Aber es hat auch unheimlich viele Vorteile.

Helga Ja, das stimmt. Ich mag ganz besonders die gesellige Seite. Kegeln ist immer lustig und man trifft öfters neue Leute, besonders wenn man auf Turniere geht.

Birgit Was, auf Turniere geht ihr auch noch? Da ist doch bestimmt eure ganze Freizeit verplant. Das wäre ganz und gar nicht nach meinem Geschmack. Ich habe gerne auch mal Zeit für mich selbst. So sehr eingebunden zu sein, würde mir überhaupt nicht gefallen.

Peter Aber du darfst auch nicht vergessen, dass der Club viele interessante Unternehmungen organisiert, die uns beiden doch viel Spaß machen. Denk doch nur mal an die Städtereisen, die wir schon unternommen haben – und schließlich ist es ja auch eine sportliche Betätigung, die man bis ins hohe Alter betreiben kann.

QUICK VOCAB

die Partnerstadt (¨-e) *twin town*
sich etwas vor | nehmen *to plan something*
das sagt uns nicht zu *that is not to our liking*
aus | treten aus (+ dat.) *to leave (a club, society, etc.)*
das Turnier (-e) *tournament*
von etwas genug haben *to have enough of something*
verplanen *to book fully, to plan every minute*
Das wäre nicht nach meinem Geschmack. *That would not be to my taste.*
die Betätigung (-en) *activity*
betreiben *to do (esp. sport), to pursue*

Übung 10 Positiv und negativ ...

Lesen Sie den Text noch einmal und ergänzen Sie die folgenden (i) vier positiven und (ii) vier negativen Aussagen.

i

a Es hat auch unheimlich ...
b Ich ______ ______ ______ die gesellige Seite.
c Ich habe ______ ______ ______ Zeit für mich.
d Der Club organisiert viele Unternehmungen, die …

ii

a Also, ich hätte davon schon …
b Das ist das einzige, was …

c Das wäre ganz und gar nicht nach ...
d So eingebunden zu sein, würde ...

Insight: Vereine/Clubs in Deutschland

Insgesamt gehören über 27 Millionen Menschen in Deutschland einem Sportverein an. Die folgenden Sportarten haben die meisten Mitglieder:

1	Fußball	6.563.977	**6**	Handball	842.070
2	Turnen	5.006.039	**7**	Deutscher Alpenverein	782.753
3	Tennis	1.586.663	**8**	Reiten	752.964
4	Sportschießen	1.462.290	**9**	Sportfischen	653.300
5	Leichtathletik	891.006	**10**	Tischtennis	616.796

Quelle: Deutscher Olympischer Sportbund: http://www.dosb.de/

Übung 11 Sagen Sie's auf Deutsch!

CD1, TR 5, 8:10

a Have you made any plans for the coming weekend?
b Splendid, we'd love to come.
c Can't you skip that for once?
d What a pity!
e That is not always to our liking.
f Well, I would have had enough of that long ago.
g That would not be at all to my taste.

Grammatik

1 Verben und Präpositionen *Verbs and prepositions*

In the **Sprachinfo**, you were introduced to verbs that are followed by a preposition. Here is a list of the most common ones:

an	denken an	*to think of/about*
	sich erinnern an	*to remember*

	glauben an	*to believe in*
	schreiben an	*to write to*
auf	sich freuen auf	*to look forward to*
	warten auf	*to wait for*
bei	sich entschuldigen bei	*to say sorry to*
für	sich entschuldigen für	*to say sorry for*
	sich interessieren für	*to be interested in*
	sich begeistern für	*to be enthusiastic about*
mit	aufhören mit	*to stop sth.*
	sprechen mit	*to talk to*
	telefonieren mit	*to phone*
nach	fragen nach	*to ask about*
	suchen nach	*to look for*
über	nachdenken über	*to think about*
	sich ärgern über	*to get annoyed about*
	sich freuen über	*to be pleased about*
	sprechen über	*to talk about*
um	sich bewerben um	*to apply for*
von	träumen von	*to dream of, about*

Note that prepositions such as **an, auf** and **über,** which can be followed by either the accusative or dative case, usually take the accusative in a verb + preposition expression:

Ich schreibe an meinen Bruder. *I'm writing to my brother.*

As you might have noticed, some verbs also go with more than one preposition and change their meaning depending on the preposition used:

Ich freue mich auf den Film. *I'm looking forward to the film.*
Ich freue mich über mein Geschenk. *I'm pleased about my present.*

Verbs can also take more than one preposition at a time:

Ich habe mit Herrn Schmidt **über** das Theaterstück gesprochen.

Insight: Reflexivpronomen

Haben Sie gemerkt, dass viele Verben mit festen Präpositionen (Ich ärgere mich über …, Ich freue mich auf …) reflexiv sind?

Hier ist eine Liste der Reflexivpronomen (*myself*, *yourself*, *him/herself*, etc.):

ich freue *mich*	wir freuen *uns*
du freust *dich*	ihr freut *euch*
Sie freuen *sich*	Sie freuen *sich*
er/sie/es freut *sich*	sie freuen *sich*

2 Präpositionalpronomen *Prepositional pronouns*

If you reply to a question in which a verb + *preposition* is used, you don't have to repeat the whole phrase. Look at the examples:

Hat er **nach** deinem Namen gefragt? *Nein, er hat nicht **danach** gefragt.*

Interessierst du dich **für** Sport? *Nein, ich interessiere mich nicht **dafür**.*

Note that you can put **da(r)-** in front of most prepositions when you want to say *in it*, *on it*, *about it*, etc. and replace the noun with a so-called prepositional pronoun:

Erinnerst du dich **an** dieses Buch? *Ja, ich erinnere mich sehr gut daran.*

Ärgerst du dich über moderne Musik? *Nein, ich ärgere mich nicht **darüber**.*

The prepositional pronoun can in most cases also go at the beginning of a phrase:

Hat er nach deinem Namen gefragt? *Nein, **danach** hat er nicht gefragt.*

2 zu + Infinitivsätze *zu + infinitive clauses*

As already explained in the **Sprachinfo**, **zu** is often needed to create an infinitive clause, as in **Ich versuche, noch Karten zu bekommen.**

Apart from a number of verbs, many expressions which consist of a **verb + noun** or a **verb + adjective** are often followed by an infinitive **+ zu.** Especially the phrases **Ich habe ...** and **Es ist ...** indicate the use of a **zu** + infinitive clause:

> Ich habe große Lust, einen Tanzkurs zu machen.
> Es ist Zeit, nach Hause zu gehen.
> Es ist verrückt, so viel Sport zu treiben.
> Ist es nicht langweilig, den gleichen Film noch einmal zu sehen?

Note also the useful German construction **um ... zu ...** *in order to*, in which **zu** + infinitive is used:

Sie treibt viel Sport, um fit zu bleiben.	*She is doing a lot of sport (in order) to stay fit.*
Ich fliege nach Budapest, um Verhandlungen mit einer ungarischen Firma zu führen.	*I'm flying to Budapest (in order) to conduct negotiations with a Hungarian firm.*

As you can see, **um** goes at the beginning of the clause and the **zu** + infinitive at the end.

TESTEN SIE SICH!

A) MEHR ÜBUNGEN

1 Dafür, daran usw.

Answer these questions, using the prompts in brackets to help you. After either **Ja** or **Nein** you should start your answer with the appropriate combination of **da(r)** + preposition.

Beispiele: Interessieren Sie sich für Fußball? (Nein – gar nicht) →
Nein, dafür interessiere ich mich gar nicht.

Erinnerst du dich an meine 18. Geburtstagsparty? (Ja – sehr gut!) →
Ja, daran erinnere ich mich sehr gut!

a Freust du dich auf deinen Urlaub in Spanien? (Ja – sehr)
b Erinnern Sie sich an meine erste Ausstellung? (Nein – leider nicht)
c Bewerben Sie sich um die Stelle? (Ja – bestimmt)
d Ärgerst du dich über das englische Wetter? (Nein – überhaupt nicht)
e Interessierst du dich für Musik? (Ja – ungeheuer)
f Hast du dich nicht über deine Geschenke gefreut? (Nein – ganz und gar nicht!)

2 Was kann man auch sagen?

Welche Ausdrücke haben eine ähnliche Bedeutung?

a Ich bin kulturinteressiert.
b Das hat mich schon immer gelangweilt.
c Das würde mir nicht gefallen.
d Ich bin gern auf dem Laufenden.
e Das schätze ich sehr.

i Ich weiß gern, was so passiert.
ii Das ist eine Sache, die wir nicht mögen.
iii Das verstehe ich nicht.
iv Ich interessiere mich für Kultur.

f	Das ist das Einzige, was uns nicht gefällt.	**v**	Das mag ich nicht.
g	Ich habe kein Verständnis dafür.	**vi**	Das fand ich schon immer langweilig.
		vii	Das ist mir viel wert.

3 Und jetzt Sie!

Übernehmen Sie die folgende Rolle und sprechen Sie mit Hilfe der englischen Hinweise über Ihre Freizeitaktivitäten. Benutzen Sie die Vokabeln, die in dieser Lektion vorgekommen sind. Die Antworten hören Sie auf der Höraufnahme.

CD1, TR 5, 9:07

Markus Was machst du denn gerne in deiner Freizeit?
Sie *Tell him that you have been swimming for a club for eight years, and that you are also a member of a bowling club.*
Markus So viel Sport – das wäre ganz und gar nicht nach meinem Geschmack! Da ist doch bestimmt deine ganze Freizeit verplant!
Sie *Tell him that sometimes you think that it is a little bit too much. However, you think it has a lot of advantages.*
Markus Was gefällt dir denn so gut daran?
Sie *Tell him that you meet a lot of people, you keep fit and you get to see a lot of new places when going to tournaments with the clubs.*
Markus Interessierst du dich denn gar nicht für Kultur?
Sie *Tell him that you are interested in culture, but that you prefer sports.*
Markus Magst du denn zum Beispiel klassische Musik oder Malerei?
Sie *Tell him that, quite honestly, you prefer modern music, and that you also like to go to the cinema.*
Markus Naja, jeder nach seinem Geschmack!

B) LESETEXT

Eine Stadt mit viel Kultur
Lesen Sie den folgenden Text über München und beantorten Sie dann die Fragen in Übungen 1 und 2

München – Weltstadt mit Herz

Sie gilt als die Weltstadt mit Herz und nach einer Umfrage der Zeitschrift Focus ist sie die Stadt, in der die meisten Deutschen leben möchten: München, mit mehr als 1,36 Millionen Einwohnern die drittgrößte Stadt Deutschlands. Ein Ort zum Wohlfühlen, der viel Lebensqualität bietet – Alpenblick, Biergärten, große Seen in unmittelbarer Nähe, elegante Shopping-Boutiquen. Der Nachteil: Neben Düsseldorf hat München die höchsten Miet- und Immobilienpreise der Bundesrepublik – ein Quadratmeter kostet mehr als €9,50.

Wirtschaftlich ist München ein Renner: Heimatstadt für BMW, Siemens, viele Banken, Versicherungen, Modefirmen und Brauereien. Täglich pendeln 417 000 Menschen. Und auch für Bücher ist München von Bedeutung: Nach New York ist es die zweitgrößte Verlagsstadt der Welt.

Kein Wunder, dass München viele Touristen anlockt: 83 Millionen Tagesbesucher und über 9,5 Millionen Übernachtungen hat die Stadt pro Jahr. Viele kommen auch wegen des kulturellen Angebotes–mehr als 60 Museen und 73 Theater bietet die Stadt. Ein Tipp: Das Deutsche Museum, das jährlich von einer Millionen Menschen besucht wird.

Andere Attraktionen sind der Englische Garten, einer der größten städtischen Gärten und die Bavaria–Filmstudios, wo unter anderem berühmte Filme wie *Das Boot* oder *Der Baader-Meinhof-Komplex* gedreht wurden. Und nicht zuletzt das Oktoberfest, das größte Bierfest der Welt.

QUICK VOCAB

die Umfrage (-n) *survey*
ein Ort zum Wohlfühlen *a place to feel at home in*
der Nachteil (-e) *disadvantage*
der Renner (-) *hit*
pendeln *to commute*
die Bedeutung (-en) *importance, significance*
der Verlag (-e) *publishing company*
an | locken *to attract*

1 Sind die folgenden Aussagen richtig oder falsch? Korrigieren Sie die falschen Aussagen.

a München ist die beliebteste Stadt in Deutschland.
b Sie ist die zweitgrößte Stadt der Bundesrepublik.
c Ökonomisch hat München keine Probleme.
d Jährlich kommen vier Millionen Besucher nach München.
e Das Oktoberfest ist das größte Bierfest der Welt.

2 Can you say in English what the following figures refer to?

a 9,50
b 60
c 73
d 417 000
e 1,36 Million
f über 9,5 Millionen
g 83 Millionen

CHECKLISTE

Now that you have completed Unit 5, can you:

1 talk about your interests, for instance culture or sport? ☐

2 express likes and dislikes? ☐

3 talk about various leisure pursuits and say what you think about them? ☐

4 use prepositions correctly with certain verbs? ☐

5 construct sentences with **zu** + infinitive? ☐

6 understand information (on attractions, the economy, inhabitants etc.) about a given city? ☐

6

Und wie ist Ihre Meinung?

In this unit you will learn how to

- ***talk about health matters and sport***
- ***ask for and express opinions***
- ***agree and disagree***
- ***use modal verbs***
- ***apply the genitive case***

Aufnahme 1

Rauchen – Pro und Contra

Elke und Jochen diskutieren über ein Rauchverbot in der Öffentlichkeit. Hören Sie sich den Dialog an und machen Sie dann die folgenden Übungen.

CD2, TR 1, 0:28

Elke Bist du der Meinung, dass das Rauchen in der Öffentlichkeit verboten werden sollte?

Jochen Ganz und gar nicht! Ich finde, die Antiraucherfanatiker sind schon zu weit gegangen mit ihren neurotischen Forderungen.

Elke Was hältst du also von dem Argument, dass jeder das Recht haben sollte, reine Luft zu atmen?

Jochen Das ist ja ein Witz! Ich als Radfahrer muss die ganzen Abgase von den vielen Autos einatmen. Wo bleibt denn da mein Recht auf reine Luft?

Elke	Da ist bestimmt 'was dran. Aber es gibt nur noch ein Unrecht mehr, wenn man sowohl Zigarettenrauch als auch Autoabgase atmen muss.
Jochen	Das ist mir egal. Solange die Autofahrer meine Luft verpesten, bestehe ich auf meinem Recht, auch in der Öffentlichkeit zu rauchen.
Elke	Und machst du dir um deine Gesundheit keine Sorgen?
Jochen	Nee, eigentlich nicht. Mir macht das Rauchen unheimlich viel Spaß.

die Öffentlichkeit (-en) *public*
ganz und gar nicht *not at all*
die Forderung (-en) *demand*
rein *pure, clean*
das Abgas (*usually pl.* **die Abgase)** *exhaust fumes*
das Recht auf *the right (to)*
Da ist bestimmt 'was dran. *There's certainly something in that.*
Es gibt nur noch ein Unrecht mehr. *Two wrongs don't make a right.*
verpesten *to pollute, foul up*
sich Sorgen machen um *to worry about*

QUICK VOCAB

Übung 1 Richtig oder falsch?

Korrigieren Sie die falschen Aussagen.

a Elke fragt, ob das Rauchen in der Öffentlichkeit verboten werden sollte.
b Jochen denkt, dass die Forderungen der Antiraucher richtig sind.
c Er selber ist auch Nichtraucher.
d Über die Autofahrer beschwert er sich aber nicht.
e Elke sagt, es ist nicht richtig, wenn man Zigarettenrauch und Abgase einatmet.
f Jochen macht sich große Sorgen um seine Gesundheit.

Übung 2 Sagen Sie's auf Deutsch!

CD1, TR 2, 3:14

Can you say these sentences in German? They all appeared in the recording.

a Not at all!
b You must be joking!
c There may well be something in that.
d I don't care.
e I really enjoy smoking.

Sprachinfo

Nach Meinungen fragen und die eigenen Meinungen äußern
Asking about and expressing opinions in German

In German there are a number of ways of asking for and expressing opinions. Some of them you probably already know. Here are the most common ones:

Wie finden Sie ... ?	*What do you think of ... ?*
Was denken Sie über (+ *acc.*) ... ?	*What do you think about ... ?*
Was halten Sie von (+ *dat.*) ... ?	*What do you think of ... ?*
Wie ist Ihre Meinung/Ansicht über ... ?	*What's your opinion/view on ... ?*
Sind Sie der Meinung/Ansicht, dass ... ?	*Are you of the opinion/view that ... ?*

Note that you could of course use the **du** *form for the questions, e.g.* Wie findest du ...? Wie ist deine Meinung über ... ?

Ich finde, .../Ich denke, .../Ich meine, ...	*I think ...*
Ich bin der Meinung/Ansicht, dass ...	*I am of the opinion view that ...*
Meiner Meinung/Ansicht nach ...	*In my opinion ...*

Note the gradual increase in formality for both the questions and the answers.

Some commonly used phrases to express agreement or disagreement are:

Das stimmt./Das stimmt nicht.
Da haben Sie recht./Da haben Sie unrecht.
Da bin ich (ganz) Ihrer Meinung./Da bin ich (ganz) anderer Meinung.
Da stimme ich mit Ihnen überein./Da muss ich widersprechen.

Note that **überein | stimmen** means *to agree* and **wider | sprechen** is *to disagree*. In English the last two sentences mean *I agree with you there and I have to disagree (with you) there.*

In **Aufnahme 1** *there are also some examples of more emotional responses to opinions, e.g.* Das ist ja ein Witz! *(You must be joking; lit. That's a joke). There are two more. Can you find them?*

Übung 3 Sagen Sie es höflicher!

Find a more polite way to express the responses given to the following statements. There is often more than one possible answer.

Beispiel: A: Rauchen sollte verboten werden.
B: Das ist ja ein Witz! →
Da bin ich anderer Meinung!/Da muss ich widersprechen!

a A: Autoabgase sind auch sehr gefährlich.
B: Da hast du recht.
b A: Man sollte weniger mit dem Auto fahren.
B: Da ist bestimmt 'was dran.
c A: Wir sollten alle mit dem Fahrrad zur Arbeit fahren.
B: Das stimmt nicht.
d A: Ich finde, du gehst zu weit mit deinen Forderungen.
B: Ach was! Ganz und gar nicht.
e A: Aber Rauchen ist doch ungesund, findest du nicht?
B: Das stimmt leider.

f A: Jeder sollte das Recht auf reine Luft haben.
B: Da hast du sicher recht.

Übung 4 Was fehlt hier?

Ergänzen Sie die folgenden Fragen.

a ______ findest du eigentlich Deutsch?
b ______ denkst du ______ d______ Politik der Regierung?
c Was halten Sie ______ d______ Idee, mehr Sport zu treiben?
d ______ Sie ______ Meinung, dass Sie gesund leben?
e Stimmen Sie mit mir ____________, dass es schwer ist, das Rauchen aufzugeben?
f ______ ist _______ An______ über ein Rauchverbot in der Öffentlichkeit?

Und wie ist Ihre Meinung? Try to find an answer for each question.

Insight: Das ist ja Quatsch!

In **Aufnahme 1** haben Sie schon einige Beispiele für umgangssprachliches Deutsch (*colloquial German*) gehört. Hier sind noch einige andere Ausdrücke:

Das ist ja Quatsch!	*What nonsense.*
Was für ein Blödsinn!	*What drivel.*
Red keinen Müll!	*Don't talk rubbish.*
Jetzt reicht's mir aber.	*Now I've had enough.*

Aufnahme 2

CD2, TR 1, 4:18

Übung 5 Sind Sie für oder gegen ein Rauchverbot?

Frau Merk sagt, was ihre Meinung über das Rauchen ist.

Hören Sie sich den Dialog an und unterstreichen Sie die richtigen Antworten.

a Frau Merk ist für/gegen ein Rauchverbot in Restaurants und Gaststätten.
b Sie findet es eine Vermutung/Verachtung/Zumutung, wenn andere Gäste rauchen.
c Viele Gäste wollen sich beim Rauchen erholen/entspannen/erregen.
d Sie ist der Meinung, Rauchen hat eine positive/neutrale/negative Einwirkung.
e Ihrer Ansicht nach sind manche Menschen anfällig/allergisch/immun gegen Rauch.
f Sie sagt, die Zahl der Restaurants mit Rauchverbot sinkt/stagniert/wächst.

QUICK VOCAB

sich aus | sprechen für *to speak in favour of*
die Zumutung (-en) *imposition, unreasonable demand*
die Einwirkung auf *effect on*
ehrlich *honestly*
meines Erachtens *in my estimation*
(nicht) zu viel verlangt *(not) asking too much*
eine Zeit lang *for a while*
die Mehrheit (-en) *majority*
die Zwischenzeit (-en) *meantime*

Übung 6 Welche Satzteile passen zusammen?

Verbinden Sie die Satzteile a–f und i–vi, die am besten zusammenpassen. Hören Sie sich dann die Aufnahme noch einmal an oder lesen Sie den Dialog hinten im Buch und überprüfen Sie Ihre Antworten.

a	Viele Gäste möchten rauchen,	**i**	dass ihr Rauchen eine negative Einwirkung hat.
b	Es ist eine Zumutung,	**ii**	die allergisch sind gegen Zigarettenrauch.
c	Solche Leute vergessen meistens,	**iii**	dass es noch eine Zeit lang dauern wird.
d	Es gibt ja Menschen,	**iv**	die das Rauchen total oder zum Teil verbieten.
e	Aber ich sehe auch ein,	**v**	wenn sie sich bei Wein oder Kaffee entspannen.
f	Es wächst die Zahl der Restaurants,	**vi**	wenn ich beim Essen durch das Rauchen gestört werde.

Insight: Rauchverbot

Das Rauchverbot in Deutschland ist Sache der Bundesländer. Darum gibt es in den verschiedenen Bundesländern unterschiedliche Regelungen. Meistens ist das Rauchen in kleinen Kneipen und Gaststätten erlaubt (wenn es dort einen separaten „Raucherraum" gibt). In Österreich und der Schweiz sind die Regelungen sehr ähnlich.

Mehr Informationen: http://www.rauchverbot.net/

Sprachinfo

Modalverben *Modal verbs*

Especially in the context of health or fitness it is important to know how to say what one can do, must do, can't do, must not do, etc.

The group of verbs which express these functions are called modal verbs. In German they are:

können *to be able to/can*, **dürfen** *to be allowed to/may*, **müssen** *to have to/must*, **sollen** *ought to/should*, **wollen** *to want to*

Note that the German equivalent of *must not* is **dürfen + nicht** or **kein:**

Hier darf man nicht rauchen.	*Here one must not (is not allowed to) smoke.*
Sie dürfen keinen Alkohol trinken.	*You must not drink any alcohol.*

Ich muss nicht in German means *I don't have to*:

Ich muss nicht mit dem Fahrrad zur Uni fahren, ich kann auch mit der Straßenbahn fahren.	*I don't have to go to the uni by bike, I can go by tram, too.*

The modal verbs in German are quite irregular. For an overview of modal verbs in the present and past simple tense, see the grammar section.

Übung 7 Wie heißt es richtig?

Setzen Sie die richtige Verbform ein.

Beispiel: Hier ______ ihr nicht parken. (dürfen) →
Hier dürft ihr nicht parken.

a ______ man hier rauchen? (dürfen)
b ______ ihr mir sagen, was das kostet? (können)
c Was? Er ______ nicht schwimmen? (können)
d Meine Ärztin sagt, ich ______ mehr Sport treiben. (sollen)
e Ich ______ ja gesünder leben, aber das ist nicht so einfach. (wollen)
f ______ du morgen mitkommen? (können)
g Ihr ______ mitkommen, wenn ihr ______, aber ihr ______ nicht. (können/wollen/müssen)

Insight: Gesundheitsversorgung

Die Gesundheitsversorgung (*health care*) in Deutschland ist auf einem sehr hohen Standard. Die meisten Deutschen gehören einer gesetzlichen Krankenkasse an (*statutory health insurance scheme*), wie zum Beispiel der Allgemeinen Ortskrankenkasse (AOK) oder der Barmer Ersatzkrankenkasse (BEK). Daneben gibt es auch zahlreiche Privatkrankenkassen.

Trotz Kürzungen im Gesundheitsbereich ist es noch vielen Menschen möglich, eine Kur in einem Kurort zu machen. Die Krankenkassen übernehmen einen großen Teil der Kosten für eine Kur. Der Name der meisten Kurorte beginnt mit „Bad", wie zum Beispiel *Bad Gandersheim* oder *Bad Harzburg*. Der bekannteste Kurort in Deutschland ist *Baden-Baden*.

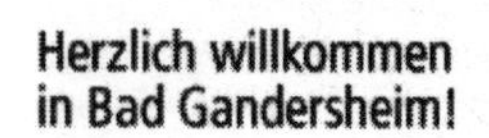

Bad Gandersheim ist einer der vielen deutschen Kurorte. Sein Heilbad bietet Linderung bei Rheuma, Kreislaufstörungen, usw.

Aufnahme 3

🔈 CD2, TR 1, 6:53

Susanne hält sich fit

Susanne tut viel für ihre Gesundheit. Sie ist sehr sportlich und Mitglied in einem Schwimmclub. Hören Sie, was sie erzählt und beantworten Sie die Fragen.

Übung 8

a Mit wie vielen Jahren hat Susanne schwimmen gelernt?
b Wie lange schwimmt sie schon für ihren Club?
c Wie viele Stunden hat sie am Anfang trainiert?
d Trainieren die Schwimmer alleine?
e Wie oft trainiert sie im Moment?
f Wozu ist Schwimmen eine gute Methode?

Hier sind einige Schlüsselwörter:

QUICK VOCAB

der Schwimmunterricht *swimming lessons*
ausgepumpt *exhausted*
sich steigern *to increase*
belasten *to strain*
das Gelenk (-e) *joint*

Martina	Sag mal, Susanne, wie lange betreibst du denn dieses Hobby schon?
Susanne	Also, meine Eltern haben mich schon mit fünf Jahren zum Schwimmunterricht geschickt, so dass ich natürlich in der Schule eine der Besten im Schwimmunterricht war. Meine Lehrerin hat mir dann geraten, in einen Schwimmclub einzutreten.
Martina	Und seit wann schwimmst du für diesen Club?
Susanna	Seit zehn Jahren schon.
Martina	Wie oft trainierst du denn da pro Woche?
Susanne	Am Anfang trainiert man zweimal pro Woche eineinhalb Stunden. Dann, je nach Alter und Leistung, steigert sich das Trainingsprogramm: dreimal, viermal, fünfmal pro Woche. Und natürlich auch längere Trainingszeiten.
Martina	Ist dir das denn niemals langweilig geworden?
Susanne	Überhaupt nicht. Erstens trainiert man ja mit den anderen Schwimmern zusammen und hat somit viel Spaß, und zweitens kommen dann ja auch die verschiedenen Wettkämpfe dazu. Da weiß man, wofür man trainiert hat. Auch wenn man nicht immer gewinnt.
Martina	Bist du denn da nicht oftmals ziemlich ausgepumpt?
Susanne	Eigentlich nicht. Das Trainingsprogramm steigert sich ja langsam, so dass ich jetzt daran gewöhnt bin, fünfmal pro Woche zu trainieren. Außerdem ist Schwimmen natürlich auch eine gute Methode, sich gesundheitlich fit zu halten. Es bringt den Kreislauf in Schwung und ist der Sport, der die Gelenke am wenigsten belastet und dabei alle Muskeln des Körpers trainiert.

QUICK VOCAB

langjährig *of many years' standing, long-standing*
betreiben *to pursue (hobbies etc.)*
ein | treten in *to join*
der Wettkampf (-¨e) *competition*
an etwas gewöhnt sein *to be used to something*
etwas in Schwung bringen *to get something going*
der Kreislauf *circulatory system**

*This aspect of health is mentioned much more frequently in German than in English. A common diagnosis by German doctors is Kreislaufstörungen (lit. circulatory disturbances).

Übung 9

Lesen Sie den Text noch einmal und ergänzen Sie.

a Wie lange betreibst ...
b Meine Lehrerin hat mir geraten, ...
c Je nach Alter und Leistung ...
d Da weiß man, ...
e Schwimmen ist eine gute Methode, sich ...
f Es bringt den Kreislauf ...
g Schwimmen belastet die Gelenke ...
h Man trainiert alle ...

Grammatik

1 Modalverben *Modal verbs*

As you are probably aware, the modal verbs in German form a group of their own and behave differently from other verbs. The five most important modals are mentioned in the **Sprachinfo**. There is one more that you also need to know: **mögen** *to like*.

Here are the present tense forms:

	dürfen *may*	können *can*	mögen *like (to)*
ich, er/sie/es	darf	kann	mag
du	darfst	kannst	magst
wir, Sie, sie	dürfen	können	mögen
ihr	dürft	könnt	mögt

	müssen *must*	sollen *ought (to)*	wollen *want (to)*
ich, er/sie/es	muss	soll	will
du	musst	sollst	willst

wir, Sie, sie	müssen	sollen	wollen
ihr	müsst	sollt	wollt

And here are the simple past tense forms:

	dürfen *may*	können *can*	mögen *like (to)*
ich, er/sie/es	durfte	konnte	mochte
du	durftest	konntest	mochtest
wir, Sie, sie	durften	konnten	mochten
ihr	durftet	konntet	mochtet

	müssen *must*	sollen *ought (to)*	wollen *want (to)*
ich, er/sie/es	musste	sollte	wollte
du	musstest	solltest	wolltest
wir, Sie, sie	mussten	sollten	wollten
ihr	musstet	solltet	wolltet

Note that for talking about the past, modal verbs usually take the simple past tense form; they occur very seldom in the present perfect tense. However, you do need to know the past participles of modal verbs. Fortunately, they are fairly straightforward:

gedurft	gekonnt	gemocht
gemusst	gesollt	gewollt

Modal verbs can sometimes be used on their own:

Du kannst sehr gut Deutsch.	*You can (speak) German very well.*
Birgit wollte gestern nach Berlin.	*Birgit wanted (to go) to Berlin yesterday.*
Ich hab's gekonnt!	*I was able (to do) it!*

But they usually need a second verb, and this goes at the end of the sentence or clause:

Karin und Gerd **mussten** gestern Abend bis 22 Uhr im Büro **arbeiten.**

To express *would like/should like* you use a special form of **mögen** (like the simple past tense but with an umlaut):

Möchtet ihr heute Abend bei uns essen?	*Would you like to eat at our place tonight?*
Ich möchte im Sommer nach New York fliegen.	*I'd like to fly to New York in the summer.*

There is more on modal verbs when used in the subjunctive form in Unit 7.

2 Der Genitiv *The genitive case*

People tend to use different kinds of language or 'registers' depending on factors such as the degree of formality or informality required in a given situation. In this unit, recordings 1 and 3 take place between friends and are therefore relatively informal. Recording 2 is an interview between strangers and therefore has a much more formal feel to it.

One of several factors that makes this recording more formal is the use of the genitive case in two instances:

Das wäre **meines Erachtens** *nicht zu viel verlangt.*
In der Zwischenzeit wächst die Zahl **der Restaurants**, *die ...*

Other examples of the genitive from this unit include:

Ich bin **der Ansicht**, *dass ...*
Ich bin ganz **Ihrer Meinung**, *dass ...*

The genitive in German often covers the meaning of the word *of* in English. It is also often used to denote possession or ownership.

The forms of the genitive are fairly easy to remember:

a The masculine and neuter singular forms follow one pattern. They require an -(e)s on the article or possessive and on the noun:

die Schwester meines Freundes *das Auto Ihres Vaters*
die Mutter des Kindes

b The feminine singular and all the plural forms follow the second pattern. They require an **-er** on the article or possessive:

der Bruder meiner Freundin *die Wohnung Ihrer Mutter*
das Haus der Eltern

Instead of using the genitive, you can often use **von** + dative. The effect is then less formal:

die Schwester von meinem Freund
die Wohnung von Ihrer Mutter
das Haus von den Eltern

3 Meinungen – mehr Beispiele *Expressing opinions – more examples*

Agreeing	
Da stimme ich mit Ihnen überein.	*I agree with you there.*
Ich teile Ihre Meinung.	*I share your opinion.*
Darüber sind wir uns einig.	*We're in agreement on that.*
Disagreeing	
Da muss ich widersprechen.	*I have to disagree (with you) there.*
Hier gehen unsere Meinungen auseinander.	*On this point we beg to differ.*
Da liegst du völlig falsch!	*You're quite wrong there!*
Conceding a point before going on to put a counter-argument	
Das mag wohl sein, aber ...	*That may well be, but ...*
Das sehe ich schon ein, aber ...	*I do see that, but ...*
Sicher, aber ...	*Sure, but ...*
Expressing lack of opinion or indifference	
Das ist mir (alles) egal.	*It's all the same to me.*
Das ist mir alles Wurscht.	*I really don't give a damn.*
Na, und?	*OK, so what?*

TESTEN SIE SICH!

A) MEHR ÜBUNGEN

1 Wie heißt das auf Deutsch?

How would you say the following phrases in German? Use the Sie-form.

a What is your opinion on … ?
b What do you think of … ? (Mention at least two possibilities)
c We have to contradict you on that.
d Is that correct in your estimation?
e Do you share my opinion?
f There is certainly something in that.
g They are quite wrong on that.
h We do see that, but …

2 Üben Sie Endungen im Genitiv

Add the appropriate endings. Note that sometimes no ending is needed.

a Die Gefahren d__ Rauchen_ sind bekannt.
b Die Tochter mein__ Bruder_ ist in einem Tennisclub.
c Der Trainer d__ Fußballmannschaft__ ist sehr populär.
d Der Vater ihr__ Mann_ war ein bekannter Sportler.
e Ich bin da ganz dein__ Meinung_.
f Mein__ Erachten_ sind die Preise für den Fitnessclub viel zu hoch.
g Die Namen mein__ beiden Brüder__ willst du wissen?
h Was sollte man denn Ihr__ Meinung nach tun?

3 Aus dem Radio: Alkoholismus in Deutschland

CD2, TR 1, 9:24

Listen to this radio broadcast and fill in the missing words.

Auf einem Kongress in (**a**) ______ hat der Präsident der deutschen Ärztekammer gestern vor den Gefahren des (**b**) ______ zunehmenden Alkoholismus gewarnt. Er wies darauf hin, dass das (**c**) ______ unbemerkt von der Öffentlichkeit ständig anwachse. Die (**d**) ______ der Alkoholtoten liege etwa (**e**) ______ so hoch wie die der Drogentoten. Insgesamt gebe es in (**f**) ______ (**g**) ______ bis (**h**) ______ Millionen Alkoholkranke. Auch die Folgeschäden (**i**) ______ Alkoholmissbrauchs, wie Leberzirrhose, Hirnabbau und verschiedene (**j**) ______erkrankungen werden nach seiner Einschätzung von den meisten (**k**) ______ verkannt.

QUICK VOCAB

die Ärztekammer (-) *chambers of doctors*
hin | weisen auf *to point out*
an | wachsen *to grow, increase*
der Folgeschaden (¨) *harmful effect*
der Missbrauch (-¨e) *abuse*
die Leberzirrhose (-n) *cirrhosis of the liver*
der Hirnabbau *brain damage (lit. brain reduction)*
verkennen *to fail to appreciate/recognize*

Insight: Nachrichtenstil im Deutschen

Haben Sie den eher formellen Stil des Radioberichts bemerkt? Typisch für viele Berichte im Radio, Fernsehen oder in der Presse ist der häufige Gebrauch des Genitivs. Zum Beispiel:

... der Präsident der deutschen Ärtzekammer (... *the President of the German Chamber of Doctors*).

Im Text gibt es noch vier weitere Beispiele. Können Sie sie finden?

4 Und jetzt Sie!

Anita und Jürgen talk about health risks related to smoking and drinking. Complete the dialogue with the help of the English prompts.

CD2, TR 1, 10:05

Jürgen Sag mal, Anita, warum hast du denn plötzlich das Rauchen aufgegeben?

Anita *Tell him that you were concerned about your health. Also, your husband is allergic to smoke.*

Jürgen Stört es dich jetzt, wenn andere Leute in der Öffentlichkeit rauchen?

Anita *You say yes, very much. Tell him that you think smoking should be forbidden in public places, especially in restaurants when people are eating.*

Jürgen War es nicht schwierig, den guten Vorsatz durchzuhalten?

Anita *You say yes. Ask him whether he has cut back on his alcohol consumption.*

Jürgen Ein wenig. Aber ich möchte es ganz aufgeben.

Anita *Ask him if he had been concerned about the harmful effects of alcohol abuse.*

Jürgen Ja. Das war auch der Grund, warum ich mich entschlossen habe, vollkommen aufzuhören. Ich habe nämlich Angst vor Krebs und Leberzirrhose.

B) LESETEXT

i Lesen Sie den Text „Acht Gesundheitstipps". Welche Überschriften fehlen? Ordnen Sie die Überschriften aus der Box dem Text zu.

(...) Regelmäßige Entspannung
(3) Frische Luft und Licht
(...) Beziehungen sind wichtig
(1) Die Ernährung
(...) Positiv denken
(...) Genussgifte – schlecht für den Körper
(...) Regelmäßiges Gehirnjogging
(...) Bewegung braucht der Körper

Acht Gesundheitstipps

1 Die Ernährung

Eines der wichtigsten Aspekte für ein gesundes Leben und eine gute Fitness ist die Ernährung. Wer sich fettarm ernährt, wenig Fleisch und regelmäßig Obst und Gemüse isst, wird bald merken, dass sich das allgemeine Wohlbefinden verbessert.

Täglich ausreichend trinken ist ein Muss für ein gesundes Leben. Hauptgetränk sollte natürlich Wasser sein, aber auch Obstsäfte oder Kräutertees sind gut.

2 ....

Wer sich vom Bürostuhl direkt auf das Sofa fallen lässt, wird bald merken, dass die Fitness deutlich nachlässt. Es muss nicht unbedingt ein Marathon sein; nur 20 bis 30 Minuten leichtes Laufen täglich reichen dem Körper schon aus.

3 Frische Luft und Licht

Frische Luft ist gesund – und das zu jeder Jahreszeit. Es muss nicht immer die Sonne scheinen, aber das Tageslicht tut der Psyche und somit dem allgemeinen Wohlbefinden gut.

4 ....

Wer arbeitet und sich regelmäßig bewegt, der braucht natürlich auch Erholungsphasen. Nur eine Harmonie von Bewegung und Erholung bringt dem Körper den größten Nutzen. Genauso wie Bewegung braucht der Körper genügend Schlaf. In der Schlafphase regeneriert sich der Körper.

5 ....

„Wer rastet, der rostet", das gilt auch für unser Gedächtnis. Deshalb sollte man die grauen Zellen regelmäßig fit halten. Dies geht schon mit einfachen Mitteln, wie zum Beispiel Kreuzworträtsel lösen.

6 ....

Dass Alkohol und Nikotin nicht gerade gut für die Gesundheit und Fitness sind, weiß heutzutage fast jeder. Hier sollte man aber nicht immer zu streng mit sich sein, denn gegen ein Gläschen Wein ist nichts einzuwenden. Bloß dürfen es nicht zu viele werden!

7 ....

Wer keine Freunde hat oder wenig Kontakt zur Familie, der fühlt sich oft sozial abgesondert und dies ist nicht gut für die Gesundheit. Daher ist ein stabiles soziales Umfeld enorm wichtig für das körperliche und geistige Wohlbefinden.

8 ....

Wer ständig mit negativen Gedanken durch das Leben geht, wird keine Freude daran haben und kann die schönen Dinge des Alltags nicht richtig genießen. Daher ist es von großer Bedeutung eine positive Lebenseinstellung zu haben.

Nach: http://www.100-gesundheitstipps.de

QUICK VOCAB

regelmäßig *regular(ly)*
die Entspannung *relaxation, recreation*
die Beziehung (-en) *relationship*
die Ernährung *nourishment, food*
der Genuss (¨e) *here indulgence*
das Gift (-e) *toxin, poison*
das Gehirn (-) *brain*
die Bewegung (-en) *movement*
fettarm *low-fat*
das Wohlbefinden *well-being*
aus | reichen *to suffice*
der Kräutertee (-s) *herbal tea*
nach | lassen *to diminish, decline*
der Nutzen *benefit*
das Gedächtnis *memory*
ein | wenden *to object*
abgesondert *cut off, isolated*
die Freude (-n) *joy*
die Lebenseinstellung (-en) *attitude to life*

ii Beantworten Sie die folgenden Fragen.

a How should one eat in order to feel good?
b Which drinks are healthy?
c What does a lack of movement lead to?
d Why are fresh air and daylight important?
e Why is sleep important?
f What suggestion is given for keeping the brain in good order?
g What is said about the occasional glass of wine?
h Why are social contacts with friends and family recommended?
i What happens to people who go through life constantly thinking negative thoughts?

Bear in mind that you should carry on working on this unit until you can answer over three-quarters of the questions correctly for all sections of the tests.

CHECKLISTE

Now that you have completed Unit 6, can you:

1 ask people for their opinions and express your own? ☐

2 agree and disagree with others using varying degrees of politeness? ☐

3 talk about health matters and keeping fit? ☐

4 name the modal verbs and use them correctly? ☐

5 use the genitive case in set phrases and to indicate belonging? ☐

6 understand information on improving your health? ☐

7

Berlin ist eine Reise wert

In this unit you will learn how to

- ***make travel arrangements and make polite requests***
- ***understand and give directions***
- ***talk about Berlin and its attractions***
- ***use prepositions and cases***
- ***form indirect questions***

Aufnahme 1

Was kostet ein Flug nach Berlin?

Silke möchte nächste Woche nach Berlin fliegen. Sie ist in einem Reisebüro und fragt, wann es Flüge gibt und was sie kosten.

Hören Sie sich den Dialog an und beantworten Sie dann die Fragen in Übung 1.

CD2, TR 1, 0:19

Silke	Guten Tag. Ich hätte gern gewusst, ob es abends nach 18.00 Uhr Flüge nach Berlin gibt.
Frau Jahn	Sonntags bis freitags kann man um 19.20 Uhr mit British Airways ab Münster/Osnabrück nach Berlin Tegel fliegen. Sonnabends ist der letzte Flug um 14.20 Uhr. An welchem Tag wollen Sie denn fliegen?
Silke	Am kommenden Freitag, wenn es geht. Um wie viel Uhr kommt die Maschine in Berlin Tegel an?

Frau Jahn	Um 20.25 Uhr. Ich sehe mal auf dem Computer nach, ob noch Plätze frei sind. (*Sie sieht auf dem Computer nach.*) Ja, Sie haben Glück, es sind noch Plätze frei. Für wie viele Personen?
Silke	Für mich alleine. Dann müsste ich auch noch wissen, ob ich Sonntagabend oder Montag früh zurückfliegen könnte.
Frau Jahn	Also, sonntagabends startet der letzte Flug um 17.40 Uhr und montags ist der erste Flug um 6.50 Uhr – Ankunft in Münster/Osnabrück um 8.00 Uhr.
Silke	Mmmh. 8.00 Uhr am Flughafen. Dann wäre ich erst gegen 9.00 Uhr im Büro. Aber ich glaube, das wäre nicht so schlimm, wenn ich noch vorher mit meiner Chefin rede. Was kostet der Hin- und Rückflug?

Übung 1 Beantworten Sie die Fragen.

a Wann möchte Silke nach Berlin fliegen?
b Um wie viel Uhr geht wochentags der letzte Flug?
c Wann kommt die Maschine in Berlin an?
d Wann möchte Silke zurückfliegen?
e Was muss sie noch tun?

QUICK VOCAB

Ich hätte gern gewusst ... *(lit.) I would have liked to know ...*
sonnabends *on Saturdays (Sonnabend is frequently used in North Germany instead of Samstag)*
nach | sehen *to have a look (to see)*
dann müsste ich wissen ... *then I would have to know ...*
die Ankunft (-¨e) *arrival*
der Hin- und Rückflug (-¨e) *return flight*

Übung 2 Wie heißt das im Text?

Finden Sie für die Wörter in kursiv die Ausdrücke im Text mit den gleichen Bedeutungen.

Beispiel: am *nächsten* Freitag → am ***kommenden*** Freitag

a wenn es *möglich* ist –
b *das Flugzeug* –
c *es gibt noch Plätze* –
d *geht* der letzte Flug –
e das wäre *kein Problem* –
f *Wie teuer ist …* –

Berliner Flughäfen					**Abflüge Live**
		Abflug		**Ankunft**	
Flug	**von**	**nach**	**Term./ Counter**	**Plan**	**Status**
4U 015	Schönefeld	Köln-Bonn	D42-D45	15:45	Gestartet
SK 680	Tegel	Kopenhagen	D82/D83	15:50	Gestartet
AF 2035	Tegel	Paris CDG	A15	15:55	Einstieg
LH 259	Tegel	Düsseldorf	A12	15:55	Gestartet
AB 6521	Tegel	Köln-Bonn	A13	16:00	Einstieg
3L 305	Tegel	Friedrichshafen	C40	16:00	Abfertigung
LH 278	Tegel	Köln-Bonn	A10	16:10	Einstieg
LH 207	Tegel	Frankfurt	A08	16:15	Einstieg
AB 6419	Tegel	Nürnberg	C48-C57	16:20	Abfertigung
BA 985	Tegel	London LHR	A04	16:25	Abfertigung
FR 8545	Schönefeld	London STN	A08	16:25	Einstieg

Sprachinfo

1 **Indirekte Fragen** *Indirect questions*

A polite way to ask a question in German – for instance when you enquire in a shop – is to use what is called in English an indirect question. Look at the following examples:

direct:	Was kostet der Flug?
indirect:	Können Sie mir sagen, was der Flug kostet?
direct:	Wann kommt die Maschine an?
indirect:	Wissen Sie, wann die Maschine ankommt?

As you can see, an indirect clause is often preceded by an introductory question, e.g. **Können Sie mir sagen, ...?** **Wissen Sie, ...?**

Direct questions which start with a verb and not a question word (**wo, wann, was,** etc.) add **ob** *whether* when transformed into an indirect question:

direct: Gibt es einen Flug nach 19.00 Uhr?
indirect: Wissen Sie, ob es einen Flug nach 19.00 Uhr gibt?

Note that in indirect questions, the verb is usually placed in last position.

There are three examples where **ob** *is used in* ***Aufnahme*** *1. Can you find them?*

2 Konjunktiv II (a) *Imperfect subjunctive (a)*

You might have wondered what form the verbs **wäre** and **hätte** are. They are examples of the subjunctive form in German called **Konjunktiv II.**

Konjunktiv II is mainly used for two purposes:

1 to indicate what might happen:

Dann wäre ich erst gegen 9.00 Uhr im Büro.	*Then I wouldn't be at the office till about 9.00 am.*

2 to add a degree of politeness:

Könnten Sie mir helfen?	*Could you help me?*

Note that verbs in the **Konjunktiv II** form frequently introduce indirect questions:

Könnten Sie mir sagen, wie spät es ist?

For more details look at the grammar section.

Übung 3 Nicht so formell, bitte!

Put the verbs in the subjunctive back into the present tense form.

Beispiel: Könnte ich Montag früh zurückfliegen? →
Kann ich Montag früh zurückfliegen?

a Wäre es möglich, die Spätmaschine zu nehmen?
b Ich müsste noch mal mit dem Reisebüro sprechen.
c Dürfte ich Ihr Telefon benutzen?
d Wissen Sie, wie teuer es mit dem Taxi wäre?
e Könnten Sie mir sagen, wo man in Berlin gut ausgehen kann?
f Hättet ihr Lust, mit ins Kino zu kommen?

Übung 4 Sagen Sie es anders!

i While on a holiday in Berlin, Caroline needs to put her knowledge of indirect questions to the test. Help her to re-formulate the following questions by using **Entschuldigung, könnten Sie mir sagen, ...** and an indirect question.

Beispiel: Wo ist die nächste Post? →
Entschuldigung, könnten Sie mir sagen, wo die nächste Post ist?

a Wie weit ist es bis in die Stadtmitte?
b Was kostet eine Tageskarte für die U-Bahn?
c Wie komme ich am schnellsten nach Charlottenburg?
d Gibt es hier in der Nähe eine Touristeninformation?
e Ist das hier vorne eigentlich die Gedächtniskirche?
f Wo kann man hier in der Nähe gut essen gehen?

ii Unfortunately none of the people asked were from Berlin. Answer each question for them, starting with the phrase **Es tut mir leid, aber ich weiß nicht, ...**

Beispiel: Wo ist die nächste Post? →
Es tut mir leid, aber ich weiß nicht, wo die nächste Post ist.

Aufnahme 2

CD2, TR 2, 3:37

Und wie komme ich zu meinem Hotel?

Am Flughafen Tegel in Berlin fragt Silke an der Information, wie sie am besten zu ihrem Hotel kommt.

Hören Sie sich den Dialog an und unterstreichen Sie die richtige Antwort.

Übung 5

a Silke sagt: „Ich habe/hatte/hätte eine Frage, bitte."
b Vom Flughafen fährt die Buslinie 108/109/110 zum Bahnhof Zoo.
c Mit dem Taxi wäre es ungefähr/mindestens/wahrscheinlich das Zehnfache.
d Ihr Hotel liegt in der Güntherstraße/Goethestraße/Güntzelstraße.
e Vom Bahnhof Zoo sind es noch zwei/drei/vier U-Bahnstationen.
f Die Bushaltestelle ist cirka 50 Meter auf der linken/rechten Seite.
g Eine Fahrkarte kann man im Bus/am Automaten/am Schalter kaufen.

QUICK VOCAB

mit der 109 *The gender is feminine, as this is an abbreviation for* **die Buslinie 109.**
Bahnhof Zoo *Short for* **Bahnhof Zoologischer Garten**, *a major intersection of the mainline railway, the* **U-Bahn** *and the* **S-Bahn**.
das Gepäck *luggage*
Es lohnt sich (nicht). *It's (not) worth it.*
cirka *about*
die Bushaltestelle (-n) *bus stop*
lösen *to buy, obtain (a ticket)*

Sprachinfo

Wegbeschreibungen und Präpositionen *Directions and prepositions*

When giving or asking for directions, prepositions are very important.

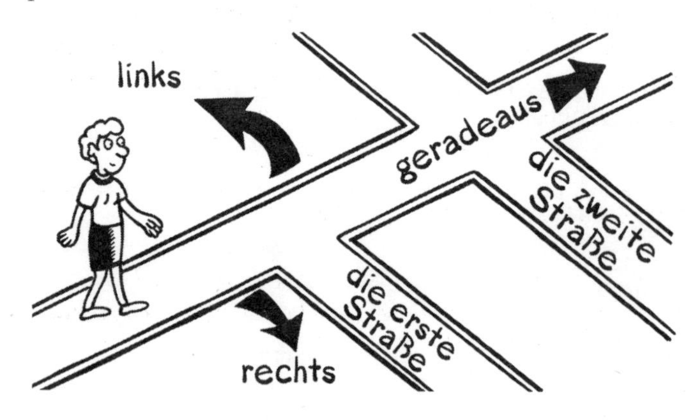

Here are some points to remember:

1 When asking for a location or building you often need to use **zu**:

Wie komme ich **zum** *Bahnhof?*

If you are actually entering a location or building you usually use **in**:

Gehen wir **ins** *Kino?*

2 You probably remember that prepositions require a certain case.

The following ***always*** need the accusative or the dative case:

accusative: **bis, durch, für, gegen, ohne, um, entlang**
dative: **aus, bei, mit, nach, seit, von, zu, gegenüber, außer**

3 There are also a number of prepositions, called **Wechselpräpositionen,** which take the accusative case when movement towards a place is implied, and the dative case when the emphasis is on location or position:

acc./dative	**an, auf, hinter, in, neben, über, unter, vor, zwischen**

Here are some examples:

accusative (**wohin?**/*where to?*)	*dative* (**wo?**/*where?*)
Gehen Sie auf die linke Seite. Wie komme ich ins Stadtzentrum?	Das Museum ist auf der linken Seite. Im Stadtzentrum kann man gut essen.

Insight: Wechselpräpositionen

Bei Wechselpräpositionen wie **an, auf, in** usw. gibt es zwei Möglichkeiten, wie man erkennen kann, ob sie den Akkusativ oder den Dativ brauchen:

1 Verben

Bestimmte Verben implizieren Bewegung und brauchen den Akkusativ. Dazu gehören:

gehen, kommen, überqueren, fahren: *Ich gehe ins Kino.*

Mit den meisten anderen Verben (**sein, liegen, sich befinden, essen** usw.) brauchen Wechselpräpositionen den Dativ: *Ich bin im Kino.*

2 Wohin oder wo?

Fragt man **wohin**, braucht man den Akkusativ: *Wohin gehst du? Ins Kino.*

Fragt man **wo**, brauchen Wechselpräpositionen den Dativ: *Wo bist du? Im Kino.*

Übung 6 Akkusativ oder Dativ?

Identify (i) the preposition in the following sentences and (ii) explain why the accusative or dative case is used.

Beispiel: Die Kneipe ist direkt neben dem Kino.

→ **i** The preposition is **neben.**
→ **ii** Because we're talking here about position (exemplified by **ist** *is*), not movement, the preposition requires the **dative.**

a Ist das der Weg zum Bahnhof?
b Gehen Sie über die Kreuzung und dann immer geradeaus.
c Wie komme ich am besten in die Stadt?
d Die Touristeninformation befindet sich im Bahnhof.
e Die Kneipe ist direkt neben der Kirche.
f Vom Flughafen nehmen Sie am besten den Zug.

Insight: Berlin

Nach dem Fall der Mauer 1989 und der Wiedervereinigung Deutschlands 1990 wurde Berlin zur Hauptstadt der Bundesrepublik Deutschland gewählt. 1999 zog auch das deutsche Parlament, der Bundestag, wieder nach Berlin und hat seinen Sitz im alten Reichstag. Der britische Architekt Norman Foster hat dem Reichtag mit einer modernen Glaskuppel ein neues Design gegeben.

Berlin ist heute eine multikulturelle Metropole mit etwa 3,4 Millionen Einwohnern. Von einem spektakulären Nachtleben über erstklassige Opernhäuser, Gallerien und Museen bis hin zu hervorragenden Sportstätten, Kinos und Geschäften bietet die Stadt für jeden Geschmack etwas.

Aufnahme 3

Berlin ist eine Reise wert!

Frau Heine ist Touristenführerin in Berlin. In einem Radiointerview erzählt sie, wie sie nach Berlin kam, warum es ihr hier gefällt und welche Tipps sie Touristen geben würde.

Hören Sie sich den Dialog an.

Übung 7 Beantworten Sie die Fragen.

a Seit wann lebt Frau Heine in Berlin?
b Was mag sie an den Berlinern?
c Wann wurde Berlin zu einer wirklichen Weltstadt?
d Was folgte nach den „Goldenen Zwanzigern"?
e Welche Kunst kann man im Brücke-Museum sehen?
f Was bietet Berlin Leuten, die zum Einkaufen kommen?

Hier sind einige Schlüsselwörter.

QUICK VOCAB

die Eigenschaft (-en) *characteristic, feature*
die Möglichkeit (-en) *possibility*
bieten *to offer*
die Teilung (-en) *division*
Es hängt davon ab ... *It depends on ...*
edel *noble*

🔊 CD2, TR 2, 6:24

Journalist Frau Heine, Sie arbeiten als Touristenführerin in Berlin. Sind Sie denn eigentlich auch eine richtige Berlinerin?

Frau Heine Nein, ich bin in Nürnberg geboren, lebe aber schon seit über 20 Jahren in Berlin. Ich habe damals an der FU, an der Freien Universität, studiert und mir hat Berlin so gut gefallen, dass ich dann nach meinem Studium gleich hier geblieben bin.

Journalist Was hat Ihnen denn so gut gefallen?

Frau Heine Nun, zum einen die Berliner selber. Ich finde, die Leute haben Humor und sagen offen, was sie denken. Das ist eine Eigenschaft, die ich sehr mag. Gut, manchmal können sie auch etwas unfreundlich wirken, aber im Allgemeinen sind die Menschen humorvoll und auch tolerant.

Journalist Hat sich denn Berlin in den Jahren stark verändert?

Frau Heine Ja, das kann man wohl sagen. Aber das war schon immer typisch für diese Stadt. Sehen Sie, im 19. Jahrhundert war Berlin eigentlich nur ein großes Dorf. Erst nach dem 1. Weltkrieg – in den „Goldenen Zwanzigern"– wurde es zu einer wirklichen Weltstadt. Danach folgten 12 Jahre Diktatur der Nationalsozialisten. Und nach dem Krieg der Wiederaufbau, 1961 der Mauerbau und die Teilung. Seit dem Fall der Mauer 1989 ist Berlin aber wieder das wirkliche Zentrum von Deutschland.

Journalist Was würden Sie denn einem Touristen empfehlen?

Frau Heine Tja, es hängt davon ab, welche Interessen jemand hat. Wer sich für Kultur interessiert, für den bietet die Stadt natürlich fantastische Möglichkeiten: Museen, wie die Neue Nationalgalerie oder das Brücke-Museum, wo man expressionistische Kunst zeigt. Wer sich für Geschichte oder für Preußen interessiert, kann zum Beispiel das Deutsche Museum besuchen. Und wer nur zum Einkaufen kommt, dem bietet Berlin fast alles – von eleganten Kaufhäusern wie dem KaDeWe und edlen Boutiquen, bis zu alternativen Läden. Und die etwas jüngeren – die können nach Kreuzberg oder zum Prenzlauer Berg gehen, wo es viele Szenekneipen, Restaurants und Clubs gibt.

Übung 8 Wie heißt das?

Finden Sie im Dialog die deutschen Wörter für:

a history
b village
c Prussia
d the Great War
e expressionist art
f 'Golden Twenties'
g re-buildung
h fall of the Wall
i shopping
j 'in' pubs

Übung 9

Lesen Sie den Text noch einmal und ergänzen Sie.

a Frau Heine ist nach ihrem Studium …
b Sie schätzt an den Berlinern, dass …
c Sie erklärt, dass Berlin erst nach …
d Nach den „Goldenen Zwanzigern" folgten …
e Seit 1961 gab es …
f Sie sagt, dass man im Brücke-Museum …
g Wer zum Shoppen kommt, dem …
h Am Prenzlauer Berg gibt es …

Grammatik

1 Indirekte Fragen *Indirect questions*

You've already seen how indirect questions can be used as a politer way of requesting information:

Könnten Sie mir sagen, wann der nächste Zug nach Berlin fährt?	*Could you tell me when the next train leaves for Berlin?*

You also saw in **Übung 4 ii** that indirect questions are often used in reply to requests for information:

Es tut mir leid, aber ich weiß nicht, wann der nächste Zug nach Berlin fährt.	*I'm sorry, but I don't know when the next train leaves for Berlin.*

Here is a reminder of the main points:

Indirect questions are introduced either by a question word (**wann**? **warum**? **wie**?, etc.) or by **ob** *whether*. As with most subordinating clauses, the verb goes to the end of the clause. And don't forget to put a comma at the start of the indirect question.

2 Konjunktiv II *Imperfect subjunctive*

Note that the **Konjunktiv II** is most often used with the verbs **haben, sein** and **werden** and with the modal verbs.

Here are the forms for **haben, sein** and **werden:**

	would have	*would be*	*would (+ second verb)*
ich, er/sie/es	hätte	wäre	würde
du	hättest	wärest	würdest
ihr	hättet	wäret	würdet
wir, Sie, sie	hätten	wären	würden

The forms for the modal verbs are as follows:

	might	*could*	*should like (to)*
ich, er/sie/es	dürfte	könnte	möchte
du	dürftest	könntest	möchtest
ihr	dürftet	könntet	möchtet
wir, Sie, sie	dürften	könnten	möchten

	would have to	*should*	*would want (to)*
ich, er/sie/es	müsste	sollte	wollte
du	müsstest	solltest	wolltest

ihr	müsstet	solltet	wolltet
wir, Sie, sie	müssten	sollten	wollten

You will recall from the **Sprachinfo** that the **Konjunktiv II** is used to say what might happen and also to add a degree of politeness:

a **Dann hätte ich zu viel Arbeit.** *Then I'd have too much work.*
Das wäre nett von Ihnen. *That would be nice of you.*
Dann würde ich nicht gehen. *Then I wouldn't go.*

b **Dürfte ich einen Bonbon haben?** *Might I have a sweet?*
Möchtest du ein Eis? *Would you like an ice-cream?*
Du solltest mehr Sport treiben. *You should do more sport.*

3 Präpositionen und Fälle *Prepositions and cases*

It is important to know which cases prepositions require in German. Here is an overview.

Accusative	**bis**	*until*
	durch	*through*
	für	*for*
	gegen	*against, around*
	ohne	*without*
	um	*around, at*
Dative	**aus**	*from, out of*
	außer	*apart from*
	bei	*at, near*
	gegenüber	*opposite*
	mit	*with, by (for means of transport)*
	nach	*after, to*
	seit	*since, for*
	von	*from*
	zu	*to*

Accusative or dative	**an**	*at, on*
	auf	*on*
	hinter	*behind*
	in	*in, into*
	neben	*near, next to*
	über	*over, above, across*
	unter	*under, among*
	vor	*in front of, before*
	zwischen	*between*
Genitive	**trotz**	*despite, in spite of*
	während	*during*
	wegen	*because of, due to*
	(an)statt	*instead of*

TESTEN SIE SICH!

A) MEHR ÜBUNGEN

1 Was fehlt?

Ergänzen Sie:

a Das Opernhaus liegt gegenüber d__ Humboldt-Universität.
b Gehen Sie über d__ Kreuzung bis z__ Goethe-Platz.
c Das Café Marina? Das liegt gleich hinter d__ Kirche.
d Z__ Museum für Deutsche Geschichte wollen Sie? Da fahren Sie am besten mit d__ U-Bahn.
e Gehen Sie hier um d__ Ecke. Da finden Sie auf d__ rechten Seite einen Supermarkt.
f Die Buchhandlung liegt zwischen d__ Bäckerei und d__ Secondhandgeschäft.
g Wenn Sie hier durch d__ Tiergarten gehen, stehen Sie fast direkt vor d__ Reichstag.

2 Und jetzt Sie!

With the assistance of the English prompts and the map overleaf, play the role of the person giving directions. Note that in German, street names ending in **-er** do not change their endings (Konstanzer Straße, Düsseldorfer Straße, etc.) but street names ending in **-isch** take the normal adjectival endings (e.g. **Gehen Sie rechts in die Bayerische Straße; Wir stehen hier in der Bayerischen Straße**).

Tourist	Entschuldigen Sie, bitte. Wie komme ich zur Pariser Straße?
Sie	*Tell him that you're now in Brandenburgische Straße. Ask whether he can see the traffic lights at the next crossroads.*
Tourist	Ja, die sehe ich.

CD2, TR 2, 8:45

Sie	Tell him to go right there into Düsseldorfer Straße. After about 300 metres he'll come to Konstanzer Straße. He should go over Konstanzer Straße, straight on for perhaps 300 metres till he gets to Bayerische Straße. Go left at this crossroads into Bayerische Straße.
Tourist	Moment, bitte. Was sagten Sie? Hier rechts, dann geradeaus bis zur Düsseldorfer Straße, über die Düsseldorfer Straße und weiter geradeaus bis zur Bayerischen Straße. Dann rechts.
Sie	Tell him, no, not right but left into Bayerische Straße. Then about one kilometre further on he'll come to Pariser Straße.
Tourist	Vielen Dank.
Sie	You say that he's welcome.

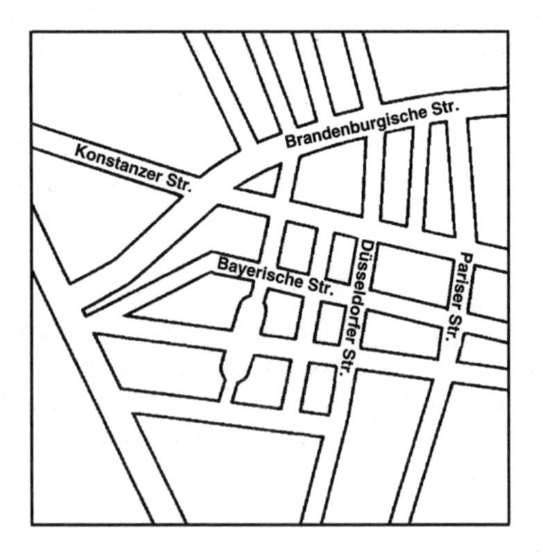

3 Berlin – früher und heute

Hier ist eine kurze Geschichte von Berlin. Welches Wort fehlt? Setzen Sie ein.

„Goldenen Zwanziger"   Mauer   Einwohnern   Stadt
Diktatur   Nachtleben   Nationalsozialisten   Wiederaufbau
Jahrhundert   Weltkrieg   Mauerbau   Angebot   Hauptstadt

Berlin ist eine alte (a) ***Stadt*** und wurde 1337 gegründet. Zu einer wirklichen Weltstadt wurde Berlin aber erst nach dem Ersten (b) .... Noch im 19. (c) .... war es lange ein großes Dorf, bis nach 1870 die Industrialisierung in Deutschland begann.

Die Zwanzigerjahre des vorherigen Jahrhunderts werden oft als die (d) .... bezeichnet. 1933 kamen die (e) .... an die Macht und es folgten 12 Jahre (f) .... Nach dem Ende des Zweiten Weltkrieges folgte der (g) .... Deutschlands und Berlins.

Ein anderes wichtiges Ereignis war der (h) .... im Jahre 1961. Für 27 Jahre war die Stadt getrennt. Seit dem Fall der (i) .... 1989 ist Berlin wieder das wirkliche Zentrum von Deutschland und seit 1990 ist es auch die offizielle (j) .... des wiedervereinigten Deutschlands.

Heute ist Berlin eine moderne, multikulturelle Metropole mit etwa 3,4 Millionen (k) .... Von einem spektakulären (l) .... über ein erstklassiges kulturelles (m) .... bis hin zu hervorragenden Einkaufsmöglichkeiten bietet die Stadt für jeden Geschmack etwas.

B) LESETEXT

Kurzreise nach Berlin

On the next two pages there is information advertising a short break in Berlin for people from the Osnabrück area. Read the text to find out what is on offer, paying special attention to the following points:

a What is included in the price of the trip.
b How the hotel is described and what it has to offer.
c What is on the itinerary for the three days in Berlin.

QUICK VOCAB

der EZ-Zuschlag (¨e) *single room supplement*
die Leistung (-en) *here: service*
die Übernachtung (-en) *night's stay*
die Versicherung *insurance*
die Stimmung (-en) *atmosphere, ambience*
aus | zeichnen *to characterise, mark out*
der Reiseverlauf (¨e) *itinerary*
zur freien Verfügung stehen *to be free/freely available*
der Bezug (¨e) *(+ gen.) moving into*
vermitteln *to provide*
ehemalig *former*
gestalten *to arrange*
zahlreich *numerous*
die Kuppel (-n) *cupola, dome*
einzigartig *unique*
betrachten *to observe*

Eine Kurzreise in die Bundeshauptstadt

Reiseinformationen
Reisetermin: 17.–19. Oktober
Reisedauer: 3 Tage
Reisepreis: 215,00 € pro Person
EZ-Zuschlag: 76,00 € pro Person

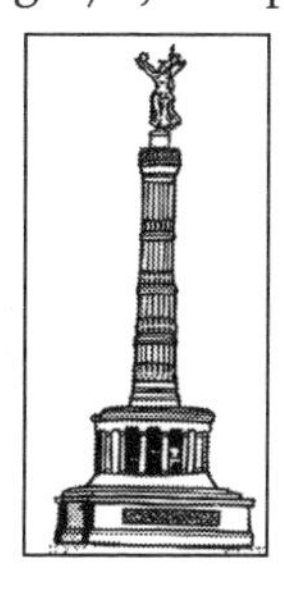

Unsere Leistungen
- Fahrt im modernen Komfortreisebus
- Frühstück auf der Hinreise
- 2 Übernachtungen im „Scandotel Castor"
- 2 × Frühstücksbüfett
- Stadtrundfahrt Berlin
- Besuch des Reichstages
- Schiffsfahrt
- Eintrittsgelder
- Versicherung

Hotel

Sie wohnen im 3-Sterne Hotel „Scandotel Castor" in zentraler Lage, nur wenige Gehminuten vom Kurfürstendamm und dem legendären Kaufhaus des Westens (KaDeWe) entfernt.

Die gute Lage, die freundliche Atmosphäre und die persönliche Stimmung zeichnen dieses Stadthotel aus.

Die 78 Zimmer sind hell und komfortabel eingerichtet und haben Dusche/WC, Radio, Telefon, Kabel-TV, Minibar und Haarfön.

Reiseverlauf

1. Tag **Anreise nach Berlin/Hotelbezug/Freizeit**
07.00 Uhr Abfahrt ZOB (Zentraler Omnibusbahnhof), Eisenbahnstraße, Osnabrück.
Sie reisen über Hannover und Magdeburg nach Berlin. Nach dem Bezug Ihres Hotels, steht Ihnen der Nachmittag zur freien Verfügung. Übernachtung in Berlin.

2. Tag Stadtrundfahrt
Eine intensive Stadtrundfahrt vermittelt Ihnen heute einen Eindruck von den Dimensionen der Stadt und ihren vielen Gesichtern. Sie lernen nicht nur das westliche Zentrum mit dem Kurfürstendamm kennen, sondern auch die „Neue Mitte“ und den ehemaligen Ostteil der Stadt. Gestalten Sie den Abend nach Ihren persönlichen Vorlieben. Gern sind wir Ihnen bei der Reservierung einer der zahlreichen Veranstaltungen in der Weltstadt behilflich. Übernachtung in Berlin.

3. Tag Besuch des Reichstagsgebäudes/Schifffahrt/Heimreise
Am Vormittag besuchen Sie den Deutschen Bundestag im Reichstagsgebäude. Sie haben hier die Gelegenheit, die weltberühmte Kuppel des Bauwerks zu besichtigen. Anschließend bieten Ihnen Berlins Wasserwege eine einzigartige Möglichkeit, die Innenstadt mit Ihren Sehenswürdigkeiten vom Schiff aus zu betrachten. Mit vielen neuen Eindrücken und Erlebnissen reisen Sie dann zurück nach Hause.

CHECKLISTE

Now that you have completed Unit 7, can you

1. make travel arrangements? ☐
2. make polite requests? ☐
3. ask for and give directions? ☐
4. talk about Berlin and its attractions? ☐
5. use prepositions with the appropriate cases? ☐
6. form indirect questions? ☐
7. understand the information contained in a travel brochure? ☐

8

Typisch deutsch?

In this unit you will learn how to
- ***discuss stereotypes and prejudices***
- ***make comparisons***
- ***report what others have said***
- ***form and use reported speech and Konjunktiv I***
- ***apply adjectival endings***

Aufnahme 1

Darren aus Großbritannien und Martin aus Deutschland unterhalten sich über typisch deutsche Eigenschaften. Was ist Darren in Deutschland aufgefallen?

Hören Sie sich die Höraufnahme an und machen Sie dann Übung 1.

CD2, TR 3, 0:33

Martin Ich habe gehört, deine Mutter ist Deutsche. Hast du denn schon früher mal in Deutschland gelebt?

Darren Nein, ich bin zum ersten Mal hier in Deutschland. Meine Mutter hat aber meistens Deutsch mit mir gesprochen und mir auch viel über deutsche Geschichte, Kultur und das tägliche Leben erzählt, worüber ich natürlich sehr froh bin. Aber weißt du, besonders neugierig war ich darauf, diese so genannten typisch deutschen Eigenschaften zu entdecken.

Martin Welche Eigenschaften meinst du denn damit?

Darren	Naja, zum Beispiel hat meine Mutter immer gesagt, dass kein Volk so fleißig sei wie die Deutschen, das würde man ja schon daran sehen, dass sie so früh morgens aufstehen. Und natürlich wäre das Wirtschaftswunder nie möglich gewesen, wenn die Deutschen nicht so arbeitsam wären!
Martin	Das glaube ich dir gern. Ja, und hat dir deine Mutter auch erzählt, dass die Deutschen so ordnungsliebend und sauber sind?
Darren	Genau! Aber da muss ich dir sagen, das habe ich auch festgestellt. Ich finde, die Häuser und Straßen in Deutschland sehen viel sauberer und gepflegter aus als in England.
Martin	Ja, manchmal habe ich das Gefühl, dass wir es ein bisschen übertreiben. Hast du denn sonst noch Unterschiede bemerkt?
Darren	Mir ist besonders aufgefallen, dass man hier in Deutschland viel mehr Aufwand betreibt, wenn es um gewisse Anlässe geht, wie zum Beispiel Weihnachten, Ostern und so weiter. Die Leute hier machen sich so viel Arbeit mit den ganzen Vorbereitungen für das Fest, wie Dekoration, Essen kochen, Kuchen und Plätzchen backen. Und auch bei Geburtstagen wird viel mehr gefeiert, und die Leute schicken sich Karten, auch wenn sie nicht zusammen feiern. Das ist in England weniger der Fall.

Übung 1 Richtig oder falsch?

Korrigieren Sie die falschen Aussagen.

a Darren war schon oft in Deutschland.
b Seine Mutter hat ihm viel über das Leben in Deutschland erzählt.
c Sie sagte ihm, dass die Deutschen sehr fleißig seien.
d Außerdem erklärte sie ihm, dass die meisten Leute spät aufstehen.
e Darren findet die Häuser in Deutschland ähnlich wie in Großbritannien.

f Ihm ist aufgefallen, dass die Menschen weniger feiern.
g Auch schickt man sich weniger Karten.

QUICK VOCAB

die Eigenschaft (-en) *characteristic*
arbeitsam *hard-working*
das Wirtschaftswunder (-) *the economic miracle*
ordnungsliebend *liking to see things neat and tidy*
gepflegt *well-kept*
übertreiben *to exaggerate*
der Aufwand *expenditure (in time/money)*
Aufwand betreiben *to make an effort*
der Anlass (-¨e) *occasion*

Übung 2 Wie sagt man das?

Lesen Sie den Text und finden Sie ein passendes Adjektiv.

Beispiel: die Leute arbeiten viel → sie sind ***fleißig***

a eine Person ist glücklich – eine Person ist ______
b die Deutschen arbeiten hart – sie sind ______
c jemand macht, was im Gesetz steht – jemand ist ______
d es gibt keinen Dreck – es ist ______
e man kümmert sich um den Garten – der Garten sieht ______ aus.

Insight: Das Wirtschaftswunder (The economic miracle)

Nach dem Ende des Zweiten Weltkrieges 1945 befand sich Deutschland in einem totalen Chaos. In vielen Städten waren Häuser, Straßen und die Fabriken zerstört. Die meisten Experten glaubten, dass es 30–40 Jahre dauern würde, bevor sich die Situation in Deutschland wieder „normalisieren" würde.

Aber schon weniger als 10 Jahre später war der Lebensstandard wieder sehr hoch, lag die Arbeitslosigkeit bei unter 1% und war Deutschland eine der führenden Industrienationen der Welt. Deshalb sprechen viele Leute von einem „Wirtschaftswunder".

Sprachinfo

Der Komparativ *The comparative*

Remember that the comparative in German is formed by adding **-er** to the adjective:

klein – Die Schweiz ist viel klein**er** als Österreich.
hektisch – Das Leben in der Stadt ist hektisch**er** als auf dem Land.

Many adjectives with only one syllable also need an umlaut in the comparative:

kalt → kälter, dumm → dümmer, groß → größer

A few adjectives and adverbs are slightly irregular:

gut → besser, hoch → höher, gern → lieber, viel → mehr

Another way of comparing things is to use the expressions **ähnlich ... wie ...** (*similarly ... to*), **genauso ... wie ...** (*just as ... as*) or **nicht so ... wie ...** (*not as ... as ...*):

Ist vieles in Deutschland nicht ähnlich teuer wie in Großbritannien?
Die Fahrt mit der Bahn ist genauso teuer wie mit dem Flugzeug.
Die Deutschen sind aber nicht so arbeitsam wie viele denken.

Übung 3 Stereotype, Stereotype!

Stereotype gibt es nicht nur zwischen verschiedenen Nationen, sondern auch in einem Land. Die folgenden Beispiele stammen aus Deutschland. Setzen Sie die Adjektive in den Komparativ.

Viele Leute denken,

a die Schwaben sind **fleißiger** als die anderen Süddeutschen. (fleißig)
b die Leute aus Bayern sind ______ als die Norddeutschen. (gastfreundlich)

c die Menschen aus Hamburg sind ______ als Ostdeutsche. (tolerant)
d Leute aus Ostdeutschland sind ______ als Leute aus Berlin. (herzlich)
e Berliner sind ______ als die Sachsen. (weltoffen)
f Menschen aus Sachsen sind ______ als Schwaben. (humorvoll)

Gibt es ähnliche Stereotype auch in Ihrem Land?

Sprachinfo

Adjektivendungen *Adjectival endings*

Adjectival endings are often seen as a difficult area in German. The problem is that they might occur in four different ways in one sentence, each time needing slightly different endings. Note the four different categories:

1 The adjective is not preceded by an article or possessive:
Trinkst du gern *deutsches* Bier?
2 The adjective follows an indefinite article or a possessive:
Sie führt ein *interessantes* Leben.
3 The adjective is preceded by a definite article:
Der *neue* Minister kommt aus Köln.
4 The adjective stands on its own:
Die Leute sind sehr *freundlich*.

The last example is the easiest one, as no endings are needed. In the other three instances you have to consider the gender, case and which – if any – article is used. But it is not as complicated as you might think, as the endings are quite often the same across categories and cases. If you practise, you will eventually get a feel for what is correct.

Here you can see how the endings for the **definite articles** go:

	masculine	*feminine*	*neuter*	*plural*
nom.	der nett**e** Mann	die nett**e** Frau	das nett**e** Kind	die nett**en** Leute

	masculine	*feminine*	*neuter*	*plural*
acc.	den nett**en** Mann	die nett**e** Frau	das nett**e** Kind	die nett**en** Leute
gen.	des nett**en** Mannes	der nett**en** Frau	des nett**en** Kindes	der nett**en** Leute
dat.	dem nett**en** Mann(e)	der nett**en** Frau	dem nett**en** Kind	den nett**en** Leuten

Insight: Adjektivendungen – bestimmter Artikel

Adjektivendungen in Deutsch wirken auf den ersten Blick sehr kompliziert. Doch gibt es Tricks, wie man sie leichter lernen kann:

1 Alle Endungen nach dem **bestimmten Artikel** (siehe Tabelle oben) sind entweder **-en** oder **-e**.
2 **-en** braucht man für alle Pluralformen, alle Endungen im Dativ und Genitiv und im Akkusativ für männliche Nomen.
3 **-e** braucht man für die übrigen Formen (Nominativ und Akkusativ Singular außer für männliche Nomen).

Übung 4 Adjektivendungen

Ergänzen Sie die richtigen Adjektivendungen nach dem bestimmten Artikel (**-e** oder **-en**). Alle Beispiele sind aus Lektionen dieses Buches.

a Die deutsch... Wirtschaft kann nicht alle Akademiker beschäftigen.
b Reisen ist einer der attraktivst... Aspekte bei meiner Arbeit.
c Ich bin gern auf dem Laufenden, was die neuest... Filme angeht.
d Das Theater finden Sie auf der link... Seite.
e Als Radfahrer muss man die ganz... Abgase von den viel... Autos einatmen.
f Berlin ist wieder das wirklich... Zentrum von Deutschland.
g Für die jünger... Leute gibt es am Prenzlauer Berg viele Szenekneipen.

Aufnahme 2

CD2, TR 3, 4:38

Ausbildung in Deutschland und Großbritannien – ein Vergleich

Hören Sie sich den Dialog an und unterstreichen Sie die richtige Antwort.

Übung 5

a Darren meint, dass Deutsche und Engländer ähnlich/unterschiedlich/sehr verschieden sind.
b Er sagt, die Ausbildung in Deutschland ist schnell/zu lang/gründlich.
c Leute ohne Abitur bekommen einen guten/schlechten Start im Berufsleben.
d In Großbritannien ist es genauso/ähnlich/weniger streng geregelt.
e In Deutschland fördert man auch Sport/Mathematik/Fremdsprachen.
f Martin meint, dass die Deutschen viel/wenig Wert auf den Doktortitel legen.
g Er glaubt, dass der Leistungsdruck in der Schule hoch/nicht so hoch ist.

Übung 6 Sagen Sie's auf Deutsch!

CD2, TR 3, 9:16

Lesen Sie jetzt die Transkription des Dialogs (am Ende des Buches), finden Sie die deutschen Ausdrücke und überprüfen Sie dann Ihre Antworten auf der Höraufnahme.

a Just take training in Germany.
b So much emphasis is put on qualifications.

c The other side of the coin is, however, the pressure to work harder.
d I don't know where this will lead.
e I think that the Germans generally tackle their leisure activities much more systematically.
f There is certainly a grain of truth in that.
g You don't strike me as the typical German.

QUICK VOCAB

die Gründlichkeit *thoroughness*
gründlich *thorough(ly)*
nimm doch nur mal ... *just take ...*
regeln *to regulate, settle*
fördern *to promote, support, foster*
Wert legen auf *to attach importance to*
die Kehrseite der Medaille *the other side of the coin*
die Leistungsanforderung (-en) *demands on performance*
der Leistungsdruck *pressure to perform, work harder*
sich erstrecken auf *(+ acc.) to stretch to*
ein Körnchen Wahrheit *a grain of truth*
Ausnahmen bestätigen die Regel *the exception proves the rule*

Sprachinfo

Indirekte Rede und Konjunktiv I *Reported speech and present subjunctive*

If you want to report what someone said – for example, if Marco said, 'The Bavarians are very hospitable' – you use what is called reported speech: Marco said that the Bavarians were very hospitable.

German often uses a specific form of the verb for this purpose:

Meine Mutter hat immer gesagt, dass kein Volk so fleißig sei wie die Deutschen.	*My mother has always said that no nation is as hard-working as the Germans.*
Er meinte, er komme morgen.	*He said he would come tomorrow.*

This is a subjunctive form of the verb and is called **Konjunktiv I.** You form it by adding the appropriate endings to the stem of a verb, whether the verb is regular or irregular:

ich komm**e**	wir komm**en**
du komm**est**	ihr komm**et**
Sie komm**en**	Sie komm**en**
er/sie/es komm**e**	sie komm**en**

The only exception is the verb **sein:**

ich sei	wir seien
du seist	ihr seid
er/sie/es sei	Sie/sie seien

If you use **dass** in reported speech, remember that the verb needs to go to the end: Marco hat gesagt, **dass** die Bayern sehr gastfreundlich **seien.**

For more information, see the grammar section later in this unit.

Übung 7 Was hat er gesagt?

Setzen Sie die folgenden Sätze in die indirekte Rede und benutzen Sie **dass + Konjunktiv I.**

Beispiel: Carola sagt: „Ich will nächstes Jahr nach New York fliegen." →
Sie sagt, dass sie nächstes Jahr nach New York fliegen wolle.

a Lothar sagt: „Das Essen in Italien schmeckt fantastisch."
b Herr Martinez meint: „In Berlin kann man sehr gut einkaufen."
c Frau Knoob findet: „Hamburg hat einen wirklich tollen Hafen."
d Gabrielas Meinung ist: „Schottland ist wirklich interessant."
e Frau Clemens findet: „In Brasilien gibt es die schönsten Strände."

Aufnahme 3

CD2, TR 3, 10:21

Vorurteile – und die Realität

Helga war im Urlaub in Großbritannien. Sie erzählt über die Klischees, die Deutsche gegenüber den Engländern haben, aber auch was Engländer über die Deutschen denken. Bevor Sie die Audioaufnahme anhören, lesen Sie bitte die folgenden Aussagen. Entscheiden Sie, ob diese Vorurteile auf England oder Deutschland zutreffen. Hören Sie sich dann den Dialog an und kreuzen Sie die Stereotype an, die Sie hören können. Hatten Sie recht?

Übung 8

Here are some commonly held views about the Germans and the British. Indicate which statements refer to which nationality. Then listen to the recording and say whether or not they appear in **Aufnahme** 3. Check your answers in the text. (E = Englisch, D = Deutsch.)

	E/D	im Dialog?
a Es ist ein kaltes, verregnetes Land.	E	☑
b Die Leute sind sehr korrekt.	☐	☐
c Dort gibt es nur Fish und Chips.	☐	☐
d Man kommt schwer mit den Leuten in Kontakt.	☐	☐
e Sie tragen alle Lederhosen.	☐	☐
f Die Leute arbeiten sehr viel und stehen früh auf.	☐	☐
g Sie sind kühl und reserviert.	☐	☐
h Alles ist perfekt organisiert.	☐	☐

Karin Und wie hat es dir in England gefallen?

Helga Also, ich muss dir sagen, es war einfach super. Ich war erst eine Woche in London und bin dann für eine Woche nach Cornwall gefahren. London ist natürlich eine tolle Stadt und in Cornwall ist die Landschaft einfach fantastisch. Ich werde auf jeden Fall in meinem nächsten Urlaub wieder nach England fahren!

Karin Ach, ich kann mich aber erinnern, dass du zu Anfang recht kritisch warst, was England und die Engländer anbelangt. Erst hast du doch gemeint, dass England ein so kaltes und verregnetes Land sei, und dass man dort nichts außer Steak & Kidney Pie und Fish & Chips zu essen bekäme. Und von den Engländern hast du gesagt, sie seien so kühl und reserviert, dass man nie mit ihnen in Kontakt käme, erst recht nicht, wenn man ihre Art von Humor nicht versteht!

Helga Naja, das waren halt so die typischen Vorurteile, die man irgendwann mal aufgeschnappt hat. Ehrlich gesagt, ich habe so viele nette Leute kennen gelernt, mit denen ich mich großartig verstanden habe. Ein paarmal war ich zum Essen eingeladen und es war ausgezeichnet. Was das Wetter anbelangt, so ist es eigentlich fast so wie in Deutschland – natürlich kann man nicht gerade einen Badeurlaub dort verbringen ...

Karin Und hast du auch irgendwelche Vorurteile gegenüber den Deutschen bemerkt?

Helga Im Großen und Ganzen nicht.

Karin Da bin ich ja froh, dass das Bild der Deutschen nicht ganz so schlecht ist, wie man annehmen könnte!

Helga Naja, es gibt natürlich auch einige Klischees, die die Engländer über die Deutschen haben, genauso wie ich vorher über die Engländer und England!

Karin Was denn zum Beispiel?

Helga Ach, zum Beispiel die Vorstellung, dass alle Deutschen so sauber und korrekt seien, so früh aufstehen und so viel arbeiten würden. Außerdem hatten sie natürlich schon von der deutschen Gründlichkeit gehört.

Aber das Beste war, dass sie gedacht haben, die Deutschen würden sich von Bratwürsten mit Sauerkraut und Schweinebraten mit Klößen ernähren!

die Landschaft (-en) *scenery, landscape*
was ... anbelangt *as far as ... is concerned*
das Vorurteil (-e) *prejudice*
die Vorstellung (-en) *idea, notion*
das Sauerkraut *pickled cabbage*
der Schweinebraten (-) *roast pork*
der Kloß (-¨e) *dumpling*

QUICK VOCAB

Übung 9 Was erzählt Helga über ihren Urlaub in England?

Answer the following questions about Helga's impressions of England. Use reported speech and the **Konjunktiv I**, as in the example, to quote what she said.

Beispiel: Was sagt Helga über Cornwall? →
Sie sagt, dass die Landschaft in Cornwall einfach fantastisch sei.

a Was meint sie zu London?
b Was dachte sie anfangs über die Engländer?
c Was sagt sie über ihre eigenen Erfahrungen mit den Leuten?
d Was denken Engländer über die Deutschen?
e Wovon glauben sie, ernähren sich die Deutschen?

Übung 10

Lesen Sie den Text noch einmal und ergänzen Sie.

a Helga fand England ...
b Anfangs jedoch dachte sie, dass die Engländer ...
c Dann hat sie aber viele ...
d Das Wetter ist ...
e Sie sagt, viele Engländer denken alle Deutschen würden morgens ...

f Es gibt das Klischee, dass sich die Deutschen von Bratwürsten ...
g Im nächsten Urlaub ...

Grammatik

1 Adjektivendungen *Adjectival endings*

As mentioned in the **Sprachinfo**, there are four categories. You have already seen that adjectives standing on their own don't need any endings and you also practised adjectival endings after the definite article.

Here are the remaining two categories.

1 The adjective is *not* preceded by an article or possessive:

	masculine	*feminine*	*neuter*	*plural*
nom.	deutsch**er** Wein	englisch**e** Musik	kalt**es** Wetter	gut**e** Ideen
acc.	deutsch**en** Wein	englisch**e** Musik	kalt**es** Wetter	gut**e** Ideen
gen.	deutsch**en** Weines	englisch**er** Musik	kalt**en** Wetters	gut**en** Ideen
dat.	deutsch**em** Wein	englisch**er** Musik	kalt**em** Wetter	gut**en** Ideen

Note that in this category, in the absence of an article or possessive, the adjective takes the endings of the definite article:

Der Wein ist gut. → Deutscher Wein ist gut.
Das Wetter ist schlecht. → Schlechtes Wetter herrscht schon seit Tagen.
Bei d**em** Wetter bleibe ich zu Hause. → Bei kalt**em** Wetter bleibe ich zu Hause.

2 **The adjective follows an indefinite article or a possessive:**

	masculine	*feminine*	*neuter*	*plural*
nom.	ein alt**er** Mann	eine alt**e** Stadt	ein schön**es** Land	meine schön**en** Bücher
acc.	ein**en** alten Mann	eine alt**e** Stadt	ein schön**es** Land	meine schön**en** Bücher
gen.	eines alt**en** Mannes	einer alt**en** Stadt	eines schön**en** Landes	meiner schön**en** Bücher
dat.	einem alt**en** Mann	einer alt**en** Stadt	einem schön**en** Land	meinen schön**en** Büchern

Note that in this category all plural endings and singular endings in the genitive and dative case take **-en**, as does the masculine accusative.

All other singular endings follow the pattern of the previous table, where the adjective takes the endings of the (absent) definite article:

das Buch → Das ist ein interessant**es** Buch.
der Film → Oh, das war kein besonder**er** Film.

For a reminder of the endings on adjectives after the definite article see the **Sprachinfo**.

Note that adjectives in the comparative or superlative – when in front of a noun – follow the pattern of the three categories described:

Die Schweizer haben den höchst**en** Lebensstandard in Europa.
Humorvoller**e** Leute wirst du kaum finden.
Bayern ist ein reicher**es** Bundesland als Bremen.

Try not to feel overwhelmed by adjectival endings in German. As pointed out previously in this unit, there are certain patterns and in fact only a few endings you need to apply. With practice you will feel more confident when dealing with adjectives in German.

2 Indirekte Rede *Reported speech*

In the **Sprachinfo** you saw that in reporting what someone said you use what is called reported speech. Here are several different examples of reported speech:

a Christiane hat gesagt, Florian Wörle ist mit Birgit Klarmann verheiratet.
b Christiane hat gesagt, dass Florian Wörle mit Birgit Klarmann verheiratet ist.
c Christiane hat gesagt, Florian Wörle sei mit Birgit Klarmann verheiratet.
d Christiane hat gesagt, dass Florian Wörle mit Birgit Klarmann verheiratet sei.

There is little if any difference in meaning between these four sentences. As you can see, in two of the sentences **dass** introduces the second clause and the verb therefore goes to the end. In two cases the verb is the one you would normally expect (**ist**) and in two other cases it is **sei**, the **Konjunktiv I** form mentioned in the **Sprachinfo**.

While you may not choose to use the **Konjunktiv I** forms yourself very often, you do need to be able to recognize them when they occur.

In the **Konjunktiv I** the irregular and mixed verbs do not undergo vowel changes. You just take the stem of the infinitive and add the appropriate endings as indicated below. Bear in mind that **sein** is an exception:

	spiel-en	*woll-en*	*werd-en*	*hab-en*	*sein*
ich	spiel-**e**	woll-**e**	werd-**e**	hab-**e**	sei
du	spiel-**est**	woll-**est**	werd-**est**	hab-**est**	sei(e)st
er/sie/es	spiel-**e**	woll-**e**	werd-**e**	hab-**e**	sei
wir	spiel-**en**	woll-**en**	werd-**en**	hab-**en**	seien
ihr	spiel-**et**	woll-**et**	werd-**et**	hab-**et**	seiet
sie/Sie	spiel-**en**	woll-**en**	werd-**en**	hab-**en**	seien

Note that the other form of the subjunctive, **Konjunktiv II**, can also be used in reported speech, particularly in the case of **haben** and **sein**:

Konjunktiv I - Petra hat gesagt, dass Köln sehr schön sei.
Konjunktiv II - Petra hat gesagt, dass Köln sehr schön wäre.
Konjunktiv I - Anna und Frank haben gesagt, dass sie bald Urlaub haben.
Konjunktiv II - Anna und Frank haben gesagt, dass sie bald Urlaub hätten.

In the second example, **Konjunktiv II** would be preferred, because the **Konjunktiv I** form happens to be the same as the normal form of the verb.

You will find an overview of **Konjunktiv II** in the next unit.

TESTEN SIE SICH!

A) MEHR ÜBUNGEN

1 Wie heißen die Endungen?

Supply the appropriate endings for the adjectives in the following sentences:

i Here the adjective is not preceded by an article or possessive:

(**a**) Französisch__ Brot schmeckt mir am besten. (**b**) Ja, aber spanisch__ Wein ist fantastisch. (**c**) Was hältst du denn von deutsch__ Wein? (**d**) Tschechisch__ Bier ist unschlagbar. (**e**) Wichtig__ Feste feiert man mit groß__ Aufwand. (**f**) Italienisch__ Anzüge sind teuer, aber sehr gut. (**g**) Ehrlich, englisch__ Kneipen sind einfach toll. (**h**) Gut__ Abend. (**i**) Gut__ Nacht.

ii Here the adjectives follow an indefinite article or a possessive:

(**a**) Für mich ist es ein sehr interessant__ Land. (**b**) Die Stadt ist durch ihren alt__ Dom weltbekannt. (**c**) Was? Er ist mit seinem alt__ Fahrrad nach Dänemark gefahren? (**d**) Von ihrer französisch__ Brieffreundin hat sie lange nichts mehr gehört. (**e**) Sie warf einen kritisch__ Blick auf die Leute. (**f**) Die Alpen sind ein beeindruckend__ Gebirge. (**g**) Haben Sie vielleicht eine englisch__ Zeitung? (**h**) Einen stark__ Kaffee, bitte. (**i**) Ich nehme noch ein klein__ Stück. (**j**) Für mich ein groß__ Bier, bitte.

iii These adjectives are mixed. Note that sometimes no ending is needed.

(**a**) Nett__ Menschen findet man überall. (**b**) Still__ Wasser sind oft tief. (**c**) Vor allem sind ihm die sauber__ Straßen aufgefallen. (**d**) Erst dachte sie, es ist ein kalt__, verregnet__

Land. (**e**) Sie ist mit ihrem jünger__ Bruder gefahren. (**f**) Wien ist die größt__ Stadt in Österreich. (**g**) Hier kann man oft klassisch__ Musik hören. (**h**) Das ist ein kompliziert__ Problem. (**i**) Vorurteile sind dumm__ .

2 Und jetzt Sie!

CD2, TR 3, 13:02

Holger und Stefanie sind zwei Deutsche, die schon lange in England leben. Oftmals begegnen sie Vorurteilen oder Klischees bezüglich Deutschlands und der Deutschen. Gerade sprechen sie über ihre Erfahrungen. Übernehmen Sie die folgende Rolle und sprechen Sie mit Hilfe der englischen Hinweise.

Holger Sag mal, Stefanie, fühlst du dich eigentlich mehr als Engländerin oder als Deutsche?

Stefanie *Tell him that you have largely adapted to the English way of life, although you have made an effort not to forget your German culture and language.*

Holger Und wirst du von den Engländern akzeptiert oder hast du auch gegen Vorurteile und Klischees anzukämpfen?

Stefanie *Tell him that you know they exist, but that luckily you find that they are more the exception than the rule. Tell him that sometimes people ask you about the typical German characteristics such as German thoroughness, or whether the Germans really get up so early in the morning and work so hard.*

Holger Und was antwortest du auf solche Fragen?

Stefanie *Tell him that mostly you laugh and say that you are very sceptical as far as these typical German characteristics are concerned, and that you think that one can find them in people of other nationalities as well.*

B) LESETEXT

Die Deutschen – die Reiseweltmeister

Die Reisebranche ist im vergangenen Jahr weiter gewachsen. Und die Deutschen sind von allen Nationen die reiselustigsten: Weltweit wurden annähernd 85 Millionen Ankünfte deutscher Touristen gezählt.

Beliebtestes Reiseziel war Italien, in das fast 12 Millionen Deutsche fuhren, dicht gefolgt von Spanien mit 10,2 Millionen Touristen. Danach folgt unser Nachbar Österreich, immerhin noch mit 9,8 Millionen.

Immer mehr Urlauber nutzen dabei das Flugzeug für ihre Auslandsreisen: Allein von April bis Oktober waren cirka 42 Millionen Menschen von deutschen Flughäfen ins Ausland gestartet, ein Plus von 3,9 Prozent gegenüber dem Vorjahr.

Aber auch immer mehr Touristen reisen nach Deutschland: Im letzten Jahr gab es rund 17,3 Millionen Übernachtungen ausländischer Gäste. Spitzenreiter unter den Gästen waren Besucher aus den Beneluxländern. Daneben kamen 1,8 Millionen Besucher aus den USA und auch viele Gäste aus Großbritannien und der Schweiz.

1 Beantworten Sie die Fragen.

- **a** Wie oft reisten die Deutschen ins Ausland?
- **b** Was waren die drei beliebtesten Reiseziele?
- **c** Welchen Trend konnte man bei den Auslandsreisen feststellen?
- **d** Wie viele Übernachtungen ausländischer Gäste gab es in Deutschland?

QUICK VOCAB

reiselustig *keen on travelling*
das Reiseziel (-e) *destination*
der Flughafen (¨) *airport*
die Übernachtung (-en) *overnight stay*
der Spitzenreiter (-) *leader, front runner*

CHECKLISTE

Now that you have completed Unit 8, can you

1 discuss stereotypes, particularly in relation to Germany? ☐

2 make comparisons? ☐

3 report what others have said? ☐

4 produce the correct forms of **Konjunktiv I** and **II** in reported speech? ☐

5 use adjectival endings correctly? ☐

6 understand information on travel trends? ☐

9

Was tun Sie für die Umwelt?

In this unit you will learn how to
- ***discuss environmental issues***
- ***talk about hypothetical situations***
- ***use Konjunktiv II and the conditional***
- ***form the passive***

Aufnahme 1

Tun wir genug für die Umwelt?

Drei Schüler unterhalten sich mit ihrem Lehrer darüber, ob wir genug für die Umwelt tun und wie man Energie sparen kann.

Hören Sie sich den folgenden Dialog an und beantworten Sie dann die Fragen in Übung 1.

Hier sind einige wichtige Vokabeln.

QUICK VOCAB

der Umweltschutz *environmental protection*
die Erforschung *research*
die Energiequelle (-n) *source of energy*
die Atomkraft *atomic energy*
weg | kommen von *to get away from*

CD2, TR 4, 0:29

Lehrer Glaubt ihr, dass Umweltschutz und Energiesparen Sache der Regierung ist, oder dass die Bürger auch etwas dafür tun müssen?

Sascha Es langt nicht, wenn ich allein etwas tue, auch die Politiker und die Industrie müssten mehr unternehmen. Man sollte mehr Geld für die Erforschung und Nutzung alternativer Energiequellen ausgeben. Außerdem wünsche ich mir mehr Informationen, wo und an welcher Stelle ich Energie noch aktiver einsparen könnte.

Lehrer Was könnte man denn zum Beispiel tun, um mehr Strom zu sparen?

Ela Das mit dem Strom ist so eine Sache. Von Atomkraft sollte man auf Dauer ganz wegkommen. Biomasse könnte doch mehr genutzt werden. Erneuerbare Energien sind meiner Meinung nach langfristig sowieso viel sinnvoller. Abgesehen davon müsste die Sonnenenergie stärker genutzt werden – das wäre vielleicht auch eine ganz gute Alternative.

Andreas Ich denke auch, dass wir allgemein einfach mehr mit Solarenergie oder anderen Energiequellen arbeiten sollten, die viel umweltfreundlicher sind.

Lehrer Wie spart ihr denn zu Hause Energie?

Sascha Wenn ich aus meinem Zimmer gehe, mache ich den Computer und das Licht aus. In der Küche haben wir nur wenige automatische Geräte, wir machen das meiste mit der Hand. Das Radio machen wir auch immmer aus, wenn wir es nicht mehr brauchen.

Ela Wir haben einen speziellen Zähler an der Heizung, der uns anzeigt, wie viel Energie wir verbrauchen. Außerdem haben wir Solarzellen auf dem Dach und Energiesparlampen im Haus. Ich glaube aber, dass allgemein noch zu wenig getan wird.

Lehrer Und was haltet ihr davon, auf das Autofahren zu verzichten, um Energie zu sparen?

Andreas Ich finde, man kann einiges an Energie sparen, wenn man mit dem Bus fährt, anstatt jeder für sich mit dem eigenen Auto. Außerdem gibt es inzwischen auch spezielles Pflanzenöl, mit dem man die Autos betreiben könnte.

Ela	Die Autos könnte man auch abschaffen. Was man da an Sprit sparen würde – das wäre eine tolle Maßnahme! Oder vielleicht Solarautos – das wäre auch super. [aus: Izzze-Blitz - Das Jugendmagazin der Stromversorger]

Übung 1 Richtig oder falsch?

Korrigieren Sie die falschen Aussagen.

a Sascha denkt, dass Politiker und Industrie genug für den Umweltschutz tun.
b Er fordert mehr Geld für die Erforschung alternativer Energien.
c Ela ist der Meinung, dass wir von Atomkraft nicht wegkommen werden.
d Zuhause sparen Ela und Sascha keine Energie.
e Ela denkt, dass im Allgemeinen nicht genug getan wird.
f Andreas meint, es wäre gut, wenn Leute mehr den Bus benutzen würden.

jemandes Sache sein *to be of someone's concern*
die Nutzung *use*
die Biomasse *biomass*
erneuerbar *renewable*
die Sonnenenergie *solar energy*
die Solarenergie *solar energy*
elektrische Geräte (pl.) *electrical appliances*
der Zähler (-) *meter*
der Sprit (coll.) *petrol*

QUICK VOCAB

Übung 2 Was passt am besten?

Lesen Sie den Dialog noch einmal und finden Sie ein Wort, das passt.

a Tun wir wirklich genug für den ______?
b Alternative ______ sollten besser erforscht werden.
c Viele denken, dass die ______ gefährlich für die Umwelt ist.

d Die Solarenergie gilt dagegen als ______.
e Auf einigen Häusern gibt es schon ______ auf den Dächern.
f Im Haus kann man zum Beispiel ______ verwenden.
g Ein anderes Wort für Benzin ist ______.

Insight: Vokabeln – Verstehen und Lernen

Wie Sie bestimmt gemerkt haben, gibt es sehr viele neue Wörter, die mit dem Thema „Umwelt" zu tun haben. So kann man ihre Bedeutung leichter verstehen:

1 Viele Wörter sind sehr ähnlich oder identisch mit den englischen Wörtern, zum Beispiel: Solar- *solar*, das Atom *atom*, die Energie *energy*.
2 Viele Wörter sind Kombinationen aus Wörtern, die Sie wahrscheinlich schon kennen, zum Beispiel: die Solarenergie, das Solarauto, die Biomasse.

Sprachinfo

Konjunktiv II (b) *Imperfect subjunctive (b)*

In the previous two units you've already learned about two situations in which the *subjunctive* form of a verb (i.e. **wäre, hätte**) is used in German: in sentences where people want to add a tone of politeness and in reported speech when a person is being quoted.

Another function of **Konjunktiv II** is to express ideas and situations which are not real but just imagined:

Dann hätte ich mehr Zeit.	*Then I would have more time.*
Das wäre vielleicht eine Alternative.	*This would perhaps be an alternative.*
Man könnte mehr Energie sparen.	*One could save more energy.*

As you can see, in addition to the verbs **haben** and **sein**, modal verbs are often in the subjunctive.

Note that the subjunctive is also used in conditional sentences to express situations in which people imagine events which are fairly hypothetical:

> Wenn ich viel Geld hätte, würde ich morgen auf die Bahamas fliegen.
> Wenn ich Bundeskanzler wäre, würde ich mehr für die Umwelt tun.

For more details, see the grammar section.

There are quite a few examples of ***Konjunktiv II*** *in the dialogue. Can you find at least ten?*

Übung 3 Kombinieren Sie.

Bilden Sie neue Wörter.

Note that sometimes more than one combination is possible: **Atommasse, Atomenergie, Atomkraft.**

-energie -masse -kraft -schutz -sparen -quellen -sparlampe -energie -zelle

a Umwelt *schutz*
b Energie______
c Energie______
d Atom______
e Energie______
f Bio______
g Sonnen______
h Solar______
i Solar______

Übung 4 Was würde Herr Paul machen, wenn er ...

Write down what Herr Paul would do under the following circumstances.

Beispiel: mehr Zeit hätte? (Chinesisch lernen) →
Wenn Herr Paul mehr Zeit hätte, würde er Chinesisch lernen.

a in der Stadt seiner Wahl leben könnte? (in San Francisco)
b im Lotto gewinnen würde? (eine Weltreise machen)
c in die Vergangenheit reisen könnte? (in die Antike fahren)
d mit einem Popstar essen gehen könnte? (am liebsten mit Madonna)
e eine bekannte Person interviewen könnte? (am liebsten Claudia Schiffer)
f in einem Film mitspielen könnte? (im neuesten James Bond-Film)

Und Sie? Was würden Sie machen? Now go through the questions again, this time answering for yourself.

Beispiel: **a** Wenn ich mehr Zeit hätte, würde ich ...
b Wenn ich in der Stadt meiner Wahl leben könnte, würde ich ...

Aufnahme 2

CD2, TR 4, 3:05

Roland – der Umweltflegel

Roland, ein junger Mann, hat im Park eine Dose auf die Wiese geworfen. Eine ältere Frau, die sehr umweltbewusst ist, konfrontiert ihn.

Hören Sie sich den Dialog an und unterstreichen Sie die richtige Antwort.

Übung 5

a Roland hat eine Coladose/Wasserdose/Bierdose auf die Wiese geworfen.

b Er sagt, die Müllarbeiter/Parkarbeiter/Parkwächter sollen etwas für ihr Geld tun.
c Außerdem hat er den Mund/den Hals/die Nase voll von all dem Recycling.
d Die Frau antwortet, Recycling ist eine sinnvolle/wichtige/gute Sache.
e Roland soll zum Kiosk/zum Container/Mülleimer rennen.
f Er könnte die Dose in die Tasche/Jacke/Hose packen.
g Roland sagt, dazu sei das Leben zu schön/amüsant/kurz.

QUICK VOCAB

der Flegel (-) *lout*
umweltbewusst *conscious of the environment*
die Auffassung (-en) *here: attitude*
ersticken *to suffocate*
die Müllhalde (-n) *rubbish tip*
schwafeln *to waffle*
die Nase voll haben *to have had enough*
jemanden auf den Arm nehmen *to pull someone's leg*
entsorgen *to dispose of*
jemanden bekehren *to convert someone*
sich täuschen *to be wrong about something*
die Moralpredigt (-en) *(moralizing) lecture*

Übung 6 Was passt zusammen?

Verbinden Sie die passenden Satzteile.

a Wenn jeder so denken würde wie Sie,
b Sind Sie auch so eine,
c Davon habe ich die Nase
d Wenn wir jetzt nichts tun,
e Für Ihre Moralpredigten
f Und jetzt lassen Sie mich

i wie sieht das Leben für unsere Kinder aus?
ii habe ich keine Zeit.
iii in Ruhe.
iv dann würden wir bald im Müll ersticken.
v die dauernd von Recycling schwafelt?
vi schon lange voll.

Übung 7 Sagen Sie's auf Deutsch!

🔊 CD2, TR 4, 6:28

Wenn Sie nicht sicher sind, wie die Ausdrücke heißen, können Sie die Transkription des Dialogs am Ende des Buches lesen. Überprüfen Sie dann Ihre Antworten auf der Höraufnahme.

a What business is that of yours?
b It's all too late anyway.
c Are you pulling my leg?
d All that nonsense ...
e Leave me alone now!

Insight: Umweltschutz

In Deutschland spielt der Umweltschutz eine große Rolle. So ist es kein Zufall, dass die Partei **Bündnis 90/Die Grünen** eine der größten und wichtigsten Umweltparteien der Welt ist.

Gegründet 1979 hat die Partei in den letzten Jahrzehnten immer mehr an Bedeutung gewonnen und ist als Koalitionspartner in vielen Stadt- und Landesparlamenten an der Regierung beteiligt. Von 1998 bis 2005 war sie mit der SPD (Sozialdemokratische Partei Deutschlands) die Regierungspartei in Deutschland.

Mehr Informationen:
http://www.gruene.de
http://www.umweltschutz.de

Sprachinfo

Wie man das Passive bildet *Forming the passive*

When talking about environmental issues or recycling you will often come across the passive. You may already be aware that the passive in German is mostly formed with the verb **werden** + a past participle:

Der Müll wird alle zwei Wochen abgeholt.	*The rubbish is collected every two weeks.*
Der Müll ist gerade abgeholt worden.	*The rubbish has just been collected.*
Sein altes Auto wurde recycelt.	*His old car was recycled.*

Here is an example from the next recording where you can see that a sentence can have more than one verb in the passive voice:

In Deutschland wird jetzt alles getrennt gesammelt und dann wieder verwertet oder umweltfreundlich entsorgt.

In Germany everything is now separated before collection (lit. *collected separated) and then recycled or disposed of in an environmentally friendly manner.*

For more information, see the grammar section later in this unit.

Aufnahme 3

Andere Länder – andere Sitten

Frau Müller hat einen neuen Untermieter, Herrn Schmitt, der seit längerer Zeit nicht mehr in Deutschland war und daher mit dem neuen Prinzip der Müllentsorgung noch nicht vertraut ist.

Hören Sie sich die Höraufnahme an und beantworten Sie dann die Fragen in Übung 8. Was ist alles neu für ihn?

Übung 8

a Hat Herr Schmitt schon von der Müllsortierung gehört?
b Wie viele Tonnen hat Frau Müller in ihrer Garage stehen?
c In welche Tonne kommt das Altpapier?
d Was – sagt Frau Müller – kann jetzt jeder machen?
e Was passiert, wenn man bei der Mülltrennung nicht mitmacht?
f Wohin kommen die Blechdosen und alte Flaschen?

CD2, TR 4, 7:03

Frau Müller Und mit der Müllsortierung wissen Sie ja Bescheid, Herr Schmitt, oder?

Herr Schmitt Ich habe schon darüber gelesen – es hört sich aber komisch an. Vielleicht habe ich es ja auch falsch verstanden? Wie Sie sich vorstellen können, hat man in Südamerika andere Sorgen, als sich um den Müll zu kümmern.

Frau Müller Ja, also hier sieht das ganz anders aus. Kommen Sie mal mit! (*Führt ihn zur Garage, wo drei verschiedene Tonnen stehen.*)

Herr Schmitt Machen Sie Witze? Wozu braucht man denn drei Tonnen? Das erscheint mir aber alles sehr merkwürdig.

Frau Müller Gar nicht! In Deutschland wird jetzt alles getrennt gesammelt und dann wiederverwertet oder umweltfreundlich entsorgt.

Herr Schmitt Das kann ich mir aber überhaupt nicht vorstellen. Wie soll denn das funktionieren?

Frau Müller Ganz einfach, Herr Schmitt. Die blaue Tonne hier ist für Papier. Die braune Tonne ist für Biomüll und der Sack ist für alle Verpackungen, die den Grünen Punkt aufweisen. Alles wird im Wechsel vierzehntägig abgeholt.

Herr Schmitt Ist das denn nicht ungeheuer zeitaufwendig?

Frau Müller Eigentlich nicht. Sie werden sich schon schnell daran gewöhnen. Auf jeden Fall kann jetzt jeder was für die Umwelt tun – auch Sie!

Herr Schmitt	Aber wäre es denn nicht besser, Müll erst gar nicht zu produzieren, als ihn dann hinterher zu sammeln und nicht zu wissen, wohin damit?
Frau Müller	Naja, natürlich. Aber mit diesem System ist zumindest mal ein Anfang gemacht. Und mitmachen müssen Sie auf jeden Fall – es kostet nämlich eine schöne Stange Geld, wenn man den Müll nicht sortiert!
Herr Schmitt	Und was ist denn eigentlich das da drüben?
Frau Müller	Ach ja, das sind die Container für Blechdosen, Glas und Altbatterien. Wenn Sie außerdem Sondermüll wie Farben oder Lacke haben, müssen Sie zur Sammelstelle fahren.
Herr Schmitt	Na, das kann ja heiter werden!

QUICK VOCAB

andere Länder, andere Sitten *when in Rome, do as the Romans do (lit. other countries, other customs)*
die Mülltrennung *separation of waste*
die Müllsortierung *sorting of waste*
die Tonne (-n) *(here) rubbish bin*
wiederverwerten *to recycle*
entsorgen *to dispose of*
eine schöne Stange Geld *a small fortune*
der Lack (-e) *varnish*
das kann ja heiter werden *(ironical) that will be fun*

Übung 9 Wie heißt das?

Finden Sie im Text die deutschen Wörter für:

a packages
b tin, can
c hazardous waste
d used batteries
e paint
f collecting point/dump

Übung 10 Lesen Sie den Dialog noch einmal und ergänzen Sie

a Herr Schmitt findet die Müllsortierung …
b In Südamerika hat man andere Sorgen, als …
c Frau Müller erklärt, dass der Müll in Deutschland …
d Alte Zeitungen kommen in …
e In die braune Tonne kommt …
f Der Rest kommt …
g Sondermüll muss zur …
h Für Glas gibt es …
i Frau Müller denkt, dass jetzt jeder …

Grammatik

1 Konjunktiv II – Übersicht *Imperfect subjunctive – summary*

In the last few units you have come across various situations in which the **Konjunktiv II** is used in German. Here is a short overview.

It is used:

1 to add a degree of politeness
2 in reported speech
3 to express hypothetical situations and ideas
4 in connection with **wenn** in conditional sentences

Remember that it is mostly **haben** and **sein** and the **modal verbs** that are used in the subjunctive. You can find a list of their forms in the grammar section of Unit 7.

For most other verbs – especially in spoken German – the **Konjunktiv II** form of **werden**, namely **würde(n)**, is used together with the infinitive:

Wenn ich im Lotto gewinnen würde, ...
Wenn du weniger rauchen würdest, ...
Wenn wir weniger Müll produzieren würden, ...

Nevertheless, you will still find other verbs in the subjunctive form, especially in written texts, such as newspaper articles or novels. To help you recognize them, here are some tips on how these verbs form the **Konjunktiv II**:

Regular verbs

The **Konjunktiv II** form of regular verbs is constructed by adding the following endings to the stem:

ich spiel-**te**	wir spiel-**ten**
du spiel-**test**	ihr spiel-**tet**
Sie spiel-**ten**	Sie spiel-**ten**
er/sie spiel-**te**	sie spiel-**ten**

Irregular verbs

The **Konjunktiv II** form of most irregular verbs is formed from their past simple tense, by adding the appropriate endings, as indicated below. Note also that an umlaut is added whenever possible:

Infinitive	*fahren*	*kommen*	*gehen*	*wissen*
Präteritum/ Simple past	*fuhren*	*kamen*	*gingen*	*wussten*
ich	führ-**e**	käm-**e**	ging-**e**	wüsst-**e**
du	führ-**est**	käm-**est**	ging-**est**	wüsst-**est**
er/sie/es	führ-**e**	käm-**e**	ging-**e**	wüsst-**e**
wir	führ-**en**	käm-**en**	ging-**en**	wüsst-**en**
ihr	führ-**et**	käm-**et**	ging-**et**	wüsst-**et**
sie/Sie	führ-**en**	käm-**en**	ging-**en**	wüsst-**en**

Here is one example for the use of **wissen** in the subjunctive:

Ich wüsste gern, wann der nächste Zug nach Berlin fährt.	*I should like to know when the next train goes to Berlin.*

Note also that the **Konjunktiv II** is used in some expressions like:

Wenn ich du wäre, würde ich ...	*If I were you, I would ...*
An deiner Stelle würde ich ...	*In your position, I would ...*

2 Das Passiv *The passive*

One area that needs frequent revision is the passive. As you saw in a **Sprachinfo** earlier the passive is formed with the verb **werden** in the appropriate tense together with the past participle of the verb in question:

Present: Das Essen wird gerade gekocht.
The meal is just being cooked.

Simple past: Das Buch wurde von Heine geschrieben.
The book was written by Heine.

Present perfect: Die Rechnung ist bezahlt worden.
The bill has been/was paid.

Note that in the present perfect passive the past participle of **werden** is simply **worden** and has no **ge-** prefix. As is usual with the present perfect in German, the present perfect form of the passive can be used for events that happened in the distant past:

Dieses Haus ist 1666 gebaut worden.
This house was built in 1666.

Remember also that **von** is the German equivalent to the preposition *by* – which you often need when you use the passive:

Von wem wurde das Buch geschrieben?
Who was the book written by?

If you want to express the meaning of *by means of* then **durch** is more appropriate:

Durch Solarzellen wird umweltfreundliche Energie erzeugt.
(*Lit.*) *Through solar cells environmentally friendly energy is generated.*

Below is some more information that you might find useful when you are dealing with the passive.

Passive of dative verbs

Verbs which in German are followed by the dative case, such as **helfen, raten, gratulieren** and **folgen**, cannot be made passive in the usual way. It is, however, possible to produce a kind of passive, if the dative object is retained:

Mir wurde von einem Freund geholfen.	*I was helped by a friend.*
Ihr wurde geraten, gesünder zu leben.	*She was advised to live more healthily.*
Ihnen wurde zu ihrer Hochzeit gratuliert.	*They were congratulated on their wedding.*

Use of **man**

The pronoun **man** is often used in German where a passive would be more common in English:

Hier spricht man Deutsch.	*German spoken here.*
Man glaubt, dass ...	*It is thought that ...*
So was macht man eben nicht.	*That sort of thing is just not done.*

TESTEN SIE SICH!

A) MEHR ÜBUNGEN

1 Geben Sie Ratschläge

Give appropriate advice for some of your friends. Use **Wenn ich du wäre** or **An deiner Stelle** to start your answer. Feel free to suggest your own solutions. The versions we give in the Key are just examples of possible answers.

Beispiel: Ich kann nachts schlecht einschlafen. →
Wenn ich du wäre, würde ich weniger Kaffee trinken.
or
An deiner Stelle würde ich Yoga machen.

- **a** Ich fühle mich oft so müde.
- **b** Ich bin durch ein Examen gefallen.
- **c** Ich bin nicht mehr mit meiner Arbeit zufrieden.
- **d** Ich habe den Eindruck, dass ich immer dicker werde.
- **e** Mein Freund/Meine Freundin sagt, dass ich einen langweiligen Musikgeschmack habe.
- **f** Mein Freund/Meine Freundin sagt, dass ich langweilig aussehe.

2 Wissen Sie noch?

Beantworten Sie die Fragen in ganzen Sätzen. Im Schlüssel finden Sie Beispiele für mögliche Antworten.

Beispiel: Was wird durch Energiesparlampen erreicht? →
Durch Energiesparlampen wird Strom gespart.

- **a** Was wird durch Solarzellen erzeugt?
- **b** Was wird mit Altglas gemacht?
- **c** Wohin werden Blechdosen gebracht?
- **d** Und wohin wird der Sondermüll gebracht?

e Wann wurde die Partei „Die Grünen" gegründet? (siehe **Insight: Umweltschutz**)
f Sind Sie der Ansicht, dass genug für die Umwelt getan wird?
g Was könnte noch für die Umwelt getan werden?

3 Und jetzt Sie!

John, ein britischer Student, der gerade in Deutschland angekommen ist, redet mit Volker, einem deutschen Studenten, über die Müllsortierung. Spielen Sie mit Hilfe der englischen Anregungen die Rolle von Volker.

CD2, TR 4, 8:58

John Du, wie funktioniert eigentlich diese Müllsortierung?
Volker *Tell him that there is a brown bin for organic waste, a blue one for paper, and a plastic bag for all packages which bear the 'Green Dot', and that everything gets collected fortnightly on a rota system.*
John Funktioniert das denn? Das kann ich mir gar nicht vorstellen. Macht denn da jeder mit?
Volker *Tell him yes, most people do join in. If you don't join in, you pay heavy fines. And there are information leaflets, and so on, available to inform the population. Ask him if there are actually many differences between Germany and England.*
John Oh ja, in England wird zwar auch etwas für die Umwelt getan, aber nicht so viel wie hier. Aber hat das alles denn überhaupt einen Sinn, oder ist es nicht schon zu spät für die Erde?
Volker *Tell him that you believe recycling is a very useful measure because if nothing is done for the environment now, what will the earth be like for children of the future?*
John Aber ist es denn nicht besser, Müll zu vermeiden, anstatt ihn hinterher zu entsorgen?
Volker *You say yes of course, but at least it's a start.*

B) LESETEXTE

Umwelt

1 Ein Viertel des Waldes deutlich krank

The short article below is about the situation in German forests. To help you understand the text, here is some of the key vocabulary:

QUICK VOCAB

deutlich *here: clearly, considerably*
schädigen *to harm, damage*
die Buche (-n) *beech tree*
die Eiche (-n) *oak tree*
das Blatt (-¨er) *leaf*
die Nadel (-n) *needle*
der Trost *consolation, comfort*

Neue Studien geben wenig Anlass zur Hoffnung. Zwar ist das Waldsterben in den letzten Jahren leicht zurückgegangen, doch sind die Zahlen immer noch schockierend: Etwa 25% aller Bäume gelten als deutlich geschädigt. Als deutlich geschädigt werden die Bäume definiert, die mindestens ein Viertel ihrer Nadeln oder Blätter verloren haben.

Obwohl es dem Wald insgesamt etwas besser geht, ist der Zustand der Eichen immer noch alarmierend: Als deutlich geschädigt gelten mittlerweile etwa 50% all dieser Bäume. Auch etwa ein Drittel aller Buchen gehört in diese Kategorie. Weniger als 40% aller Bäume sind noch gesund. Besonders schlimm sind die Quoten in Rheinland-Pfalz, Bayern und Hessen. Ein kleiner Trost: Der Anteil des Waldes an der Gesamtfläche der Bundesrepublik ist mit etwa 30% konstant geblieben.

Now try to find out the main points of the text:

a Has the situation with regard to Germany's forests worsened or improved in the last few years?

b What percentage of trees are regarded as damaged?
c When is a tree defined as being damaged?
d Which trees are especially badly hit?

2 Mülltrennung

The second reading comprehension passage is about what young Germans think should be done to reduce the amount of rubbish that is generated. Read the texts and do the exercise on the following page.

Danilo, 14

Das mit der Mülltrennung finde ich voll okay. Ist ja auch wirklich keine große Aktion, die Sachen in verschiedene Mülleimer zu werfen. Letztendlich machen wir das ja für uns, denn wenn es keine Rohstoffe mehr gibt, können wir nicht überleben.

Julian, 11

Wir haben nur Getränke in Mehrwegflaschen, Joghurt in Gläsern und andere Dinge mit möglichst wenig Verpackung. Schon bei uns auf der Grundschule haben wir gelernt, wie wichtig Mülltrennung und vor allem Müllvermeidung ist, um Rohstoffe zu sparen.

Denise, 13

Ich werfe nie Müll auf die Straße und fände es gut, wenn jeder bewusster mit der Umwelt umgehen würde. Verpackungen sind oft viel zu aufwendig. Bei Geburtstagsgeschenken möchte man schon eine schöne Verpackung haben, aber da gibt es ja auch Möglichkeiten, diese wieder zu verwerten.

QUICK VOCAB

der Mülleimer *rubbish bin*
der Rohstoff (-e) *raw material*
die Mehrwegflasche (-n) *reusable bottle*
die Verpackung (-en) *packaging*
die Vermeidung *avoidance*
bewusst *conscious*
um | gehen mit *to deal with*
aufwendig *lavish*
die Mülltrennung *sorting of rubbish*

Wer sagt das? Und wie heißt das im Text?

Beispiel: Wir benutzen nur Flaschen, die man wiederverwenden kann. →
Julian: Wir haben nur Getränke in Mehrwegflaschen.

a Es wäre gut, wenn man mehr für die Umwelt machen würde.
b Die Lehrer haben uns erklärt, wie wichtig die Mülltrennung ist.
c Den Müll zu sortieren ist keine große Arbeit.
d Ich bin für die Mülltrennung.

CHECKLISTE

Now that you have completed Unit 9, can you

1 discuss environmental issues? ☐

2 give at least six examples of environment-related vocabulary? ☐

3 talk about hypothetical situations, for instance what you would do if you won the lottery? ☐

4 use the imperfect subjunctive and form conditional sentences? ☐

5 use the passive in the present, simple past and present perfect tenses? ☐

6 understand short texts relating to the environment? ☐

10

Deutschland heute

In this unit you will learn how to
- ***talk about newspapers and magazines***
- ***do a quiz on the German political structure***
- ***express an opinion on economic issues***
- ***form relative clauses***
- ***identify adjectival and weak nouns***

Aufnahme 1

CD2, TR 5, 0:24

Frankfurter Rundschau

die tageszeitung

Mindener Tageblatt

Herr Hinschken arbeitet als Journalist in Hamburg. Im folgenden Interview spricht er über die wichtigsten Zeitungen und Zeitschriften in der Bundesrepublik Deutschland.

Hören Sie, was er sagt, und beantworten Sie dann die Fragen in Übung 1.

QUICK VOCAB

das Blatt (-¨er) *here: paper*
das Qualitätsblatt (-¨er) *quality paper, broadsheet*
die Boulevardzeitung (-en) *tabloid*
die Auflage (-n) *here: circulation*
die Zeitschrift (-en) *magazine, journal*

Der deutschsprachige Zeitungsmarkt ist einer der größten der Welt. Insgesamt gibt es fast 400 Tageszeitungen in Deutschland, mit einer täglichen Druckauflage von etwa 30 Millionen Exemplaren.

Anders als zum Beispiel in Großbritannien dominieren Lokal- und Regionalzeitungen den Markt. Diese Zeitungen berichten ausführlich über Ereignisse in der entsprechenden Region, haben aber auch Welt- und Wirtschaftsnachrichten. Jemand, der beispielsweise in Hamburg lebt, wird also vielleicht das *Hamburger Abendblatt* kaufen, das sehr detailliert darüber berichtet, was in Hamburg und in der Umgebung von Hamburg passiert, in dem es aber auch ausführliche Berichte über Ereignisse in Deutschland, im Ausland und zum Beispiel Wirtschafts- und Kulturnachrichten gibt.

Wer sich noch weiter informieren möchte, wird dann vielleicht noch eine der überregionale Zeitungen lesen, die man in ganz Deutschland bekommen kann: die *Süddeutsche Zeitung*, die *Frankfurter Rundschau*, die *Frankfurter Allgemeine Zeitung* oder *Die Welt*. Die letzten beiden gelten als konservativ, während die *Süddeutsche Zeitung* und die *Frankfurter Rundschau* eher linksliberal sind.

All diese Zeitungen könnte man als Qualitätsblätter bezeichnen. Daneben gibt es dann die so genannten Boulevardzeitungen.

Am bekanntesten ist dabei die *Bild*-Zeitung, die eine Auflage von etwa 4,5 Millionen hat und damit die am meisten verkaufte Zeitung in Deutschland ist.

Außer Tageszeitungen gibt es auch noch Sonntags- und Wochenzeitungen. Die bekanntesten Wochenzeitungen sind *Die Zeit* und *Die Woche*, die beide aus Hamburg kommen. Sonntagszeitungen spielen eine weit geringere Rolle als in Großbritannien, da die meisten Redaktionen einen Ruhetag haben und viele Zeitungen sonntags nicht erscheinen.

Neben Zeitungen gibt es natürlich auch einen riesigen Zeitschriftenmarkt. Gewinner der letzten Jahre waren vor allem Computerzeitschriften, Magazine für Essen und Trinken und Zeitschriften über Motorsport. Bekannt sind aber auch Nachrichtenmagazine, wie *Focus* oder *Der Spiegel*, der schon seit 1947 auf dem Markt ist.

Wer gerne liest, für den ist das Internet eine wahre Fundgrube: Mittlerweile gibt es Hunderte von Zeitungen und Zeitschriften, von einem Lokalblatt wie der *Schweriner Volkszeitung* bis zum *Spiegel* oder *Stern*.

Übung 1

a Wie viele verschiedene Zeitungen erscheinen täglich in Deutschland?
b Was ist typisch für Lokal- und Regionalzeitungen?
c Wo steht die *Frankfurter Allgemeine Zeitung* politisch?
d Wie hoch ist die Auflage der *Bild*-Zeitung?
e Was für Zeitschriften haben in den letzten Jahren viele neue Leser gewonnen?
f Seit wann gibt es das Nachrichtenmagazin *Der Spiegel*?

QUICK VOCAB

das Ereignis (-se) *event*
marktdominierend *dominating the market*
regional *regional*
überregional *national, nationwide*

ausführlich *detailed*
gelten als *to be regarded as*
das Exemplar (-e) *copy*
die Redaktion (-en) *editorial staff, editorial board*

Übung 2 Was passt am besten?

Lesen Sie das Interview noch einmal und finden Sie ein Wort, das passt.

a Es gibt fast 400 _____ in Deutschland.
b Marktdominierend sind die Lokal- und _____.
c Ein Beispiel für eine _____ Zeitung ist die *Süddeutsche Zeitung*.
d Politisch ist die *Süddeutsche Zeitung* eher _____.
e Die *Bild*-Zeitung ist die meistverkaufte _____.
f Sie hat eine _____ von etwa 4,5 Millionen _____.
g *Focus* und *Der Spiegel* sind bekannte _____.
h Man kann Hunderte von _____ und _____ im Internet lesen.

Insight: Kurznamen für Zeitungen

Namen von Zeitungen sind oft sehr lang. Es ist deshalb üblich, dass man Kurznamen benutzt, zum Beispiel wenn man am Kiosk eine Zeitung kauft. Hier sind einige Beispiele:

Frankfurter Allgemeine Zeitung	FAZ
Frankfurter Rundschau	FR
Hamburger Morgenpost	Mopo
Hannoversche Allgemeine Zeitung	HAZ
Süddeutsche Zeitung	SZ
die tageszeitung	taz
Westdeutsche Allgemeine Zeitung	WAZ

Da **Zeitung** weiblich ist (*die* **Zeitung**), sagt man: **Eine Bild, bitte** oder **Ich möchte eine HAZ.**

Sprachinfo

Relativsätze *Relative clauses*

A relative clause is a type of subordinate clause, in which more information about a specific item in the main clause is given. Here are three examples:

Bekannt ist auch *Der Spiegel*, der seit 1947 auf dem Markt ist.
Am bekanntesten ist die *Bild*, die eine Auflage von etwa 4,5 Millionen hat.
Focus ist ein Nachrichtenmagazin, das aus Berlin kommt.

As you can see, the second clause refers directly to the noun in the first part and provides you with more details: for example, about *Bild*, which has a circulation of about 4.5 million, or about *Der Spiegel*, which has been on the market since 1947.

A relative clause is usually introduced by a relative pronoun (equivalent to 'who', 'that' or 'which' in English). In the nominative case the pronouns are quite straightforward:

der for masculine, **das** for neuter and **die** for feminine and plural nouns

You probably won't be surprised to find that in a relative clause – as with most subordinate clauses – the verb goes to the end.

There are two examples of relative plural clauses in ***Aufnahme*** *1. Can you find them?*

Übung 3 Wie heißen die Zeitungen?

Wissen Sie die vollen Namen für die folgenden Abkürzungen?

Beispiel: FR → ***Frankfurter Rundschau***

a taz – ______
b FAZ – ______
c Mopo – ______
d SZ – ______
e WAZ – ______

Übung 4 Verbinden Sie!

a Überregionale Zeitungen sind Zeitungen,
b Lokalzeitungen sind Blätter,
c Die FAZ ist eine Zeitung,
d Wochenzeitungen sind Zeitungen,
e Boulevardblätter sind Zeitungen,
f Der Spiegel ist ein Nachrichtenmagazin,

i die einmal pro Woche erscheinen.
ii die oft viel Sex und Crime haben.
iii das es seit 1947 gibt.
iv die man in ganz Deutschland kaufen kann.
v die aus Frankfurt kommt.
vi die viel über die eigene Region berichten.

Aufnahme 2

CD2, TR 5, 3:04

Deutschland-Quiz

In der nächsten zwei Übungen können Sie Ihr Wissen über Deutschland testen. Lesen Sie zunächst die acht Quizfragen und entscheiden Sie dann jeweils, welche Antwort stimmt. Hören Sie sich dann die Audioaufnahme an und überprüfen Sie, ob Sie recht hatten.

NB *Some of the details provided in* **Aufnahme 2** *might of course change; for example, the number of MPs in the Bundestag varies from election to election. For up-to-date information on various aspects of Germany, see* http://www.deutschland.de or http://www.bundestag.de

Übung 5

1 Flächenmäßig ist Deutschland
- **a** größer als Frankreich
- **b** etwa so groß wie Frankreich
- **c** deutlich kleiner als Frankreich.

2 Deutschland hat eine Grenze mit
- **a** 8 Ländern
- **b** 9 Ländern
- **c** 10 Ländern.

3 Das Parlament heißt
- **a** Bundesrat
- **b** Bundestag
- **c** Reichstag.

4 Abgeordnete gibt es
- **a** 498
- **b** 556
- **c** 656.

5 Bundesländer gibt es
- **a** 12
- **b** 14
- **c** 16.

6 Die meisten Menschen wohnen in
- **a** Bayern
- **b** Berlin
- **c** Nordrhein-Westfalen.

7 Die meiste politische Macht hat
- **a** der Bundespräsident
- **b** der Bundeskanzler
- **c** der Bundestags-präsident.

8 Die politische Struktur ist
- **a** föderalistisch
- **b** zentralistisch
- **c** dezentralisiert.

QUICK VOCAB

bevölkerungsreich *densely populated*
flächenmäßig *in area*
der Ballungsraum (¨-e) *conurbation*
der/die Abgeordnete* *member of parliament*
verfassungsgemäß *constitutional*
das Grundgesetz (-e) *Basic Law/the German constitution*
ernennen *to appoint*
entlassen *to dismiss*
der Grundpfeiler (-) *cornerstone*

*for the plural forms see the **Sprachinfo.**

Übung 6

Beantworten Sie die folgenden Fragen.

- **a** Welches ist das größte Bundesland?
- **b** Wie heißt das kleinste?
- **c** Wie werden Hamburg und Bremen genannt?
- **d** Wie oft gibt es Wahlen zum Bundestag?
- **e** Was für Aufgaben hat der Bundespräsident?
- **f** Was ist ein Grundpfeiler der politischen Struktur Deutschlands?

Insight: Informationen über Österreich und die Schweiz

In Aufnahme 2 haben Sie einige wichtige Fakten über Deutschland erfahren.

Wenn Sie ähnliches über Österreich wissen wollen, besuchen Sie bitte die folgende Website: http://www.austria.info/at/oesterreich-fakten/

Dort finden Sie Informationen über die Geschichte, die Bevölkerung, das politische System, Kunst und Kultur, sowie viele anderen Themen.

Informationen über die Schweiz, von der Bevölkerung über geografische Fakten bis hin zum Umweltschutz und zur Wirtschaft finden Sie unter: http://www.swissworld.org/de/

Übung 7 Sagen Sie's auf Deutsch!

CD2, TR 5, 8:10

a Welcome to a new edition of ...
b Our first topic today is Germany.
c Now, just imagine a map of Europe ...
d As you know, Germany consists of 16 Bundesländer.
e If I would ask you ...
f Altogether there are nine countries ...
g But how many members does the Bundestag actually have?
h More about this in the next week.

Sprachinfo

Besondere Nomen (1) *Adjectival nouns*

You may have noticed in the vocabulary list that **der/die Abgeordnete** *member of parliament* is asterisked as being a bit different from other nouns. It is in fact one of several nouns in German that take endings like adjectives:

Other nouns that behave like this include:

der/die Deutsche *German* — **der/die Kranke** *sick person, patient*

der/die Bekannte *acquaintance* — **der/die Verlobte** *fiancé(e)*

For further details, see the grammar section.

Aufnahme 3

CD2, TR 5, 9:25

Im folgenden Interview spricht Frau Matthiesen von der Industrie- und Handelskammer (Chamber of Commerce) über die wirtschaftliche Situation in Deutschland.

Hören Sie sich die Höraufnahme an und entscheiden Sie, ob die folgenden Aussagen richtig oder falsch sind. Korrigieren Sie dann die falschen Aussagen.

Übung 8

a Deutschland ist eine der führenden Industrienationen der Welt.
b Der Motor der Wirtschaft waren die Banken und Versicherungen.
c Deutschland importiert mehr als es exportiert.
d Die USA sind der wichtigste Handelspartner.
e In Deutschland werden nicht genug neue Jobs geschaffen.
f Viele Firmen denken noch nicht global genug.

Journalist Frau Matthiesen, die Bundesrepublik gehört zu den international führenden Industrienationen. In welchen Bereichen ist die deutsche Wirtschaft denn besonders stark?

Matthiesen	Nun, traditionell im produzierenden Gewerbe, das für Jahrzehnte sozusagen das Herz und der Motor der deutschen Wirtschaft war. Als erstes wäre hier natürlich die Autoindustrie zu nennen, mit Betrieben wie Volkswagen, BMW und natürlich Mercedes-Chrysler, die alle weltweit bekannt sind. Neben der Automobilindustrie spielen andere Wirtschaftszweige wie der Maschinenbau oder auch die chemische Industrie eine große Rolle.
Journalist	Wie wichtig ist denn der Export für die deutsche Industrie?
Matthiesen	Deutschland ist primär ein exportorientiertes Land. Nehmen Sie zum Beispiel die Autoindustrie, die mehr als 60 % ihrer Produkte ausführt. Jeder dritte Arbeitsplatz in Deutschland ist vom Export abhängig.
Journalist	Und welches sind die wichtigsten Handelspartner Deutschlands?
Matthiesen	Am wichtigsten sind die Länder der EU, in die annähernd 60 % der Ausfuhren gehen. Nordamerika und der asiatisch-pazifische Raum spielen etwa eine gleich wichtige Rolle.
Journalist	Die deutsche Wirtschaft hat in den letzten Jahren aber auch mit vielen Problemen zu kämpfen gehabt.
Matthiesen	Richtig. Insbesondere ist die hohe Arbeitslosigkeit ein Grund zur Besorgnis. Hier gibt es strukturelle Defizite in Deutschland. Daneben ist es uns auch nicht gelungen, im Dienstleistungssektor ähnlich viele neue Arbeitsplätze zu schaffen wie etwa die USA oder Großbritannien.
Journalist	Und wie sehen Sie die Zukunft für die deutsche Wirtschaft?
Matthiesen	Im Zuge der Globalisierung wird es für die Betriebe immer wichtiger werden, international präsent zu sein. Viele Firmen, vor allem in der Autoindustrie, aber auch die Banken und Versicherungen haben das verstanden und ihre internationale Präsenz verstärkt. Ich bin daher recht optimistisch, was die Zukunft angeht.

Übung 9 Wie heißt das?

Finden Sie die deutschen Wörter für:

a manufacturing industry
b mechanical engineering
c chemical industry
d service sector
e branches of industry
f trading partner
g export
h globalization

die Industrienation (-en) *industrialized nation*
der Betrieb (-e) *business, factory*
aus | führen *to export*
annähernd *almost*
der Grund (¨-e) *reason*
zur Besorgnis *for concern*
im Zuge von *in the wake of*
verstärken *to reinforce, to increase*

QUICK VOCAB

Übung 10

Hören Sie sich den Dialog noch einmal an und ergänzen Sie.

a Der Motor der deutschen Wirtschaft war …
b Weltweit bekannt sind Betriebe wie …
c Andere wichtige Wirtschaftszweige sind …
d Die wichtigsten Handelspartner Deutschlands …
e Ein Grund zur Besorgnis …
f Im Dienstleistungssektor …
g Im Zuge der Globalisierung müssen Betriebe…
h Frau Matthiesen ist aber …

Grammatik

1 Relativsätze *Relative clauses*

As you learned in the **Sprachinfo**, relative clauses provide more information about an item in the main clause and they are usually introduced by a relative pronoun.

You saw that in the **nominative** case the pronouns are: **der, die, das,** and **die** in the plural.

In the **accusative** case there is a change for masculine nouns only:

m: Das ist Peter, **den** ich noch aus der Schule kenne.

In the **genitive** case, the case of possession, the German words for the equivalent of whose are:

m: Das ist Marcus, **dessen** Tochter Journalistin ist.
f: Ist das nicht Helga, **deren** Tochter in den USA lebt?
n: Das ist das Kind, **dessen** Eltern aus Bern kommen.
pl: Das sind die Studenten, **deren** Tests sehr gut waren.

In the **dative** case the pronouns are: **dem** for masculine and neuter, **der** for feminine and **denen** for the plural:

m: Das ist Herr Kaiser, **dem** ich 100 Euro geliehen habe.
f: Das ist Petra, **der** ich das Buch über New York gegeben habe.
n: Das ist das Kind, **dem** ich geholfen habe.
pl: Das sind die Leute, **denen** wir gestern begegnet sind.

Here is an overview:

	masc.	*fem.*	*neuter*	*plural*
nom.	der	die	das	die
acc.	den	die	das	die
gen.	dessen	deren	dessen	deren
dat.	dem	der	dem	denen

As in English, relative pronouns are commonly used together with *prepositions*:

Das war die Firma, *bei* **der** ich ein Praktikum gemacht habe.
Das sind Ulrike und Edda, *von* **denen** ich dir schon viel erzählt habe.

Don't forget that in a relative clause the verb goes to the end. Note that you also have to put a comma at the start of the relative clause. You also need a comma at the end of the relative clause if this appears – as it often does – in the middle of the main clause:

Meine Freundin, die in Berlin wohnt, kommt morgen nach Hannover.

2 Besondere Nomen *(1) Adjectival nouns*

As you saw in the **Sprachinfo**, some nouns behave like adjectives in the endings they take.

Here are a few more adjectival nouns:

der/die Angestellte *employee*
der/die Erwachsene *adult, grown-up*
der/die Reisende *traveller*
der/die Fremde foreigner, stranger
der/die Verwandte *relative*

This overview may help to remind you of the endings needed:

	masculine	*feminine*	*plural*
nom.	der Verwandte/mein Verwandter	die/meine Verwandte	die/meine Verwandten
acc.	den/meinen Verwandten	die/meine Verwandte	die/meine Verwandten
gen.	des/meines Verwandten	der/meiner Verwandten	der/meiner Verwandten
dat.	dem/meinem Verwandten	der/meiner Verwandten	den/meinen Verwandten

3 Besondere Nomen *(2) Weak nouns*

In this unit you met the nouns **der Journalist** *journalist* and **der Präsident** *president*. These belong to a group of nouns called 'weak nouns'. They tend to take -(**e**)**n** in all cases except the nominative singular:

Nominative:	Ein Journalist sollte eigentlich die Wahrheit schreiben.
Accusative:	Kennst du den Journalist**en**?
Genitive:	Hier ist das neue Buch des Journalist**en**.
Dative:	Mit diesem Journalist**en** möchte niemand zusammenarbeiten.

Other frequently found nouns in this group include:

der Architekt, der Assistent, der Direktor, der Fotograf, der Franzose, der Herr, der Junge, der Kandidat, der Kollege, der Kunde, der Mensch, der Nachbar, der Soldat, der Student, der Tourist.

Note that **Herr** adds **-n** in the singular, but **-en** in the plural:

Kennst du Herr**n** Schröder?	Guten Tag, meine Damen und Herr**en**!

TESTEN SIE SICH!

A) MEHR ÜBUNGEN

1 Üben Sie Relativsätze

Bilden Sie Relativsätze, wie in dem folgenden Beispielsatz. Beginnen Sie alle Sätze mit **Das ist Herr Franke, …**

Beispiel: Er kommt aus Stuttgart. →
Das ist Herr Franke, der aus Stuttgart kommt.

a Er arbeitet als Journalist.
b Seine Frau ist auch Journalistin.
c Sein Sohn studiert in den USA.
d Er fährt einen roten Ferrari.
e Er trägt meistens italienische Anzüge.
f Man sieht ihn auf vielen Partys.
g Von ihm bekomme ich noch € 200,–.

2 Welches Wort passt am besten?

gewählt Handelspartner Macht Demokratie Export Bundeskanzler ~~Europas~~ Bundestag Wirtschaftszweige Aufgaben Einwohner Abgeordnete Bundespräsident

Deutschland liegt im Zentrum (a) ***Europas*** und hat mehr als 81,5 Millionen (b) ______. Es ist eine parlamentarische (c) ______. Das Parlament heißt der (d) ______, in dem mehr als 600 (e) ______ sitzen. Es wird alle vier Jahre (f) ______. Die größte politische (g) ______ hat der Chef der Regierung, der (h) ______. Das Staatsoberhaupt, der (i) ______, erfüllt dagegen nur repräsentative (j) ______.

Wirtschaftlich hängt Deutschland stark vom (k) ______ ab. Bedeutende (l) ______ sind die Automobilindustrie und die chemische Industrie. Die wichtigsten (m) ______ sind die Länder der EU.

Using the text on Germany as a model, write a similar description about your country.

3 Und jetzt Sie!

Spielen Sie die Rolle eines deutschen Journalisten, der über verschiedene Aspekte der deutschen Wirtschaft befragt wird.

CD2, TR 5, 11:42

Reporter	Die Bundesrepublik Deutschland ist eine der führenden Industrienationen der Welt. Welche Industriezweige sind denn besonders wichtig?
Sie	*Say that the manufacturing industry is very important. Say it is the driving force of German industry.*
Reporter	Gibt es denn noch andere bedeutende Wirtschaftszweige?
Sie	*Say that the chemical industry and mechanical engineering are also quite important.*
Reporter	Und welche Bedeutung haben die Banken und Versicherungen?
Sie	*Say that banks and insurance companies also play a big role.*
Reporter	Kann man sagen, dass viele Bereiche primär exportorientiert sind?
Sie	*Say yes. Explain that the car industry for instance exports more than 60% of its products. Say that a third of all jobs depend on export.*
Reporter	Und was sind die wichtigsten Handelspartner?
Sie	*Say that the most important trading partners are the countries of the EU.*
Reporter	Und was denken Sie über die weitere wirtschaftliche Entwicklung?
Sie	*Say you think that globalization will become more and more important. Say that overall you are quite optimistic.*

B) LESETEXT

Lesen Sie den Text über Frankfurt und das Bundesland Hessen und beantworten Sie die folgenden Fragen.

Frankfurt – das Herz von Hessen

Keine andere Stadt in Deutschland hat so eine Skyline wie Frankfurt am Main. Die Stadt mir den vielen Banken und der großen Kulturszene ist das Zentrum von Hessen. Doch das Bundesland in der Mitte von Deutschland hat auch anderes zu bieten.

Jörg Fuhrmann arbeitet als Investmentbanker bei der DZ BANK in Frankfurt. „Obwohl wir unseren Hauptkundenstamm in Deutschland haben, arbeiten wir natürlich auch auf internationaler Ebene. Da ist es ganz normal, dass man sehr viel auf Englisch kommuniziert." Für den 38-Jährigen ist das kein Problem, da er zwei Jahre bei der Barclays-Bank in London gearbeitet hat.

Was ihm an Frankfurt gefällt, ist die Tatsache, dass hier Menschen aus der ganzen Welt leben und arbeiten. „Der Ausländeranteil beträgt über 30 Prozent, so vielfältig ist sonst keine Stadt in Deutschland", sagt der Banker, der eigentlich aus Hannover stammt, sich nun aber ganz als Frankfurter fühlt.

Fuhrmann gefällt auch das kulturelle Angebot, das Frankfurt bietet: „Neben den Museen, Theatern und einer lebendigen

Literaturszene, bin ich auch von der Frankfurter Oper total begeistert," erzählt er mit großer Freude. Daneben hat Frankfurt noch einen anderen Vorteil. „Da der Flughafen nicht weit von der Innenstadt entfernt liegt, ist es einfach, meine Termine mit unseren Kunden und Geschäftspartnern im Ausland wahrzunehmen."

Die Rhein-Main-Gegend mit Frankfurt als Zentrum ist der Jobmotor von Hessen. Neben der Finanzwelt und dem Flughafen sind hier auch chemische und pharmazeutische Unternehmen wie Höchst und Merck zu Hause. Auch der Maschinenbau spielt eine große Rolle. In den letzten Jahren haben sich zudem neue innovative Unternehmen im Bio- und Umweltbereich in Hessen angesiedelt.

Doch Hessen hat auch eine ganz andere Seite. Wenige Kilometer von den großen Städten entfernt gibt es malerische Dörfer und kleine Städtchen, wo das Leben noch in aller Ruhe verläuft. Das weiß auch Jörg Fuhrmann, der am Wochenende gern Ausflüge in die Umgebung von Frankfurt unternimmt. „Mein Geheimtipp ist Marburg", sagt er. Marburg ist eine alte Universitätsstadt mit einer gemütlichen Altstadt, vielen Cafés, Buchläden und Kneipen. „In Marburg ist alles weniger hektisch und haben die Leute noch Zeit. Das ist manchmal ein guter Kontrast zu meinem Leben in Frankfurt", erklärt er.

QUICK VOCAB

der Hauptkundenstamm (-¨e) *main client base*
das Ebene (-n) *level*
betragen *to amount to*
vielfältig *diverse*
begeistert von *enthusiastic about*
wahr | nehmen *to keep (appointments)*
das Unternehmen (-) *enterprise, company*
sich an | siedeln *to settle, become established*
malerisch *picturesque*
verlaufen *(here) to take its course, go on*
gemütlich *cosy, homely, snug*

Beantworten Sie die Fragen.

- **a** Does Jörg Fuhrmann have clients only in Germany?
- **b** Why does he have no problems with communicating in English?
- **c** What does Jörg particularly like about Frankfurt and how does it compare with other German cities in this respect?
- **d** What does Jörg think about the range of cultural activities on offer in Frankfurt?
- **e** Frankfurt also has a third advantage, as far as Jörg is concerned. What is it?
- **f** What are the main industries to be found in the Rhine–Main area?
- **g** But what quite different aspect does Hessen have?
- **h** What is Jörg's secret tip and why does he particularly like it?

CHECKLISTE

Now that you have completed Unit 10, can you

1 talk about newspapers and magazines? ☐

2 answer questions on the German political structure? ☐

3 answer questions on aspects of the German economy? ☐

4 give a short overview of the political and economic structure of your country? ☐

5 form relative clauses? ☐

6 identify adjectival and weak nouns? ☐

7 understand a text containing information about one of the German states? ☐

Congratulations on completing *Perfect your Geman!*

We hope you have enjoyed working your way through the course. We are always keen to receive feedback from people who have used our course, so why not contact us and let us know your reactions? We'll be particularly pleased to receive your praise, but we should also like to know if you think things could be improved. We always welcome comments and suggestions and we do our best to incorporate constructive suggestions into later editions.

You can contact us through the publishers at:

Teach Yourself Books, Hodder Headline Ltd,
338 Euston Road, London NW1 3BH
www.teachyourself.com

We hope you will want to build on your knowledge of German and have made a few suggestions to help you do this in the reference section after the **Key to the exercises**.

Alles Gute!

Heiner Schenke and Paul Coggle

Key to the exercises

Unit 1

1 **a** F. Die Arbeit macht ihr viel Spaß. **b** F. Sie hat vier Jahre in Bristol gelebt. **c** F. Sie ist seit fast zehn Jahren verheiratet. **d** F. Er ist selbstständig (und hat ein kleines Architektenbüro in Köln). **e** F. Sie geht zu einem Englischkurs für Fortgeschrittene. **2 a** halbtags **b** Spaß **c** verheiratet **d** selbstständig **e** fließend **f** interessiert. **Sprachinfo** There are **4 ja/nein questions a** Frau Peters, können Sie ein bisschen über sich erzählen? **b** Und sind Sie berufstätig? **c** Sind Sie denn verheiratet? **d** Und haben Sie ein Hobby? and **2 w-questions a** Und welche Sprachen sprechen Sie? **b** Was macht denn Ihr Mann? **Sprachinfo** to study at: studieren an; *to be married to:* verheiratet sein mit **3 a** in **b** aus **c** aus **d** an **e** als **f** in **g** seit **h** aus **i** in **j** als **4 a**-iv **b**-vi **c**-v **d**-i **e**-vii **f**-ii **g**-iii

5

Name	*Alter*	*Familienstand*	*Wohnort*	*Beruf*	*Hobbys*
Martin	32	geschieden	Apolda, in Thüringen	Krankenpfleger	Kino, Skifahren
Petra	44	verheiratet	Salzburg, in Österreich	Hotelfachfrau	Geschichte, Lesen
Max	22	ledig/single	Lübeck, in Norddeutschland	Student der Mathematik	Bungeespringen, Surfen

6 1. b 2. a 3. b 4. c 5. b. **7 a** Können Sie sich bitte kurz vorstellen? **b** Was sind Sie von Beruf? **c** Was machen Sie in Ihrer Freizeit? **d** Was für Hobbys haben Sie? **e** Ich gehe gern ins Kino. **f** In den Ferien gehe ich surfen. **8 a** die **b** die **c** die **d** das **e** der **f** der **g** das **h** das **i** die. **9 a** Ja, sie fährt das erste Mal nach Berlin. **b** Seine Freundin wohnt in Berlin. **c** Er wohnt in Hannover. **d** Sie studiert Film (an der Hochschule der Künste). **e** Sie studiert Medizin und möchte Kinderärztin werden. **f** Sie möchte ihr das Berliner Nachtleben zeigen. **g** Er findet, dass die meisten Leute sehr offen sind./Er findet die meisten Leute sehr offen. **10 a** ... schon seit langem besuchen. **b** ... aus Hannover. **c** ... ganz schön kostspielig. **d** ... sie einen Studienplatz an der HdK bekommen hat. **e** ... Kinderärztin werden. **f** ... alte Schulfreundin von ihr. **g** ... Menschen aus der ganzen Welt treffen. **h** ... sehr lebendig.

Testen Sie sich!

A) Mehr Übungen

der	*die*		*das*
Mittwoch	Woche	Sprache	Silber
Sonntag	Natur	Pension	Gold
Sommer	Landschaft	Fußballmannschaft	Gymnasium
Winter	Region	Freundschaft	Mädchen
Dezember	Passion	Nationalität	Märchen
Schnaps	Rose	Identität	Tanzen
Wein	Temperatur	Intelligenz	Schwimmen
Ferrari			
Audi			

2 **a** Berufe **b** Kurse **c** Gäste **d** Schnäpse **e** Züge **f** Kneipen **g** Städte **h** Häuser **i** Restaurants **j** Büros. 3 **a** Kommen Sie aus Berlin? **b** Wo sind Sie aufgewachsen? **c** Welche Sprachen sprechen Sie? **d** Was *sind Sie von* Beruf? **e** Sind Sie verheiratet? **f** Haben Sie Kinder?

4

- Ja, natürlich. Mein Name ist Matthias Brandt und ich bin 1955 in Hannover geboren, aber seit 20 Jahren wohne ich in Berlin.
- Ja, ich bin selbstständig. Ich bin Architekt.
- Ja, und ich habe eine Tochter, Steffi. Sie ist Studentin und studiert an der Universität Heidelberg.
- Ich gehe gern ins Kino und ich lese gern. Ich interessiere mich auch für Sprachen.
- Ja, die Menschen in Berlin sind sehr freundlich und die Stadt ist wirklich interessant.

B) Lesetext

1 **a** Er ist 18 Jahre alt. **b** Er hat ihn seit zwei Monaten. **c** Ja, seine Hobbys sind Computerspielen, Internetsurfen, Chatten. **d** Er hat es seit einer Woche. **e** Das Auto (die Kiste) frisst (braucht) so viel Benzin. **f** Später möchte er gern als Programmierer arbeiten (vielleicht bei Siemens).

Unit 2

1 **a** F. Er steht gegen halb acht auf. **b** R. **c** F. Es ist nur zehn Minuten zu Fuß. **d** F. Normalerweise isst er in der Mensa. **e** R. **f** F. Abends bleibt er zu Hause./ Abends liest er die Zeitung, schaut Nachrichten im Fernsehen, manchmal noch

einen Film. Gewöhnlich liest er oder hört Radio oder eine Schallplatte. **2 a** aufstehen **b** frühstücken **c** stattfinden **d** laufen **e** einkaufen gehen **f** beginnen **g** besuchen. **Insight:** Lorenz Müller uses: normalerweise, meistens, manchmal, gewöhnlich. **3 a** Zuerst mache ich 15 Minuten Yoga. **b** Zum Frühstück trinke ich Orangensaft und esse ein Croissant mit Marmelade. **c** Normalerweise gehe ich gegen acht Uhr aus dem Haus. **d** Meistens arbeiten wir bis 18.00 Uhr. **e** Am Wochenende besuchen wir öfters Freunde oder gehen essen. **f** Manchmal fahren mein Freund und ich am Wochenende zum Windsurfen an den Starnberger See. **4** Normalerweise steht Herr Müller um halb acht auf. Dann frühstückt er. Danach arbeitet er zu Hause am Schreibtisch. Anschließend fährt oder geht er zur Arbeit. Mittags isst er in der Mensa. Später gibt er Seminare an der Universität. Abends liest er oder hört er Musik.

5 a bis um Mitternacht **b** gegen eins, halb zwei **c** geht sie ins Bett **d** um neun, halb zehn **e** Orangensaft oder Grapefruitsaft **f** vier Uhr nachmittags **g** Englischstunden **h** viermal im Jahr. **6 1** b **2** c **3** a **4** c **5** b. **7 a** Es kommt darauf an ... **b** gegen eins. **c** Ich stelle mich schnell unter die Dusche. **d** eine Scheibe Toast. **e** ab und zu. **f** höchstens viermal im Jahr. **g** zu Weihnachten. **h** bei Geburtstagen. **8** Here are 10 possible combinations. If you found more, please check your answers in the glossary or in a dictionary: anfangen, abwaschen, abräumen, stattfinden, mitgehen, abholen, zumachen, einladen, ausmachen, einkaufen. **9 a** fangen ... an/finden ... statt. **b** bereitet ... vor. **c** waschen ... ab. **d** räumt ... ab. **e** findet ... statt. **f** sehen ... fern. **g** lädt ... ein. **h** auffrischen. **10 a** Sie steht um 7 Uhr auf. ✓ **b** Zum Frühstück isst sie Croissants. ✗ **c** Nach dem Frühstück liest sie Zeitung. ✓ **d** Sie besucht gerne eine ihrer Freundinnen. ✓ **e** Meistens isst sie in einem Restaurant zu Mittag. ✗ **f** Sie strickt einen Pullover für ihre Urenkelin. ✗ **g** Sie sieht nicht gern Unterhaltungssendungen. ✓ **h** Sie geht gegen 22 Uhr ins Bett. ✗ **11 a** ... langweilig? **b** ... um 7 Uhr auf. **c** ... auf meinem Balkon. **d** ... für Politik. **e** ... zu Mittag. **f** ... in die Umgebung. **g** ... zu stricken. **h** ... gar kein Interesse.

Testen Sie sich!

A) Mehr Übungen

1 b stellen **c** abwaschen **d** laufen **e** treiben **f** geben **g** aufräumen **h** stricken **i** arbeiten **j** übersetzen **k** machen **l** auffrischen. **2 a** Claudia fährt im Winter mit der U-Bahn zur Universität. **b** Kommst du heute Abend mit ins Kino? **c** Theo und Anke gehen in der Mittagspause zu Fuß ins Restaurant. **d** Manfred fährt nachmittags mit seinem Auto zu seinem Freund ins Krankenhaus. **e** Hans Martinek geht oft nach der Arbeit ins Fitnesscenter. **f** Frau Tiedke kauft abends noch schnell im Supermarkt ein. **g** Die Fuhrmanns wollen nächstes Wochenende eine Radtour an die Ostsee machen. **3 1** f **2** b **3** h **4** g **5** j **6** a **7** c **8** e **9** i **10** d

4

- Während der Woche stehe ich gewöhnlich gegen sieben Uhr auf, am Wochenende meistens gegen halb zehn.
- Normalerweise hole ich Brötchen von der Bäckerei. Dann koche ich Kaffee und esse Brötchen mit Marmelade und Butter und trinke ein Glas Saft. Gewöhnlich lese ich auch die Zeitung.
- Meistens fahre ich mit dem Auto und nur selten mit dem Bus.
- Gewöhnlich habe ich zwischen 12.30 Uhr und 13.15 Uhr Mittagspause. Meistens esse ich in meiner Firma und nur gelegentlich esse ich in einem Restaurant zu Mittag.
- Gewöhnlich schaue ich Nachrichten im Fernsehen, lese ein Buch oder höre Radio.
- Manchmal besuche ich Freunde oder meine Eltern, gehe gelegentlich spazieren oder mache die Arbeit, die während der Woche liegen geblieben ist. Sonntags mache ich manchmal Tagesausflüge in die Umgebung.

B) Lesetext

a The percentage of Germans who can start the day free of stress. **b** 60% go by car. Some just find it more convenient, others live so far out of town that there is no other possibility for them than using their own car. **c** By public transport, rail or bus. **d** A good feeling that they are doing something for the environment. **e** They need to travel more than 25 km to work.

Unit 3

1 **a** Bei der Deutschen Bank. **b** Es ist schwierig, Arbeit zu finden. **c** Ungefähr 1,8 Millionen. **d** Englisch. **e** Nach Florenz, in Italien. **2 a** bestehen **b** Stellung **c** überfüllt **d** aufnehmen **e** mache Gebrauch von (meinen Englischkenntnissen). 3 **a** F. Für Akademiker in Deutschland bestehen Schwierigkeiten, Arbeit zu finden. **b** F. Birgit kennt sehr viele Leute, die studiert haben und jetzt arbeitslos sind. **c** R. **d** R. **e** F. Birgit macht in ihrem Beruf jeden Tag von ihren Englischkenntnissen Gebrauch. **Sprachinfo** Heinz says: Hast du das aufgeben müssen? and not Musstest du das aufgeben? **4 a** gearbeitet **b** studiert **c** beworben **d** passiert **e** verbracht **f** gegangen **g** geworden **h** gefahren **i** besucht **j** verkauft. Verbs which take *sein* are: **d** passieren **f** gehen **g** werden **h** fahren. 5 **a** Dort habe ich auch die Schule besucht. **b** Mit 19 Jahren habe ich das Abitur bestanden. **c** Danach habe ich eine Lehre angefangen. **d** Ich habe mich bei der Dresdner Bank beworben. **e** Es gab viele Bewerber, aber ich hatte Glück. **f** Ich durfte auch 3 Monate in einer Zweigstelle in New York arbeiten. **g** Dort habe ich viel gelernt und konnte auch mein Englisch verbessern. **h** Vor einem halben Jahr habe ich meine Banklehre abgeschlossen. **6 a** Dort besuchte ich auch die Schule. **b** Mit 19 Jahren bestand ich das Abitur. **c** Danach fing ich eine Banklehre an. **d** Ich bewarb mich bei der Dresdner Bank. **e** Es gab

viele Bewerber, aber ich hatte Glück. **f** Ich durfte auch 3 Monate in einer Zweigstelle in New York arbeiten. **g** Dort lernte ich viel und konnte auch mein Englisch verbessern. **h** Vor einem halben Jahr schloss ich meine Banklehre ab. 7 **a** Kindergarten **b** Grundschule **c** Hauptschule **d** Realschule **e** Gymnasium **f** Berufsschule **g** das Abitur **h** Staatsexamen. 8 **a** Peter wird nächsten Sommer in die Schule kommen. **b** Das Seminar wird um 16.00 Uhr anfangen. **c** Frau Dr. Martini wird die Vorlesung halten. **d** Susanne wird ihre Lehre bei der Telekom machen. **e** Ich werde meinen Sprachkurs in Madrid machen. **f** Ich werde in zwei Wochen meinen neuen Job anfangen. 9 **a** F. Vera studiert Anglistik in vierten Semester. **b** R. **c** F. Ilona will Ende nächsten Semesters das Staatsexamen ablegen. **d** F. Sie wird sich beim Umweltministerium bewerben. **e** R. **f** R. 10 There are two examples: **a** Ich werde mich ... bewerben. **b** ..., wird hoffentlich wieder Nachfrage bestehen.

11 **a** Ist hier noch frei? **b** Ich studiere Anglistik im dritten Semester. **c** Du hast aber Glück! **d** Ende nächsten Semesters will ich das Staatsexamen ablegen. **e** Und was möchtest du (dann) werden? **f** Und was hast du vor? **g** Ich möchte Gymnasiallehrerin für Englisch werden. **h** Es hat viel Spaß gemacht.

Testen Sie sich!

A) Mehr Übungen

1 **a** machen **b** bewerben **c** studieren **d** durchführen **e** treffen **f** lesen **g** besuchen **h** unterrichten **i** diskutieren **j** schreiben **k** ablegen **l** feiern. 2 Verbs which do not take ge- are: bewerben, besuchen, diskutieren, studieren, unterrichten. 3 **a** Morgen besuchen wir unsere Eltern. **b** Am Dienstag arbeite ich im Garten. **c** Demnächst lassen wir das Haus renovieren. **d** Ich fange bald mit meinem Englischkurs an. **e** Im Oktober fahren wir nach England. **f** Im September kommt Martin in die Schule. **g** In zwei Wochen fange ich meinen Job als Bedienung an. **h** Übermorgen gehe ich zum Friseur. **i** Am Wochenende gehen wir zum Windsurfen. **j** Übrigens, das Abendessen ist gleich fertig!

4

- Ich wollte eigentlich studieren, aber ich wollte auf keinen Fall arbeitslos werden. Deshalb will ich eine Lehre machen.
- Ich möchte unbedingt eine Schreinerlehre machen. Aber die Leute mit Hauptschulabschluss oder mittlerer Reife haben da größere Chancen.
- Ich weiß, dass sich immer mehr Leute mit Abitur um diese Stellen bewerben. Aber ich möchte lieber kreativ arbeiten als einen Bürojob machen.
- Dann möchte ich Biologie studieren und Lehrer werden. Hoffentlich wird dann wieder Nachfrage nach Lehrern bestehen, wenn ich mit dem Staatsexamen fertig bin.

B) Lesetext

i a Richtig. **b** Falsch. Er hat seine Lehre in der Elektrobranche hinter sich. (Er hat seine Lehre in der Elektrobranche schon beendet.) **c** Falsch. Er spielt Saxofon aber nur sehr einfache Sachen auf dem Klavier. (Er kann nicht so gut Klavier spielen). **d** Falsch. Antonio glaubt, dass es schwer ist, als Musiklehrer sein Geld zu verdienen. **ii a** i) Grammar school music teachers earn good money. ii) The many holidays are also not bad. **b** Antonio could benefit from his earlier training. **c** Whether he thinks that he could pass on his knowledge of the saxophone and piano. **d** Because as a student you can earn quite a lot of money from giving music lessons. **e** Above all he has to do something that interests him.

Unit 4

1 a Sie geht dort zu einem IngenieurKongress. **b** Sie sind immer noch eine Minderheit. **c** Er arbeitet seit sieben Jahren bei seiner Firma. **d** Die Firma stellt Werkzeugmaschinen her. **e** Er fliegt nach Budapest, um dort Verhandlungen mit einer ungarischen Firma zu führen. **f** Er möchte mehr Zeit für seine Frau und Kinder haben. **g** Beide reisen gern. **2 a** bilden **b** herstellen **c** beschäftigt **d** im Allgemeinen **e** zufrieden. **Sprachinfo a** Ja, wenn man so ein bisschen genauer hinschaut, findet man heutzutage Frauen in fast jedem Beruf. **b** Und was sind Sie von Beruf, wenn ich fragen darf? **c** Zeitmangel ist ja eines der größten Probleme, wenn man berufstätig ist. **3 a** Frau Kubig kommt aus Stuttgart und sie ist Bauingenieurin. **b** Sie fährt nach Wien, denn sie möchte einen Kongress besuchen. **c** Herr Krause ist kein Ingenieur, sondern er ist leitender Angestellter. **d** Seine Arbeit gefällt ihm, denn er lernt viele neue Dinge. **e** Er reist viel, aber Geschäftsreisen nehmen viel Zeit in Anspruch. **f** Trinken Sie noch Kaffee oder brauchen Sie jetzt einen Schnaps? **g** Machen Sie jetzt die nächste Übung oder möchten Sie eine Pause machen? **4** Herr Johnson lernt Deutsch, weil ... **a** er geschäftlich oft in München ist. **b** er Verhandlungen auf Deutsch führen muss. **c** er die Süddeutsche Zeitung lesen möchte. **d** er gern Weine aus Rheinhessen trinkt. **e** seine Freundin aus Berlin kommt. **5 a** Deutsch als Fremdsprache **b** sehr gut **c** die Bezahlung **d** Gymnasiallehrer **e** Zivildienst **f** anstrengend **g** Sozialarbeiter **6** 1 -c 2 -b 3 -c 4 -b **7 a** Lange nicht gesehen. **b** Und was machst du jetzt für eine Arbeit? **c** im Allgemeinen **d** Sie haben es nötig ... **e** wenn das so ist **8 a** Normalerweise arbeitet sie von neun Uhr morgens bis halb fünf oder fünf Uhr abends. **b** Die Arbeitsatmosphäre ist sehr gut. Mit ihren Kollegen arbeitet sie gut im Team zusammen. **c** Ihr gefällt es, dass ihr Job sehr kreativ ist und ihr gefällt die Arbeit im Team. **d** Ihr gefällt nicht, dass sie oft unter Termindruck arbeiten muss. **e** Sie verdient etwa 3000,- Euro brutto. **f** In ein paar Jahren möchte sie sich selbstständig machen.

9 a Termindruck **b** Bezahlung **c** Teilzeitkraft **d** Vollzeitkraft **e** Urlaubsgeld **f** Weihnachtsgeld **g** Rentenversicherung **h** selbstständig **i** Verantwortung **j** Herausforderung **10 a** ... einer PR-Firma. **b** ... ist generell sehr gut. **c** ... für Humor. **d** ... langweilig. **e** ... zufrieden. **f** ... Termindruck arbeiten muss. **g** ... selbstständig machen. **h** ... richtige Herausforderung.

Testen Sie sich!

A) Mehr Übungen

1 i The job titles are: Bauingenieur, leitender Angestellter, Angestellter und Beamter **ii a** Arzt › Ärztin, Koch › Köchin, Rechtsanwalt › Rechtsanwältin, Tierarzt › Tierärztin, Zahnarzt › Zahnärztin **b** Krankenpfleger › Krankenschwester (although die Krankenpflegerin is increasingly being used nowadays). **2 a** Friseurin **b** Ärztin **c** Klempner **d** Lehrerin **e** Kellner **f** Apothekerin **g** Übersetzer **h** Landwirt **i** Psychologin **j** Aktienhändlerin **k** Architektin. **3 i a** Herr Krause fliegt oft nach Budapest, weil er dort geschäftlich zu tun hat. **b** Claudia gefällt ihr Beruf, obwohl sie oft unter Termindruck arbeiten muss. **c** Sie arbeitet gern im Team, weil ihre Kollegen alle Sinn für Humor haben. **d** Sie möchte sich selbstständig machen, obwohl das mehr Stress bedeutet. **e** Claudia möchte eine eigene Firma gründen, weil dies eine Herausforderung ist. **ii a** Weil er dort oft geschäftlich zu tun hat, fliegt Herr Krause oft nach Budapest. **b** Obwohl sie oft unter Termindruck arbeiten muss, gefällt Claudia ihr Beruf. **c** Weil ihre Kollegen alle Sinn für Humor haben, arbeitet sie gern im Team. **d** Obwohl das mehr Stress bedeutet, möchte sie sich selbstständig machen. **e** Weil dies eine Herausforderung ist, möchte Claudia eine eigene Firma gründen.

4

- Ich bin Bauingenieurin und bin im Allgemeinen sehr zufrieden mit meinem Beruf. Mir gefällt besonders, dass ich soviel reisen kann. Aber natürlich ist Zeitmangel eines meiner größten Probleme. Und was machst du jetzt?
- Das stelle ich mir aber sehr schwierig vor. Was willst du jetzt machen?
- Gute Idee! Zur Zeit werden ja viele Stellen angeboten, die auf diesem Gebiet Kenntnisse verlangen. Ich wünsche dir viel Glück dabei.

B) Lesetext

1 Personal data, schooling, higher education, placements, work experience, special skills, IT skills. **2 a** Ihre Kindheit verbrachte Maria in München. **b** Ihr Abitur machte sie 1999. **c** Sie studierte von Oktober 1999 bis Juni 2005. **d** Nach ihrem Studienabschluss arbeitete sie bei Unilever in Hamburg. **e** Sie ist Referentin für Personalfortbildung (bei Hapag-Lloyd).

Unit 5

1 **a** R. **b** R. **c** F. Sie findet Sport langweilig. **d** F. Sie sagt, dass es in München sehr viele Möglichkeiten gibt. **e** R. **f** F. Sie interessiert sich für Theater, geht aber auch regelmäßig in Ausstellungen. **2 a** Ich interessiere mich eben für alles, was ... **b** Was ich ganz toll finde, ist ... **c** Ich schätze die Klassiker... **d** Im Allgemeinen ziehe ich ... vor. **e** Das interessiert mich nicht. **f** Sport hat mich schon immer gelangweilt. 3 **a**-vi **b**-vii **c**-ii **d**-v **e**-iv **f**-i **g**-viii **h**-iii. **4 b** an **c** an/über **d** um **e** mit/über **f** mit **g** mit/über **h** von **i** auf **5 a** Ärgern Sie sich über das Wetter? **b** Verstehen Sie sich gut mit Ihren Kollegen? **c** Glauben Sie an Ufos? **d** Interessieren Sie sich für Kunst? **e** Können Sie sich für Techno-Musik begeistern? **f** Freuen Sie sich auf die Ferien? **6 a** Führerschein **b** dritten **c** Turnieren **d** schwimmt **e** Leute **f** eingebunden **g** flexibel **7** 1 b 2 c 3 a 4 b **Sprachinfo a** Er sagt, es ist eine gute Gelegenheit, neue Leute kennen zu lernen. **b** Sebastian meint, es würde ihm nicht gefallen, so eingebunden zu sein. **c** Er zieht es vor, seine Freizeit flexibel zu gestalten. **d** Nein, es gefällt mir zu trainieren. **8 a** ... tanzen zu gehen. **b** ... bald meinen Führerschein zu machen. **c** ... ein Bier zu trinken. **d** ... nachher ins Restaurant zu gehen. **e** ... noch Karten für das Konzert zu bekommen. **f** ... meine Freizeit selbst zu gestalten. **9 a** F. Sie geben nächstes Wochenende eine große Party. **b** F. Sie fahren mit ihrem Kegelclub nach England. **c** R. **d** F. Ihr gefällt es, dass man öfters neue Leute trifft. **e** R. **f** F. Sie haben schon Städtereisen mit dem Club gemacht. **10 i a** ...viele Vorteile. **b** mag ganz besonders **c** auch gern mal **d** ... uns beiden doch viel Spaß machen. **ii a** ... längst genug. **b** ... uns beiden nicht so gefällt. **c** ... meinem Geschmack. **d** ... mir überhaupt nicht gefallen. **11 a** Habt ihr nächste Woche schon was vor? **b** Toll, da kommen wir gern. **c** Könnt ihr das nicht mal ausfallen lassen? **d** So ein Pech. **e** Das sagt uns auch nicht immer zu. **f** Also, ich hätte schon längst genug. **g** Das wäre ganz und gar nicht nach meinem Geschmack.

Testen Sie sich!

A Mehr Übungen

1 **a** Ja, darauf freue ich mich sehr. **b** Nein, daran erinnere ich mich leider nicht. **c** Ja, darum bewerbe ich mich bestimmt. **d** Nein, darüber ärgere ich mich überhaupt nicht. **e** Ja, dafür interessiere ich mich ungeheuer. **f** Nein, darüber habe ich mich ganz und gar nicht gefreut. **2 a**-iv **b**-vi **c**-v **d**-i **e**-vii **f**-ii **g**-iii

3

- Ich schwimme seit acht Jahren für einen Club und bin auch Mitglied in einem Kegelclub.
- Manchmal denke ich ja auch, dass es ein bisschen zu viel ist. Aber es hat auch eine Menge Vorteile.

- Man trifft viele Leute. Man hält sich auch fit und sieht viele neue Orte, wenn man mit den Clubs auf Turniere geht.
- Doch, ich interessiere mich für Kultur, aber ich mag Sport lieber.
- Ehrlich gesagt ziehe ich moderne Musik vor und ich gehe auch gerne ins Kino.

B) Lesetext

1 **a** R. **b** F. Sie ist die drittgrößte Stadt Deutschlands. **c** R. **d** F. München hat 85 Millionen Tagesbesucher und drei bis vier Millionen Übernachtungen pro Jahr. **e** R. **2 a** Euros per square metre for rent in Munich. **b** Number of museums. **c** Number of theatres. **d** Number of daily commuters. **e** Inhabitants of Munich. **f** Overnight stays per year. **g** Day-trippers to Munich.

Unit 6

1 **a** R. **b** F. Er sagt, die Antiraucherfanatiker sind schon viel zu weit gegangen. **c** F. Er ist Raucher. **d** F. Er sagt, sie verpesten die Luft. **e** R. **f** F. Er macht sich keine Sorgen. **2 a** Ganz und gar nicht! **b** Das ist ja ein Witz! **c** Da ist bestimmt etwas dran. **d** Das ist mir egal. **e** Mir macht das Rauchen unheimlich viel Spaß. 3 Here are some possible answers: **a** Da bin ich ganz deiner Meinung. Da stimme ich mit dir überein. **b** Da bin ich Ihrer Meinung. **c** Da bin ich anderer Meinung./Da muss ich widersprechen. **d** Nein. Da bin ich (ganz) anderer Meinung. **e** Da bin ich deiner Ansicht. Da stimme ich mit dir überein. **f** Da bin ich ganz deiner Meinung./Da stimme ich mit dir überein. **4 a** Wie **b** Was denkst du über die Politik … **c** von der **d** Sind Sie der … **e** darin überein **f** Wie ist deine/Ihre Ansicht … **5 a** für **b** Zumutung **c** entspannen **d** negative **e** allergisch **f** wächst **6 a**-v **b**-vi **c**-i **d**-ii **e**-iii **f**-iv **7 a** Darf **b** Könnt **c** kann **d** soll **e** will **f** Kannst **g** könnt, wollt, müsst **8 a** Sie hat mit fünf Jahren schwimmen gelernt. **b** Seit zehn Jahren. **c** Am Anfang hat sie zweimal eineinhalb Stunden, also drei Stunden trainiert. **d** Nein, sie trainieren mit anderen zusammen. **e** Im Moment trainiert sie fünfmal pro Woche. **f** Es ist eine gute Methode, sich gesundheitlich fit zu halten. **9 a** … du dieses Hobby denn schon? **b** … in einen Schwimmclub einzutreten. **c** … steigert sich das Trainingsprogramm. **d** … wofür man trainiert. **e** ... gesundheitlich fit zu halten. **f** … in Schwung. **g** … am wenigsten. **h** ... Muskeln des Körpers.

Testen Sie sich!

A) Mehr Übungen

1 **a** Wie ist Ihre Meinung/Ansicht über ….? **b** Wie finden Sie …?/Was halten Sie von …?/Was denken Sie über …? **c** Da müssen wir Ihnen widersprechen.

d Stimmt das Ihres Erachtens? **e** Teilen Sie meine Meinung? **f** Da ist bestimmt 'was dran. **g** Da liegen sie völlig falsch. **h** Das sehen wir schon ein, aber ... . **2 a** des Rauchens **b** meines Bruders **c** der Fußballmannschaft **d** ihres Mannes **e** deiner Meinung **f** Meines Erachtens **g** meiner beiden Brüder **h** Ihrer Meinung **3 a** Berlin **b** stark **c** Problem **d** Zahl **e** zehnmal **f** Deutschland **g** anderthalb **h** zwei **i** jahrelangen **j** Krebs **k** Menschen

There are four more examples of the genitive: **i** ... den Gefahren des stark zunehmenden Alkoholismus ... **ii** Die Zahl der Alkoholtoten ... **iii** ... die der Drogentoten **iv** ... die Folgeschäden jahrelangen Alkoholmissbrauchs ...

4

- Ich habe mir Sorgen um meine Gesundheit gemacht. Außerdem ist mein Mann allergisch gegen Rauch.
- Ja, sehr sogar. Ich bin der Meinung, dass das Rauchen in der Öffentlichkeit verboten werden sollte. Besonders in Restaurants, wenn Leute essen.
- Oh, ja. Hast du eigentlich deinen Alkoholkonsum gedrosselt?
- War das, weil du dir Sorgen um die Folgeschäden des Alkoholmissbrauchs gemacht hast?

B) Lesetext

i 2 Bewegung braucht der Körper; **4** Regelmäßige Entspannung; **5** Regelmäßiges Gehirnjogging; **6** Genussgifte – schlecht für den Körper; **7** Beziehungen sind wichtig; **8** Positiv denken. **ii a** One should have a low-fat diet, eat little meat and plenty of fruit and vegetables. **b** Water, fruit juices and herbal teas. **c** A significant drop in fitness. **d** They are good for the psyche and thus for general well-being. **e** The body regenerates itself during sleep. **f** Solving a crossword puzzle. **g** There's nothing to object to about that. It just mustn't be too many. **h** Because without them one often feels socially isolated and this is not good for one's health. **i** They will have no joy in life and cannot properly enjoy the beautiful everyday things in life.

Unit 7

1 a Sie möchte nächsten Freitag nach Berlin fliegen. **b** Um 19.20. c Um 20.25. **d** Sie möchte am Montagmorgen zurückfliegen. **e** Sie muss noch mit ihrer Chefin sprechen. **2 a** wenn es geht **b** die Maschine **c** es sind noch Plätze frei **d** startet der letzte Flug **e** das wäre nicht so schlimm **f** Was kostet ... **Sprachinfo a** Ich hätte gern gewusst, ob es abends nach 18.00 Uhr Flüge nach Berlin gibt. **b** Ich sehe mal auf dem Computer nach, ob noch Plätze frei sind. **c** Dann müsste ich auch noch wissen, ob ich Sonntagabend oder

Montag früh zurückfliegen könnte. 3 **a** Ist es möglich, die Spätmaschine zu nehmen? **b** Ich muss noch mal mit dem Reisebüro sprechen. **c** Darf ich Ihr Telefon benutzen? **d** Wissen Sie, wie teuer es mit dem Taxi ist? **e** Können Sie mir sagen, wo man in Berlin gut ausgehen kann? **f** Habt ihr Lust, mit ins Kino zu kommen? 4 **i** Entschuldigung, könnten Sie mir sagen, ... **a** ... wie weit es bis in die Stadtmitte ist? **b** ... was eine Tageskarte für die U-Bahn kostet? **c** ... wie ich am schnellsten nach Charlottenburg komme? **d** ... wo es hier in der Nähe eine Touristeninformation gibt? **e** ... ob das hier vorne eigentlich die Gedächtniskirche ist? **f** ... wo man hier in der Nähe gut essen gehen kann? **ii** Es tut mir leid, aber ich weiss nicht, ... **a** .... wie weit es bis in die Stadtmitte ist. **b** ... was eine Tageskarte für die U-Bahn kostet. **c** ... wie Sie am schnellsten nach Charlottenburg kommen. **d** ... wo es hier in der Nähe eine Touristeninformation gibt. **e** ... ob das hier vorne eigentlich die Gedächtniskirche ist. **f** ... wo man hier in der Nähe gut essen gehen kann. 5 **a** hätte **b** 109 **c** ungefähr **d** Güntzelstraße **e** drei **f** rechten **g** im Bus **6 a i** zu **ii** always takes the dative **b i** über **ii** because of 'gehen' it takes the accusative **c i** in **ii** because of 'kommen' it takes the accusative **d i** in **ii** it takes the dative because 'befinden' puts the emphasis on location **e i** neben **ii** it requires the dative because of 'sein' i.e. location **f i** von **ii** 'von' always takes the dative 7 **a** Sie lebt seit über 20 Jahren in Berlin. **b** Sie sagt, dass die Berliner Humor haben und sagen, was sie denken. **c** Nach dem 1. Weltkrieg. **d** Es folgten 12 Jahre Diktatur. **e** Im Brücke-Museum wird expressionistische Kunst gezeigt. **f** Es bietet sehr viel – von eleganten Kaufhäusern bis hin zu alternativen Läden. **8 a** Geschichte **b** Dorf **c** Preußen **d** der 1. Weltkrieg **e** expressionistische Kunst **f** die „Goldenen Zwanziger" **g** Wiederaufbau **h** der Fall der Mauer **i** Einkaufen **j** Szenekneipen 9 **a** ... in Berlin geblieben. **b** ... sie Humor haben und offen sagen, was sie denken. **c** ... dem 1. Weltkrieg zu einer Weltstadt wurde. **d** ... 12 Jahre Diktatur der Nationalsozialisten. **e** ... die Teilung der Stadt. **f** ... expressionistische Kunst sehen kann. **g** ... bietet Berlin fast alles. **h** ... viele Szenekneipen, Restaurants und Clubs.

Testen Sie sich!

A) Mehr Übungen

1 **a** der **b** die, zum **c** der **d** Zum, der **e** die, der **f** der, dem **g** den, dem

2

- Wir sind hier in der Brandenburgischen Straße. Sehen Sie die Ampel an der nächsten Kreuzung?
- Dort biegen Sie rechts in die Düsseldorfer Straße. Nach ungefähr 300 Metern kommen Sie zur Konstanzer Straße. Gehen Sie über die Konstanzer Straße, ungefähr 300 Meter geradeaus, bis Sie zur Bayerischen Straße kommen. Biegen Sie an dieser Kreuzung links in die Bayerische Straße.

- Nein, nicht rechts, sondern links in die Bayerische Straße. Dann ungefähr einen Kilometer weiter kommen Sie zur Pariser Straße.
- Bitte schön.

3 **a** Stadt **b** Weltkrieg **c** Jahrhundert **d** „Goldenen Zwanziger" **e** Nationalsozialisten **f** Diktatur **g** Wiederaufbau **h** Mauerbau **i** Mauer **j** Hauptstadt **k** Einwohnern **l** Nachtleben **m** Angebot.

B) Lesetext

Your own version should include these points, but does not have to be exactly the same as this one: **a** What you get: Coach travel. Breakfast on the outward journey. Two nights in the "Scandotel Castor". Two breakfast buffets. Berlin city tour. Visit to the Reichstag. Boat. Entrance fees. Insurance. **b:** The "Scandotel Castor" is a 3-star hotel in a central location, just a few minutes walk from the Kurfürstendamm and the legendary KaDeWe department store. What distinguishes the hotel is its good location, friendly atmosphere and personal ambience. Its 78 bright and comfortably appointed rooms each have a shower/WC, radio, telephone, cable TV, minibar and hair-dryer. **c** Day 1: depart for Berlin, travel via Hanover and Magdeburg. After occupying rooms, the afternoon is free. Overnight stay in Berlin. Day 2: A bus tour providing an impression of the dimensions of Berlin and its many faces. Visiting not only the western centre with the Kurfürstendamm but also the 'new centre' and the former eastern part of the city. The evening is free (for people to do what they want). Overnight stay in Berlin. Day 3: In the morning visit to the German parliament in the Reichstag. There's a chance to see the world-famous cupola of this building. Berlin's waterways offer a unique opportunity to see the city centre's sights from a boat. Then the return trip home (with many new impressions and experiences).

Unit 8

1 **a** F. Er ist zum ersten Mal in Deutschland. **b** R. **c** R. **d** F. Sie sagte ihm, dass die Deutschen sehr früh aufstehen. **e** F. Er findet, dass die Straßen und Häuser in Deutschland viel sauberer und gepflegter aussehen. **f** F. Er meint, dass die Leute sich sehr viel Arbeit machen, wenn sie ein Fest vorbereiten und dass Geburtstage viel mehr gefeiert werden. **g** F. Er sagt, die Leute schicken sich sogar Karten, wenn sie nicht zusammen feiern. Das ist in England weniger der Fall. 2 **a** froh **b** arbeitsam **c** ordnungsliebend **d** sauber **e** gepflegt 3 **b** gastfreundlicher **c** toleranter **d** herzlicher **e** weltoffener **f** humorvoller 4 **a** -e **b** -en **c** -en **d** -en **e** -en, -en **f** -e **g** -en 5 **a** unterschiedlich **b** gründlich **c** guten **d** weniger **e** Fremdsprachen **f** viel Wert **g** hoch 6 **a** Nimm doch nur mal die Ausbildung in Deutschland. **b** So viel Wert wird auf Qualifikationen gelegt. **c** Die Kehrseite der Medaille ist allerdings der Leistungsdruck. **d** Ich weiß nicht, wohin das noch führen soll. **e** Ich glaube, dass die Deuschen im

Allgemeinen ihre Freizeitaktivitäten viel systematischer angehen. **f** Da ist sicher ein Körnchen Wahrheit dran. **g** Du erscheinst mir nicht wie der typische Deutsche. **7 a** Lothar sagt, dass das Essen in Italien fantastisch schmecke. **b** Herr Martinez meint, dass man in Berlin sehr gut einkaufen könne. **c** Frau Knoob findet, dass Hamburg einen wirklich tollen Hafen habe. **d** Gabriela ist der Meinung, dass Schottland wirklich interessant sei. **e** Frau Clemens findet, dass es die schönsten Strände in Brasilien gebe. **8** Here opinions may sometimes differ, but we suggest the following: **b** D **c** E **d** E **e** D **f** D **g** E **h** D. On the recording a, b, d, f and g are mentioned. **9 a** Sie meint, dass London eine schöne Stadt sei. **b** Sie dachte, dass die Engländer kühl und reserviert seien. **c** Sie sagt, dass sie nette Leute kennen gelernt habe. **d** Sie denken, dass die Deutschen sehr sauber und korrekt seien. **e** Sie glauben, dass sie sich nur von Bratwürsten mit Sauerkraut und Schweinebraten mit Klößen ernähren. **10 a** ... einfach super. **b** kühl und reserviert seien. **c** ... nette Engländer kennen gelernt. **d** ... eigentlich fast so wie in Deutschland. **e** ... früh aufstehen. **f** ... mit Sauerkraut und Schweinebraten mit Klößen ernähren. **g** ... will sie auf jeden Fall wieder nach England fahren.

Testen Sie sich!

A) Mehr Übungen

1 i a -es **b** -er **c** -em **d** -es **e** -e, em **f** -e **g** -e **h** -en **i** -e **ii a** -es **b** -en **c** -en **d** -en **e** -en **f** -es **g** -e **h** -en **i** -es **j** -es **iii a** -e **b** -e **c** -en **d** -es, -es **e** -en **f** -e **g** -e **h** -es **i** -
2

- Ich habe mich weitgehend an die englische Lebensart angepasst, obwohl ich mich bemüht habe, meine deutsche Kultur und Sprache nicht zu vergessen.
- Ich weiß, dass sie existieren, aber glücklicherweise sind sie mehr die Ausnahme als die Regel. Manchmal fragen mich die Leute über die typisch deutschen Eigenschaften, wie die deutsche Gründlichkeit, oder ob die Deutschen wirklich so früh aufstehen und so hart arbeiten.
- Meistens lache ich und sage, dass ich sehr skeptisch bin, was diese typisch deutschen Eigenschaften anbelangt. Ich glaube, man kann sie auch in Menschen anderer Nationalität entdecken.

B) Lesetext

a Sie reisten 85 Millionen Mal. **b** Italien vor Spanien und Österreich. **c** Immer mehr Touristen fliegen. **d** Im letzten Jahr gab es rund 17,3 Millionen Übernachtungen.

Unit 9

1 a F. Er meint, dass die Politiker und die Industrie mehr unternehmen müssten. **b** R. **c** F. Sie ist der Meinung, dass wir ganz von der Atomkraft wegkommen sollten. **d** F. Beide sparen sehr viel Energie im Haus. **e** R. **f** R. **2** **a** Umweltschutz **b** Energien **c** Atomkraft **d** umweltfreudlich **e** Solarzellen **f** Energiesparlampen **g** Sprit **Sprachinfo** Here are examples from the text: **a** ... auch die Politiker und die Industrie müssten mehr unternehmen. **b** Man sollte mehr Geld ... **c** ... wo und an welcher Stelle ich Energie noch aktiver einsparen könnte. **d** Von Atomkraft sollte man auf Dauer ... **e** Biomasse könnte doch ... **f** Abgesehen davon müsste die Sonnenenergie ... **g** ... das wäre vielleicht auch eine ganz gute Alternative ... **h** ... (mit) anderen Energiequellen arbeiten sollten. **i** ... mit dem man die Autos betreiben könnte. **j** Die Autos könnte man auch abschaffen. **k** Was man da an Sprit sparen würde ... **l** ... das wäre eine tolle Maßnahme! **m** ... das wäre auch super. **3** Possible answers: **a** Umweltschutz **b** Energiequellen **c** Energiesparlampe **d** Atomkraft **e** Energiesparen **f** Biomasse **g** Sonnenenergie **h** Solarenergie **i** Solarzelle Also possible: Atommasse, Atomenergie, Sonnenschutz **4** **a** Wenn Herr Paul in der Stadt seiner Wahl leben könnte, würde er am liebsten in San Francisco leben. **b** Wenn er im Lotto gewinnen würde, würde er eine Weltreise machen. **c** Wenn er in die Vergangenheit reisen könnte, würde er in die Antike fahren. **d** Wenn er mit einem Popstar essen gehen könnte, würde er am liebsten mit Madonna essen gehen. **e** Wenn er eine bekannte Person interviewen könnte, würde er am liebsten Claudia Schiffer interviewen. **f** Wenn er in einem Film mitspielen könnte, würde er gerne im neuesten James Bond-Film mitspielen. **5** **a** Bierdose **b** Parkarbeiter **c** Nase **d** sinnvolle **e** Container **f** Tasche **g** kurz **6** **a**-iv **b**-v **c**-vi **d**-i **e**-ii **f**-iii **7** **a** Was geht Sie das denn an? **b** Ist doch sowieso alles schon zu spät. **c** Wollen Sie mich auf den Arm nehmen? **d** Dieser ganze Quatsch mit ... **e** Und jetzt lassen Sie mich in Ruhe. **8** **a** Er hat davon gelesen. **b** Sie hat drei Tonnen zu Hause in ihrer Garage. **c** Das Altpapier kommt in die blaue Tonne. **d** Sie sagt, dass jetzt jeder etwas für die Umwelt tun kann. **e** Man muss Geld bezahlen. **f** Sie kommen in spezielle Container. **9** **a** Verpackungen **b** Blechdose **c** Sondermüll **d** Altbatterien **e** Farbe **f** Sammelstelle **10** **a** ... komisch **b** ... sich um den Müll zu kümmern. **c** ... getrennt gesammelt und dann wieder verwertet oder umweltfreundlich entsorgt wird. **d** ... die blaue Tonne. **e** ... der Biomüll. **f** ... in einen Sack. **g** ... Sammelstelle gebracht/gefahren werden. **h** ... einen Container. **i** ... etwas für die Umwelt tun kann.

Testen Sie sich!

A) Mehr Übungen

1 The following are only sample answers: **a** Wenn ich du wäre, würde ich mehr Sport machen. **b** An deiner Stelle würde ich mehr studieren. **c** Wenn ich du wäre, würde ich mich um eine neue Stelle bewerben. **d** Wenn ich du wäre, würde ich weniger Süßigkeiten essen. **e** Wenn ich du wäre, würde ich mal die Charts hören. **f** An deiner Stelle würde ich mal zum Friseur gehen. **2** **a** Durch Solarzellen wird Energie erzeugt. **b** Altglas wird wieder verwertet. **c** Blechdosen werden zum Container gebracht. **d** Der Sondermüll wird zur Sammelstelle gebracht. **e** „Die Grünen" wurden 1979 gegründet. **f** Ich bin der Meinung, dass nicht genug/genügend für die Umwelt getan wird. **g** Man könnte zum Beispiel mehr mit öffentlichen Verkehrsmitteln fahren. Man könnte im Haus Energie sparen. Außerdem wäre es möglich, ...

3

- Also, es gibt eine braune Tonne für Biomüll, eine blaue für Papier und einen Plastiksack für alle Verpackungen, die den Grünen Punkt haben. Alles wird im Wechsel vierzehntägig abgeholt.
- Ja, die meisten Leute machen mit. Wenn man nicht mitmacht, muss man saftige Strafen zahlen. Es gibt ja auch Aufklärungsblätter und so weiter, um die Bevölkerung zu informieren. Gibt es eigentlich große Unterschiede zwischen Deutschland und England?
- Ich glaube, dass Recycling eine sehr sinnvolle Sache ist. Denn wenn wir jetzt nichts für die Umwelt tun, wie sieht dann die Welt für die Kinder in der Zukunft aus?
- Natürlich, aber es ist zumindest ein Anfang gemacht.

B) Lesetexte

1: Ein Viertel des Waldes deutlich krank **a** It has improved slightly. **b** 25%. **c** When it has lost a quarter of its needles or leaves. **d** Oaks. **2**: Mülltrennung **a** Denise: ... fände es gut, wenn jeder bewusster mit der Umwelt umgehen würde. **b** Julian: Schon bei uns auf der Grundschule haben wir gelernt, wie wichtig Mülltrennung und vor allem Müllvermeidung ist ... **c** Danilo: Ist ja auch wirklich keine große Aktion, die Sachen in verschiedene Mülleimer zu werfen. **d** Danilo: Das mit der Mülltrennung finde ich voll okay.

Unit 10

1 **a** Täglich erscheinen etwa 400 Zeitungen in Deutschland. **b** Anders als in Großbritannien dominieren sie den Zeitungsmarkt. **c** Politisch ist die *Frankfurter Allgemeine Zeitung* eher konservativ. **d** Die Bild hat eine Auflage von etwa 4,5 Millionen. **e** Computerzeitschriften, Magazine für Essen und Trinken und Zeitschriften über Motorsport. **f** Den Spiegel gibt es seit 1947. **2 a** Tageszeitungen **b** Regionalzeitungen **c** überregionale **d** linksliberal **e** Boulevardzeitung **f** Auflage, Exemplaren **g** Nachrichtenmagazine **h** Zeitungen, Zeitschriften **Sprachinfo a** Wer sich noch weiter informieren möchte, wird dann vielleicht noch eine der überregionalen Zeitungen lesen, die man in ganz Deutschland bekommen kann. **b** Die bekanntesten Wochenzeitungen sind *Die Zeit* und *Die Woche*, die beide aus Hamburg kommen. **3 a** die *tageszeitung* **b** *Frankfurter Allgemeine Zeitung* **c** *Hamburger Morgenpost* **d** *Süddeutsche Zeitung* **e** *Westdeutsche Allegemeine Zeitung* **4 a**-iv **b**-vi **c**-v **d**-i **e**-ii **f**-iii

5 1-c 2-b 3-b 4-c 5-c 6-c 7-b 8-a **6 a** Das größte Bundesland ist Nordrhein-Westfalen. **b** Das kleinste Bundesland ist Bremen. **c** Hamburg und Bremen werden auch Stadtstaaten genannt. **d** Wahlen gibt es alle vier Jahre. **e** Der Bundespräsident hat vor allem repräsentative Aufgaben. **f** Das föderalistische Prinzip ist ein Grundpfeiler der politischen Struktur Deutschlands.
7 **a** Herzlich willkommen zu einer neuen Ausgabe von ... **b** Unser erstes Thema heute ist Deutschland. **c** Nun, stellen Sie sich einmal die Europakarte vor ... **d** Wie Sie wissen, besteht Deutschland aus 16 Bundesländern. **e** Wenn ich Sie fragen würde ... **f** Insgesamt sind es neun Länder ... **g** Aber wie viele Abgeordnete hat der Bundestag eigentlich? **h** Mehr darüber in der nächsten Woche. **8 a** R. **b** F. Der Motor der deutschen Wirtschaft war das produzierende Gewerbe. **c** F. Deutschlands Wirtschaft exportiert mehr. **d** F. Die wichtigsten Handelspartner sind die Länder der EU. **e** R. **f** F. Viele Firmen haben ihre internationale Präsenz verstärkt. **9 a** das produzierende Gewerbe **b** Maschinenbau **c** chemische Industrie **d** Dienstleistungssektor **e** Wirtschaftszweige **f** Handelspartner **g** Export/Ausfuhr **h** Globalisierung
10 **a** ... das produzierende Gewerbe. **b** ... Volkswagen, BMW und Mercedes-Chrysler. **c** ... die chemische Industrie und der Maschinenbau. **d** ... sind die Länder der EU. **e** ... ist die hohe Arbeitslosigkeit. **f** ... sind nicht so viele Jobs geschaffen worden, wie in den USA oder in Großbritannien. **g** ... international präsent sein. **h** ... optimistisch.

Testen Sie sich!

A) Mehr Übungen

1 Das ist Herr Franke, ... **a** der als Journalist arbeitet. **b** dessen Frau auch Journalistin ist. **c** dessen Sohn in den USA studiert. **d** der einen roten Ferrari fährt. **e** der meistens italienische Anzüge trägt. **f** den man auf vielen Partys sieht. **g** von dem ich noch €200 bekomme. **2 b** Einwohner **c** Demokratie **d** Bundestag **e** Abgeordnete **f** gewählt **g** Macht **h** Bundeskanzler **i** Bundespräsident **j** Aufgaben **k** Export **l** Wirtschaftszweige **m** Handelspartner

3

- Das produzierende Gewerbe ist sehr wichtig. Es ist der Motor der deutschen Industrie.
- Auch die chemische Industrie und der Maschinenbau sind sehr wichtig.
- Die Banken und Versicherungsfirmen spielen auch eine große Rolle.
- Ja. Die Autoindustrie zum Beispiel exportiert mehr als 60% ihrer Produkte.
- Ein Drittel aller Arbeitsplätze hängt vom Export ab.
- Die wichtigsten Handelspartner sind die Länder der EU.
- Ich denke, dass die Globalisierung immer wichtiger werden wird. Insgesamt bin ich sehr optimistisch.

B) Lesetext

a No. His main client base is in Germany, but he works at an international level as well. **b** Because he spent two years working for Barclays in London. **c** He likes the fact that people from all over the world live and work here. Over 30% of the inhabitants are foreign, which means that Frankfurt has the highest level of diversity of any German city. **d** He likes it. In addition to the museums, theatres and a lively literary scene, he is also very enthusiastic about the Frankfurt Opera. **e** Because the airport is not far from the city centre, it's easy to keep his appointments with clients and business partners. **f** In addition to finance and the airport there are also chemical and pharmaceutical companies like Höchst and Merck. Mechanical engineering also plays an important role. And in recent years new and innovative companies in the fields of bio- and environmental technology have established themselves. **g** Only a few kilometres from the cities there are picturesque villages and small towns where life goes on peacefully. **h** His secret tip is Marburg. It's an old university town with a cosy 'old town' area, lots of cafés, bookshops and pubs. Everything is less hectic there and people can still take their time. That is sometimes a welcome contrast to Jörg's life in Frankfurt.

Listening comprehension transcripts

Unit 1 Aufnahme 2

Moderator	Herzlich willkommen, liebe Zuschauer, zu einer neuen Ausgabe von Super-Preis, das Superquizspiel, wo Sie mit einem Schlag 20 000 Mark gewinnen können. Zuerst zu unseren Kandidaten. Kandidat 1. Können Sie sich bitte kurz vorstellen?
Martin	Ja, ich bin der Martin, bin 32, geschieden und komme aus Apolda.
Moderator	Nicht alle Zuschauer werden wissen, wo das liegt. Können Sie uns das kurz erklären?
Martin	Das liegt im Freistaat Thüringen, in der Nähe von Weimar.
Moderator	Gibt es denn etwas Besonderes dort?
Martin	Wir haben ein Bockbierfest dort, das ist ziemlich bekannt.
Moderator	Was machen Sie denn beruflich, Martin?
Martin	Ich bin Krankenpfleger im örtlichen Krankenhaus.
Moderator	Das ist wahrscheinlich ein zeitraubender Job. Bleibt Ihnen denn da noch Zeit für irgendwelche Hobbys?
Martin	Nicht so viel. Aber ich gehe gern ins Kino und fahre sehr gern Ski.
Moderator	So, das war unser erster Kandidat, Martin. Applaus, bitte. Und schnell weiter zu unserer zweiten Kandidatin, Petra.
Petra	Mein Name ist Petra Wunderlich. Ich bin 44 Jahre alt, verheiratet und komme aus Salzburg in Österreich.
Moderator	Ja, Salzburg kennt ja nun fast jeder, Mozart, die Mozartkugeln und so weiter. Was sind Sie denn von Beruf, Petra?

Petra	Ich bin Hotelfachfrau. Mit meinem Mann führe ich eine kleine Pension, die „Pension zur Post". Wir haben 20 Betten.
Moderator	Und was machen Sie in Ihrer Freizeit?
Petra	Nun, viel Zeit bleibt uns nicht, da wir das ganze Jahr über Gäste haben. Ich interessiere mich aber sehr für Geschichte und wenn ich Zeit habe, lese ich.
Moderator	Danke, danke. Applaus, bitte. Schnell zu Kandidaten Nummer 3.
Max	Ja, ich bin der Max, 22 Jahre jung und single. Noch zu haben also …
Moderator	Und woher kommen Sie?
Max	Ich komme aus Norddeutschland, aus Lübeck.
Moderator	Und was machen Sie beruflich, Max?
Max	Ich bin Student. Ich studiere Mathematik.
Moderator	Und in Ihrer Freizeit? Was für Hobbys haben Sie?
Max	Ich liebe es gefährlich, mache Bungeespringen und in den Ferien gehe ich surfen.
Moderator	Gut. Das war Max. Danke schön. Und damit können wir nun mit der ersten Runde anfangen. Also …

Unit 2 Aufnahme 2

Martina	Corinna, du bist 22 Jahre alt, wohnst seit zwei Jahren in München und arbeitest als Kellnerin. Wie sieht eigentlich dein Tagesablauf aus?
Corinna	Es kommt darauf an, ob ich Frühschicht oder Spätschicht arbeiten muss. Wir haben nämlich in der Gaststätte, wo ich arbeite, bis um Mitternacht durchgehend geöffnet. Wenn ich Spätschicht mache, komme ich erst gegen eins, halb zwei nach Hause. Ich stelle mich dann schnell unter die Dusche und gehe sofort ins Bett. Am nächsten Tag stehe ich dann meistens erst um neun oder halb zehn auf. Zum Frühstück trinke ich ein Glas Orangen- oder Grapefruitsaft und manchmal esse ich auch eine Scheibe Toast mit Marmelade oder Honig.
Martina	Da hast du dann ein paar Stunden Freizeit, oder?

Corinna	Ja. Bis vier Uhr nachmittags kann ich machen, was ich will. Einmal in der Woche bringe ich meine Wäsche zum Waschsalon. Ab und zu räume ich mein Zimmer auf. Aber das nimmt nicht allzu viel Zeit in Anspruch.
Martina	Was machst du also mit deiner Freizeit?
Corinna	Zweimal in der Woche – montags und mittwochs – habe ich Englischstunden. Da wir in der Gaststätte so viele Ausländer haben, versuche ich meine Englischkenntnisse aufzufrischen. Sonst gehe ich mit meinem Freund ins Kino oder wir fahren nach Starnberg zum Windsurfen auf dem Starnberger See.
Martina	Und wie oft siehst du deine Eltern?
Corinna	Höchstens viermal im Jahr zu Weihnachten und bei Geburtstagen. Die wohnen ja in Würzburg, was ziemlich weit weg ist.
Martina	Und wie ist es mit dem Essen? Bekommst du deine Mahlzeiten hier im Restaurant umsonst?
Corinna	Oh, ja. Das versteht sich von selbst. In meinem Zimmer habe ich nur eine Kochnische mit einer Heizplatte und einem kleinen Kühlschrank.

Unit 4 Aufnahme 2

Gerd	Du, Heiko! Lange nicht gesehen! Wie geht's dir?
Heiko	Hallo, Gerd! Gut, danke.
Gerd	Und was machst du jetzt für eine Arbeit?
Heiko	Ich unterrichte Deutsch als Fremdsprache im Sprachinstitut in der Herder-Straße.
Gerd	Und wie gefällt dir deine Arbeit?
Heiko	Im Allgemeinen sehr gut. Meine Studenten sind alle motiviert und fleißig, da sie es nötig haben, so schnell wie möglich die deutsche Sprache zu erlernen. Das Einzige, was mir nicht so gut gefällt, ist die Bezahlung.
Gerd	Wenn das so ist, kannst du denn daraus einen richtigen Beruf machen? Oder hast du noch etwas ganz anderes vor?

Heiko	Naja, ich bin natürlich auf der Warteliste für eine Lehramtsstelle. Du weißt ja, dass ich eigentlich Gymnasiallehrer für Deutsch und Latein werden möchte. Aber da es momentan so viele Anwärter gibt, werde ich wohl noch mindestens ein bis zwei Jahre warten müssen. Und was machst du eigentlich zur Zeit?
Gerd	Ich mache gerade meinen Zivildienst in einem Heim für körperlich und geistig behinderte Kinder.
Heiko	Und was hast du danach vor?
Gerd	Ich möchte Sozialarbeiter werden. Im Raum Frankfurt werden zur Zeit viele Stellen für Sozialpädagogen angeboten.
Heiko	Das ist sicher auch kein einfacher Job! Auf jeden Fall wünsche ich dir viel Glück dabei.

Unit 5 Aufnahme 2

Sebastian	Mensch, ich bin vielleicht froh, dass die Sommerferien übermorgen anfangen!
Jochen	Und ich erst! Was hast du denn eigentlich so geplant?
Sebastian	Also, ich werde meinen Führerschein anfangen. Meine Eltern haben mich endlich in der Fahrschule angemeldet und in zwei Wochen geht's los.
Jochen	Bist du denn vorher schon mal gefahren?
Sebastian	Wo denkst du hin! Ich will doch nicht riskieren, dass mir die Fahrerlaubnis für zwei Jahre entzogen wird! Das ist übrigens dem Peter passiert, und jetzt hat er das neue Auto zu Hause stehen, das ihm seine Eltern schon vorher gekauft hatten und kann nicht damit fahren …
Jochen	Wie viele Stunden glaubst du denn, dass du brauchen wirst?
Sebastian	Naja, zwanzig ist ja so der Durchschnitt – und wenn ich nicht durchfalle, müsste ich meinen Deckel Anfang des neuen Schuljahres schon haben! – Und was hast du denn eigentlich vor?

Jochen	Meine Eltern haben mir versprochen, dass ich meinen dritten Tanzkurs machen kann. Da freue ich mich schon total drauf.
Sebastian	Bist du da etwa immer noch dabei? Ich habe ja auch einen gemacht, vor etwa drei Jahren, aber einer hat mir gereicht. Ich gehe sowieso nur in die Disco und da brauche ich ja so was nicht – höchstens mal bei meiner Hochzeit und bis dahin habe ich wahrscheinlich schon wieder alle Schritte vergessen! Hast du denn eine Partnerin für den Kurs?
Jochen	Ja, du kennst doch die Sybille, oder? Wir haben schon den ersten und zweiten Kurs zusammen gemacht und nach dem dritten wollen wir in den Tanzclub eintreten und auch auf Turniere gehen.
Sebastian	Da muss man doch ziemlich oft trainieren, oder? Glaubst du denn nicht, dass dir das zu viel wird?
Jochen	Ach, außer dem Tanzen und dann noch meinem Schwimmtraining, mache ich eigentlich nichts weiter in meiner Freizeit. Und es ist ja eine gute Gelegenheit, neue Leute kennen zu lernen und sich auch fit zu halten.
Sebastian	Sicherlich. Aber das wäre mir ehrlich gesagt zu viel. So eingebunden zu sein, würde mir überhaupt nicht gefallen. Ich persönlich ziehe es vor, meine Freizeit flexibel zu gestalten. Außerdem bin ich eher kulturinteressiert – Sport hat mich eigentlich schon immer gelangweilt.

Unit 6 Aufnahme 2

Elke	Entschuldigen Sie bitte die Störung, aber darf ich Sie fragen, ob Sie für oder gegen ein Rauchverbot in Restaurants und Gaststätten sind?
Frau Merk	Ich bin auf jeden Fall dafür. Ich finde, es ist eine Zumutung, wenn ich beim Essen durch das Rauchen von anderen Gästen gestört werde.

Elke	Viele Gäste hier in der Gaststätte sagen aber, dass sie gerade dann rauchen möchten, wenn sie sich bei einem Glas Wein oder einer Tasse Kaffee entspannen.
Frau Merk	Ja, das mag wohl sein. Solche Leute vergessen aber meistens, dass ihr Rauchen eine negative Einwirkung auf ihre Mitmenschen hat. Und es gibt ja Menschen, die einfach allergisch sind gegen Zigarettenrauch.
Elke	Ja, aber sagen Sie ganz ehrlich. Kann man wirklich ein totales Rauchverbot in allen Restaurants und Gaststätten verhängen?
Frau Merk	Das wäre meines Erachtens nicht zu viel verlangt. Aber ich sehe auch ein, dass es noch eine Zeit lang dauern wird, bis diese Idee von der Mehrheit akzeptiert wird. Und in der Zwischenzeit wächst die Zahl der Restaurants, die das Rauchen entweder total oder zum Teil verbieten.

Unit 7 Aufnahme 2

Silke	Ich hätte eine Frage, bitte. Wie komme ich am besten in die Stadt?
Dame	Mit dem Bus. Vom Flughafen fahren Sie mit der 109 bis zum Bahnhof Zoo.
Silke	Und wie teuer wär's mit einem Taxi?
Dame	Das würde Sie ungefähr das Zehnfache der Busfahrt kosten. Wenn Sie aber viel Gepäck haben, lohnt es sich vielleicht, mit einem Taxi zu fahren.
Silke	Nein, viel Gepäck habe ich nicht. Bloß muss ich vom Bahnhof Zoo noch ein bisschen weiter fahren. Mein Hotel liegt nämlich in der Güntzelstraße.
Dame	Kein Problem! Vom Zoo sind es nur drei U-Bahn-Stationen bis zur Güntzelstraße.
Silke	Wo ist die Bushaltestelle?
Dame	Durch diesen Ausgang, dann nach links. Zirka 50 Meter geradeaus. Da sehen Sie dann die Haltestelle auf der rechten Seite.
Silke	Und wo kann ich eine Fahrkarte lösen?
Dame	Im Bus beim Fahrer.

Unit 8 Aufnahme 2

Martin	Ja, was die typisch deutschen Eigenschaften angeht, glaubst du, dass die Engländer wirklich so verschieden von den Deutschen sind?
Darren	Wahrscheinlich nicht. Aber die Kultur und die Mentalität sind irgendwie doch unterschiedlich. Ich finde zum Beispiel, dass dieses Klischee von der deutschen Gründlichkeit gar nicht so falsch ist.
Martin	Tatsächlich? Das musst du mir aber näher erläutern!
Darren	Naja, nimm doch nur mal die Ausbildung hier in Deutschland: man muss in diesem Land nicht unbedingt Abitur gemacht haben, um eine gute Stellung zu bekommen. Wer Hauptschulabschluss oder mittlere Reife gemacht hat, bekommt in der Lehre eine gründliche Ausbildung, sowohl praktisch als auch theoretisch, und macht eine richtige Abschlussprüfung, die ihm einen guten Start ins Berufsleben gibt.
Martin	Aber ist das in England nicht genauso?
Darren	Es ist weniger streng geregelt. Natürlich, wenn man A-Levels oder einen Universitätsabschluss hat, macht man zumeist ein gutes Training, aber ansonsten haben die Leute nicht so eine gründliche Ausbildung. Ich meine, in Deutschland macht man ja sogar als Verkäufer in einer Bäckerei oder Metzgerei eine dreijährige Ausbildung! Das gibt es in England kaum.
Martin	Und wie sieht es mit der Schulbildung in England aus?
Darren	Ja, die ist schon sehr gut. Aber zum Beispiel habe ich festgestellt, dass man in Deutschland Fremdsprachen viel mehr fördert, was ja heutzutage ungeheuer wichtig ist. Und dann finde ich auch, dass hier so viel Wert auf Qualifikationen gelegt wird. Es genügt nicht, wenn man zum Beispiel eine Fremdsprache spricht, um einen Job zu bekommen. Nein, man muss gleich einen entsprechenden Nachweis erbringen, dass man eine Prüfung oder Ausbildung in diesem Fach gemacht hat.

Martin	Da hast du allerdings Recht! Es ist dir wahrscheinlich auch schon aufgefallen, dass man hier ungeheuer viel Wert auf Titel legt, zum Beispiel auf den Doktortitel! Früher war das selbstverständlich noch extremer. Die Kehrseite der Medaille ist allerdings, dass die Leistungsanforderungen und der Leistungsdruck schon in den Schulen so hoch sind und in der Arbeitswelt noch viel höher. Man weiß gar nicht, wohin das noch führen soll!
Darren	Aber die Gründlichkeit erstreckt sich nicht nur auf den Arbeitsbereich. Ich finde, dass die Deutschen im Allgemeinen ihre Freizeitaktivitäten viel systematischer angehen als die Engländer. Sehr viele Leute betreiben ihr Hobby in einem Club und Talente werden sofort gefördert.
Martin	Mmmh ... ich weiß nicht so recht. Das ist zwar alles nicht ganz falsch, was du da festgestellt hast. Aber ich bin doch sehr skeptisch, was diese typisch deutschen Eigenschaften angeht. Sicherlich ist da ein Körnchen Wahrheit dran, aber ich glaube, man kann all diese Eigenschaften auch bei Menschen anderer Nationalität feststellen.
Darren	Na, ich bin nicht so sicher! Du erscheinst mir zwar auch nicht wie der typische Deutsche.

Unit 9 Aufnahme 2

Bürgerin	Entschuldigung, aber warum werfen Sie denn Ihre leere Bierdose auf die Wiese? Da vorne ist doch ein Abfalleimer!
Roland	Häh? Was geht Sie das denn an? Und außerdem, die Parkarbeiter, die sollen auch mal was arbeiten, dafür werden sie ja schließlich bezahlt, von meinen Steuern!
Bürgerin	Also, Sie haben vielleicht eine Auffassung – wenn jeder so denken würde wie Sie, dann würden wir bald im Müll ersticken und der Park wäre eine Müllhalde.

Roland Ach, sind Sie etwa auch so einer, der dauernd von Umwelt und Recycling schwafelt? Davon habe ich die Nase schon lange voll. Wem nützt das denn überhaupt? Ist doch sowieso alles schon zu spät. Und dieser ganze Quatsch mit dieser Müllsortierung – da habe ich in meiner Freizeit ehrlich Besseres zu tun als daran zu denken, was in welche Tonne kommt.

Bürgerin Recycling ist eine sehr sinnvolle Sache – wenn wir jetzt nichts für die Umwelt tun, wie sieht denn dann das Leben für unsere Kinder aus? Und wenn wir schon von Recycling reden: Dosen werden jetzt auch getrennt gesammelt!

Roland Wollen Sie mich jetzt auf den Arm nehmen? Soll ich jetzt etwa zum Container rennen, nur um eine einzige Blechdose wegzuwerfen? Das können Sie ja machen, wenn Sie wollen!

Bürgerin Sie könnten die Dose ja in Ihre Tasche packen und später entsorgen. Damit hätten Sie zum einen die Wiese sauber gehalten und zum anderen 'was für die Umwelt getan.

Roland Wenn Sie glauben, dass Sie mich bekehren können, haben Sie sich getäuscht. Das Leben ist kurz genug und ich will mich amüsieren. Für Ihre Moralpredigten habe ich keine Zeit. Und jetzt lassen Sie mich in Ruhe!

Bürgerin Ich sehe schon, Sie sind einer von denen, die erst saftige Geldstrafen zahlen müssen, bevor Sie irgendetwas tun! Und das ist dann zum Glück wirklich nicht meine Sache!

Unit 10 Aufnahme 2

Unser erstes Thema heute ist Deutschland. Sie wissen sicherlich, dass Deutschland mit seinen über 81,5 Millionen Einwohnern der bevölkerungsreichste Staat in Europa ist – sieht man einmal von Russland ab – aber wie ist das flächenmäßig? Ist Deutschland auch größer als Großbritannien, größer als Frankreich? Nun, stellen Sie sich einmal die Europakarte vor – Deutschland in der Mitte,

Großbritannien als Insel – nun, es ist tatsächlich um einiges größer als Großbritannien – das Vereinigte Königreich umfasst 244 100 km² und Deutschland 357 022 km² – aber im Vergleich zu Frankreich – nun, da kann man zu Recht von der „Grande Nation“ sprechen: mit 543 000 km² ist es mehr als doppelt so groß wie Großbritannien und auch um einiges größer als Deutschland.

Von der Bevölkerungsdichte her leben wir hier also ziemlich zusammengedrängt, verglichen mit unseren europäischen Nachbarn. Aber wer sind eigentlich unsere Nachbarn? Haben Sie schon mal darüber nachgedacht, mit wie vielen Ländern Deutschland eine Grenze hat? Nun, wahrscheinlich fangen Sie jetzt an zu zählen, Dänemark im Norden, Polen ja ... Lassen Sie sich ein wenig Zeit und in der Zwischenzeit wenden wir uns unseren eigenen Ländern zu. Wie Sie wissen, besteht Deutschland ja aus 16 Bundesländern, einschließlich der Stadtstaaten Hamburg und Bremen und auch Berlin. Wenn ich Sie fragen würde, welches Bundesland die meisten Einwohner hat, so werden die meisten sicherlich nicht lange zögern und Nordrhein-Westfalen sagen, das tatsächlich mit dem Ballungsraum Ruhrgebiet mit fast 18 Millionen Menschen unangefochten vor Bayern mit etwas mehr als 12 Millionen liegt. Die wenigsten Einwohner hat im Übrigen Bremen, mit etwa 700 000. Doch wissen Sie auch, welches Bundesland flächenmäßig am größten ist? Nun, ich nehme an, dass dies viele unserer süddeutschen, genauer unserer bayrischen Hörer wissen werden, denn tatsächlich ist Bayern das größte Bundesland. Nordrhein-Westfalen – im Übrigen – liegt flächenmäßig nur an vierter Stelle, noch hinter Niedersachsen und Baden-Württemberg.

Aber lassen Sie uns auf unser Problem zurückkommen, mit wie vielen Staaten Deutschland eine gemeinsame Grenzen hat, und wenn Sie mittlerweile mit dem Zählen aufgehört haben und bei 10 angekommen sind ... dann haben Sie sich verzählt! Insgesamt sind es nämlich neun Länder: Dänemark im Norden, die Niederlande, Belgien, Luxemburg und Frankreich im Westen, die Schweiz und Österreich im Süden und die Tschechische Republik und Polen im Osten.

Diese einzigartige Mittellage Deutschlands war historisch natürlich nicht ganz unproblematisch, womit wir auch bei einem anderen Thema angelangt wären: der Politik.

Sie werden wissen, dass die wichtigsten politischen Entscheidungen im Bundestag – unserem Parlament – gefällt werden. Aber wie viele Abgeordnete hat der Bundestag eigentlich? Mehr als 500? Weniger als 500? Nun, es sind weit mehr: 656. Und durch unser Wahlsystem kann die Anzahl sogar noch steigen. Und diese 656 Abgeordneten wählen dann den Bundeskanzler, der dann seine Minister benennt und somit die größte politische Macht besitzt. Der Bundespräsident – anders als zum Beispiel in den USA – hat dagegen weitgehend nur repräsentative Aufgaben: Er prüft, ob Gesetze verfassungsgemäß zustande gekommen sind, ernennt und entlässt Bundesrichter und Bundesbeamte und ernennt und entlässt auch die Bundesminister, die vom Bundeskanzler vorgeschlagen wurden.

Diese Reduzierung der Macht lag den Vätern unseres Grundgesetzes besonders am Herzen, genauso wie ein anderer Aspekt: das föderalistische Prinzip, das ein Grundpfeiler unserer politischen Struktur ist. Aber darüber mehr in der nächsten Woche.

So, damit sind wir zum Ende unseres ersten Teiles gekommen, und bevor Sie uns, liebe Zuhörerinnen und Zuhörer, direkt anrufen können – spielen wir schnell noch ein paar Takte Musik ...

Taking it further

Now that you have worked your way through *Perfect your German* you may want to take your German further. In this section we offer you a few suggestions for helping you achieve your goals.

It's a good idea to decide which of the four skills (listening and speaking, reading and writing) it is that you want to develop and then adopt a systematic approach. While development of one skill will to some extent assist the development of the other three, there really is no substitute for listening in order to improve your listening skills, speaking in order to improve your oral skills, and so on.

Listening

There is a wealth of German-language listening material to be found on the internet from radio and TV stations to podcasts and videos. It's best to concentrate on short clips to start with. You might, for instance, try the **'Heute 100 sec'** news summary on the **www.zdf.de site**. Listen for the general gist on the first hearing and then try to pick up more and more detail until you have understood everything. You may need to look up key words that you have not been able to understand in context. As you gain confidence in your listening skills, you might want to move on to some of the programmes that are available on the ZDF Mediathek menu.

Speaking

Find German native-speakers who are willing for you to try out your German on them. If you cannot find anyone in your home area, then you will either need to make a trip to a German-speaking country or to find a German-speaking partner on the internet.

Reading

Try tackling short articles in German newspapers or magazines (e.g. *Bild*-Zeitung, *Stern*, *Focus*). Again, the internet can help you find articles and information that might interest you. Use a German-language search engine or portal such as:

http://www.google.de
http://de.yahoo.com

You may also want to tackle some German literature. It's a good idea to start with short stories. There are several collections of short stories in parallel text form, i.e. in the German original, but with an English translation on the opposite page. In this way you will gradually increase your vocabulary and may even reach the point where you feel able to tackle Goethe's *Faust* in the original!

Writing

For writing, as for speaking, you really need a German native-speaker to read what you have written and make constructive suggestions for improvement. It is a good idea to make the exercise as realistic as possible by exchanging information and ideas either with a traditional pen-friend or with an internet partner using 'instant messaging'. This way you will be able to help your partner improve his/her English as you improve your German.

Websites

http://www.goethe.de The *Goethe Institut* is represented in most countries and staff may be able to inform you about German-language courses in your area. They will also have information on short intensive courses in Germany.

http://www.austria.org or **http://www.austria.org.uk** for information about Austrian life and culture.

http://www.swissinfo.ch for information about Swiss life and culture.

Viel Spaß beim Weiterlernen!

Common irregular verbs

Here is a list of commonly used irregular verbs in German, most of which are featured in *Perfect your German*. It is not intended to be complete, but should help you to familiarize yourself with the most important forms.

*indicates that these verbs normally form their perfect tense with *sein*.

infinitive	present tense vowel change 3rd person sing.	simple past	past participle
anfangen *to start*	fängt an	fing an	angefangen
anrufen *to telephone*		rief an	angerufen
aufstehen *to get up*		stand auf	aufgestanden*
beginnen *to begin*		begann	begonnen
bieten *to offer*		bot	geboten
binden *to bind, tie*		band	gebunden
bleiben *to stay*		blieb	geblieben*
brechen *to break*	bricht	brach	gebrochen
brennen *to burn*		brannte	gebrannt
bringen *to bring*		brachte	gebracht
denken *to think*		dachte	gedacht
einladen *to invite*	lädt ein	lud ein	eingeladen
empfehlen *to recommend*	empfiehlt	empfahl	empfohlen

infinitive	present tense vowel change 3rd person sing.	simple past	past participle
entscheiden *to decide*		entschied	entschieden
essen *to eat*	isst	aß	gegessen
fahren *to go (by vehicle), to drive*	fährt	fuhr	gefahren*
fallen *to fall*	fällt	fiel	gefallen*
finden *to find*		fand	gefunden
fliegen *to fly*		flog	geflogen*
geben *to give*	gibt	gab	gegeben
gehen *to go*		ging	gegangen*
gelingen *to succeed*		gelang	gelungen*
gelten *to be regarded*	gilt	galt	gegolten
geschehen *to happen*	geschieht	geschah	geschehen*
haben *to have*		hatte	gehabt
halten *to hold, keep*	hält	hielt	gehalten
heißen *to be called*		hieß	geheißen
helfen *to help*	hilft	half	geholfen
kennen *to know, be acquainted with*		kannte	gekannt
kommen *to come*		kam	gekommen*
lassen *to let, to leave*	lässt	ließ	gelassen
laufen *to run, walk*	läuft	lief	gelaufen*
leiden *to suffer*		litt	gelitten
liegen *to lie*		lag	gelegen*

infinitive	present tense vowel change 3rd person sing	simple past	past participle
nehmen *to take*	nimmt	nahm	genommen
nennen *to name*		nannte	genannt
raten *to advise*	rät	riet	geraten
reißen *to tear*		riss	gerissen
reiten *to ride*		ritt	geritten*
rennen *to run*		rannte	gerannt*
riechen *to smell*		roch	gerochen
schaffen *to create*		schuf	geschaffen
scheinen *to seem; to shine*		schien	geschienen
schlafen *to sleep*	schläft	schlief	geschlafen
schlagen *to hit*	schlägt	schlug	geschlagen
schließen *to shut, close*		schloss	geschlossen
schneiden *to cut*		schnitt	geschnitten
schreiben *to write*		schrieb	geschrieben
schwimmen *to swim*		schwamm	geschwommen*
sehen *to see*	sieht	sah	gesehen
sein *to be*	ist	war	gewesen*
singen *to sing*		sang	gesungen
sitzen *to sit*		saß	gesessen
sprechen *to speak*	spricht	sprach	gesprochen
springen *to jump*		sprang	gesprungen*
stehen *to stand*		stand	gestanden
steigen *to climb, to rise*		stieg	gestiegen*
sterben *to die*	stirbt	starb	gestorben*
tragen *to carry, wear*	trägt	trug	getragen

infinitive	present tense vowel change 3rd person sing.	simple past	past participle
treffen *to meet*	trifft	traf	getroffen
treiben *to do (esp. sport)*		trieb	getrieben
treten *to step*	tritt	trat	getreten*
trinken *to drink*		trank	getrunken
tun *to do*		tat	getan
verbergen *to hide*	verbirgt	verbarg	verborgen
vergessen *to forget*	vergisst	vergaß	vergessen
vergleichen *to compare*		verglich	verglichen
verlieren *to lose*		verlor	verloren
vermeiden *to avoid*		vermied	vermieden
wachsen *to grow*	wächst	wuchs	gewachsen*
waschen *to wash*	wäscht	wusch	gewaschen
werben *to advertise*	wirbt	warb	geworben
werden *to become*	wird	wurde	geworden*
werfen *to throw*	wirft	warf	geworfen
wissen *to know*	weiß	wusste	gewusst
ziehen *to move*		zog	gezogen*
zwingen *to force, compel*		zwang	gezwungen

Glossary of grammatical terms

This glossary covers the most important grammar terminology used in this book.

adjectives Adjectives are used to provide more information about nouns. In English they can stand on their own after a verb, such as *to be* or *to seem*, or they can appear in front of a noun: The car is new. The new car wasn't cheap. Note that in German endings are needed on adjectives that come before a noun:

Das Auto ist *neu*. Das *neue* Auto war nicht billig.

adverbs Adverbs provide more information about **a** verbs: Wayne ran *quickly* down the stairs and **b** adjectives: I was *completely* exhausted.

In English, adverbs often (but not always) end in -ly. In German, adverbs often have the same form as adjectives:

Deine Arbeit ist *gut*. Your work is *good*.
Du hast das sehr *gut* gemacht. You did that very *well*.

articles In German there are three definite articles: **der** (masculine), **die** (feminine) and **das** (neuter). The indefinite articles are **ein** (masculine), **eine** (feminine) and ein (neuter). (See also **gender**.)

auxiliary verbs Auxiliary verbs are used as a support to the main verb, e.g. I *am* working; he *has* gone. The most important verbs in German are **haben, sein** and **werden**. These are used in the formation of the present perfect tense and of the passive:

Ich *habe* gerade einen sehr guten Film gesehen. I *have* just seen a good film.
Die neue Schule *wurde* 1998 gebaut. The new school *was* built in 1998.

cases The four cases in German are: the *nominative*, the *accusative*, the *genitive* and the *dative*. Cases are used in German to express relationships between the various parts of the sentence.

Nominative – this is the case that indicates the subject of the sentence.

Der *Mann* kauft einen Computer. *The man* buys a computer.

Accusative – this is the case that indicates the direct object of the sentence:

Der Mann kauft *einen Computer*. The man buys *a computer*.

Dative – this is the case that indicates the indirect object of the sentence:

Wir haben den Computer *meinem Bruder* gegeben. We gave the computer *to my brother*.

Genitive – this is the case that indicates possession:

Das ist der Computer *meines Bruders*. That's *my brother's* computer.

Note that **prepositions** in German are followed by the accusative, dative or genitive case.

comparative When we make comparisons, we need the comparative form of the **adjective**. In English this usually means adding *-er* to the adjective or putting *more* in front of it: This shirt is *cheaper* than that one. This blouse is *more* expensive than that one.

In German *-er* is added to the adjective to form the comparative:

Dieses Hemd ist *billiger* als das da. Diese Bluse ist *teurer als die da*.

(See also **superlative**.)

conditional The conditional mood is used to express a hypothetical situation or state which is subject to a condition. For instance, the sentence 'Peter would visit his mother, if he had a car.' tells us that Peter does not visit his mother and that he doesn't have a car (real situations). For him to visit his mother (as yet a hypothetical situation) he would have to have a car (condition). The conditional in German follows a similar pattern, using subjunctive forms of the verbs:

Peter *würde* seine Mutter *besuchen*, wenn er ein Auto *hätte*.

conjunctions Conjunctions join words or clauses together. In German, a distinction is made between co-ordinating *conjunctions* and *subordinating conjunctions*. Co-ordinating conjunctions such as **und** *and*, **aber** *but* and **oder** *or* simply join two main clauses together and do not affect the word order:

Anna kommt aus München und ist 21 Jahre alt. Anna comes from Munich and is 21 years old.

Subordinating conjunctions include such words as **wenn** *when(ever)*, *if*, **weil** *because*, **obwohl** *although* and **seitdem** *since* and send the verb to the end of the clause:

Er kann nicht kommen, *weil* er krank ist. He can't come, *because* he is ill.

Other subordinating conjunctions are: **während** *while*, **nachdem** *after*, **da** *as*, **ob** *whether* and **dass** *that*. (See **subordinate clause.**)

demonstratives Words such as *this*, *that*, *these*, *those* are called demonstratives or *demonstrative adjectives*:

This book is interesting. ***Dieses* Buch ist interessant.**
These exercises are very difficult. ***Diese* Übungen sind sehr schwierig.**

In German **dieser** (masculine), **diese** (feminine and plural,) **dieses** (neuter) are the most commonly used demonstratives.

gender In German, there are three genders, *masculine*, *feminine* and *neuter*: **der Tisch** *the table*, **die Lampe** *the lamp*, **das Haus** *the house*. In German, nouns have a gender irrespective of sex. For instance, the gender of the word for girl (**das Mädchen**) is neuter.

imperative The imperative is the form of the verb used to give orders or commands: *Help* me, please. In German, there are three main forms of the imperative, because of the various forms of address. ***Helfen*** **Sie mir, bitte!** (**Sie** form); **Hilf mir, bitte!** (du form); **Helft mir, bitte!** (ihr form).

infinitive The infinitive is the form of the verb that you will find entered in the dictionary. In English, the infinitive is usually preceded by the word 'to', e.g. *to go*, *to play*. In German, the infinitive usually ends in **-en**: **gehen** *to go*, **spielen** *to play*, **machen** *to do*, etc.

irregular verbs see **verbs**

Konjunktiv I, Konjunktiv II see **subjunctive**

modal verbs Verbs which express concepts such as permission, obligation, possibility, etc. (*can*, *must*, *may*) are referred to as modal verbs. Verbs in this category cannot in general stand on their own. Modal verbs in German include **wollen** *to want to*, **können** *to be able to*, **dürfen** *to be allowed to*.

nouns Nouns are words like *house* **Haus**, *bread* **Brot** and *beauty* **Schönheit**. They are often called 'naming words'. A useful test of a noun is whether you can put *the* in front of it: e.g. *the house*, *the bread*. Nouns in German have one of three **genders** and take a capital letter.

object The term object expresses the 'receiving end' relationship between a noun and a verb. Look at the following sentence:

The dog bit the postman. **Der Hund biss den Postboten.**

The postman is said to be the object of the sentence, as he is at the receiving end of the action.

Sentences such as: *My mother gave my wife an expensive ring* have both a *direct object* (an expensive ring) and an indirect object (my wife) – indirect because the ring was given to my wife. In German the direct object requires the *accusative case* and the indirect object the *dative case*: **Meine Mutter gab *meiner Frau*** (dative) ***einen teuren*** **Ring** (accusative).

(See also **subject**.)

---

passive voice Most actions can be viewed in two different ways:

1 The dog bit the postman. *Active voice*
2 The postman was bitten by the dog. *Passive voice*

In German you will also find both the active and passive voice. The passive is normally formed with the verb **werden** rather than with the verb **sein**:

1 Der Hund biss den Postboten.
2 Der Postbote *wurde* **vom Hund gebissen.**

---

personal pronouns Personal pronouns refer, as their name suggests, to persons. In German they are: **ich** *I*; **du** *you* (informal singular), **Sie** *you* (formal singular); **er**, **sie**, **es** *he*, *she*, *it*; **wir** *we*; **ihr** *you* (informal plural), **Sie** *you* (formal plural); **sie** *they*. (See also **pronouns**.)

---

plural see **singular and plural**

---

possessives Words such as **mein** *my*, **dein** *your* (informal), **Ihr** *your* (formal), **ihr** *her*, **sein** *his* are given the term *possessives* or *possessive adjectives*, because they indicate who something belongs to.

---

prepositions Words like **in** *in*, **auf** *on*, **zwischen** *between*, **für** *for* are called prepositions. Prepositions often tell us about the position of something. They are normally followed by a noun or a pronoun:

a This present is *for* you.
b *Despite* the weather I am going to walk.
c Your book is *on* the table.

In German prepositions require the use of a **case**, such as the accusative, genitive or dative:

a **Dieses Geschenk ist** *für dich*. (accusative)
b *Trotz des* **Wetters gehe ich zu Fuß**. (genitive)
c **Dein Buch liegt** *auf dem Tisch*. (dative)

---

pronouns Pronouns fulfil a similar function to nouns and often stand in the place of nouns mentioned earlier.
The *lamp* (noun) is modern. It (pronoun) is ugly. **Die *Lampe* ist modern. *Sie* ist hässlich.**
Note that in German the pronoun has to be the same gender as the noun which it stands for (**die Lampe** → sie). (See **nouns**.)

---

relative clauses Relative clauses are *subordinate clauses* which usually provide more information about a noun or phrase in the main clause. (See **subordinate clause**.) They are usually introduced by a relative pronoun, a word like *whom*, *whose*, etc. in English and like **der**, **deren**, etc. in German:

Do you know the man (whom) we saw in the bakery?
Kennst du *den* Mann, den wir in der Bäckerei gesehen haben?
The woman whose husband works with me had an accident yesterday. **Die Frau, *deren* Mann mit mir arbeitet, hatte gestern einen Unfall gehabt.**

Note that it is not possible in German, as it often is in English, to omit the relative pronoun.

---

singular and plural The terms singular and plural are used to make the contrast between 'one' and 'more than one': *book/books* **Buch/Bücher**, *dog/dogs* **Hund/Hunde**; *hat/hats* **Hut/Hüte**.

Most plural forms in English are formed by adding an -s, but not all: *child/children*, *woman/women*, *mouse/mice*.
There are many different plural forms in German. Here are just three: **Kind/Kind*er*, Frau/Frau*en*, Maus/M*ä*use.**
Some nouns do not normally have plurals and are said to be uncountable: **das Obst** *fruit*; **die Luft** *air*.

---

subject The term 'subject' expresses a relationship between a noun and a verb. Look at the sentence 'The dog bit the postman'. Here the dog is said to be the subject of the verb to *bite*, because it is the dog that is doing the biting.
In German the subject of the sentence needs to be in the *nominative case*: ***Der Hund* biss den Postboten.**

---

subjunctive The subjunctive mood has all but disappeared from use in modern English. It appears in set expressions, such as 'If I were you.' and 'God *forbid*.' In German there are two forms of the subjunctive:

a Konjunktiv I which is formed from the present tense form of the verb and which is mainly used in reported speech.

Christiane hat gesagt, dass Florian jetzt mit Birgit verheiratet *sei*. *Christiane said that Florian is now married to Birgit.*

b Konjunktiv II which is formed from the past simple form of the verb and which is mainly used for indicating that an activity, event or state is hypothetical, possible or perhaps not true.

Ich *würde* mich freuen, wenn du kämest. *I would be glad if you came.*

---

subordinate clauses Subordinate clauses are linked to a main clause and normally can't stand on their own: *He goes home because it is late*.
In German subordinating clauses are usually introduced by a subordinating **conjunction** (*dass*, *weil* etc.):

Er geht nach Hause, weil es spät ist.

Other types of subordinate clauses covered in this book are **relative clauses** and **indirect questions**:

Weißt du, *wer* heute Abend kommt? *Do you know who is coming this evening?*

A subordinate clause is separated from the main clause by a comma or commas.

superlative The superlative is used for the most extreme version of a comparison:

a This shirt is the *cheapest* of all.
b This blouse is the *most* expensive of all.

The superlative in German follows a similar pattern:

a Dieses Hemd ist das *billigste* von allen.
b Diese Bluse ist die *teuerste* von allen.

(See also **comparative**.)

tense Most languages use changes in the verb form to indicate an aspect of time. These changes in the verb are traditionally referred to as tense, and the tenses may be *present*, *past* or *future*. Tenses are often reinforced with expressions of time:

Present: *Today* I am staying at home. ***Heute* bleibe ich zu Hause.**
Past: *Yesterday* I went to London. ***Gestern* bin ich nach London gefahren./*Gestern* fuhr ich nach London.**
Future: *Tomorrow* I'll be flying to Berlin. ***Morgen* werde ich nach Berlin fliegen.**

The German tenses dealt with in this book are the present (*das Präsens*), the simple past (*das Präteritum*), the present perfect tense (*das Perfekt*) and the future tense (*das Futur*).

verbs Verbs often communicate actions, states and sensations. So, for instance, the verb *to play* **spielen** expresses an action, the verb ***to exist* existieren** expresses a state and the verb ***to see* sehen** expresses a sensation. A verb may also be defined by its role in the sentence or clause and usually has a **subject**. It may also have an **object**.

Verbs in German can be *regular* (often called *weak verbs*), or irregular (*strong* or *mixed verbs*). A list of the most common irregular verbs is provided in the previous part of this reference section.

German–English glossary

This glossary is intended to help you recall and use some of the most important words that you have met during the course. It is not intended to be comprehensive.

~ indicates that this verb or its root form can be found in the **List of common irregular verbs.**

I indicates that a verb is separable (e.g. **ab I bauen**).

With job titles, nationalities, etc., the female version is usually given in an abbreviated form, e.g. **der Akademiker** (-)**/die -in.** In the plural, feminine nouns ending in **-in** add **-nen,** e.g. **die Akademikerin, die Akademikerinnen.**

Abkürzungen (abbreviations):

acc. – accusative, adj. n. – adjectival noun, coll. – colloquial, dat. – dative, neut. – neuter, gen. – genitive, plur. – plural, wk. n. – weak noun

ab und zu *now and again*
ab I fahren~ *to depart*
die Abfahrt (-en) *departure*
die Abgase *(plural) exhaust fumes*
der/die Abgeordnete (-n) (adj. n.) *member of parliament*
abgesehen von + dat. *apart from*
ab I hängen von + dat. *to depend on*
abhängig von + dat. *dependent on*
ab I holen *to pick up, collect*
das Abitur *school-leaving examination, taken at age 18+*
ab I legen *to sit, take (an exam)*
ab I räumen *to clear up/away*
ab I schaffen *to abolish, get rid of*
ab I schließen~ *to finish (one's studies)*
der Abschluss (-¨e) *leaving exam*
die Abteilung (-en) *department*

ab | waschen *to wash up, do the dishes*
achtlos *heedless(ly), without caring*
ähnlich *similar(ly)*
der Akademiker (-)/die -in *graduate*
der/die Alkoholkranke (-n) (adj. n.) *person who is ill from alcohol-related problems*
allerhand *all sorts (of things)*
allgemein *general*
im Allgemeinen *in general*
allzu viel *too much*
als Nächstes *next*
das Alter *age*
die Ampel (-n) *traffic lights*
an | belangen *to concern*
  Was … anbelangt, … *in so far as … is concerned*
an | bieten~ *to offer*
andere *other, different*
  andere Länder, andere Sitten *when in Rome, do as the Romans do; lit. different countries, different customs*
anders *different(ly)*
anderthalb *one and a half*
an | fallen~ *to come up (of work)*
der Anfang (-¨e) *beginning*
  von Anfang an *from the start*
an | fangen *to begin, commence*
der Anfängerkurs (-e) *beginners course*
an | gehen~ *to concern*
  Das geht dich nichts an. *That doesn't concern you.*
der/die Angestellte (-n) (adj. n.) *employee*
die Anglistik *English language and literature*
die Angst (-¨e) *fear, anxiety*
an | kommen~ *to arrive*
  gut ankommen *to be well received*
die Ankunft (-¨e) *arrival*
der Anlass (-¨e) *occasion, reason*
an | melden *to register,*
annähernd *almost*
an | nehmen~ *to assume*
sich an | passen an (+ acc.) *to adapt to*
sich etwas an | schauen *to watch, look at something*
anschließend *afterwards, subsequently*
ansonsten *otherwise*
der Anspruch (-¨e) auf (+ acc.) *right to*
  in Anspruch nehmen~ *to take up (of time, energy, etc.)*
anstatt (+ gen.) *instead of*
der Anteil (-e) *proportion*
an | wachsen~ *to grow, increase*
der Anwärter/die -in *candidate (for a job)*
die Anzahl *number*
arbeitsam *hard-working*
die Arbeitsagentur (-en) *job centre*
die Arbeitslosigkeit *unemployment*
der Arbeitsplatz (-¨e) *workplace; job*

der Architekt (wk. n.)/die -in *architect*
sich ärgern (über + acc.) *to be annoyed (about)*
der Arm (-e) *arm*
jdn auf den Arm nehmen~ *to pull someone's leg (coll.)*
der Artikel (-) *article*
die Ärztekammer (-n) *chamber of doctors*
der Assistent (wk. n.)/die -in *assistant*
atmen *to breathe*
die Atomkraft *nuclear power*
die Auffassung (-en) *view, attitude*
auf I frischen *to freshen up, to polish up*
auf I geben~ *to drop, give up*
auf I gießen *to pour on*
auf I hören *to stop, cease*
auf I polieren *to brush up*
auf I räumen *to clear up*
auf I stehen~ *to get up*
der Aufwand *expense (in time/money)*
aufwendig *lavish*
die Ausbildung (-en) *training*
ausfallen lassen~ *to skip*
der Ausflug (-¨e) *excursion, trip*
aus I führen *to export*
ausführlich *detailed*
die Ausgabe (-n) *edition*
der Ausgang (-¨e) *exit, way out*
aus I geben~ *to spend (of money)*
aus I gehen~ *to go out*
ausgepumpt (coll.) *exhausted*
ausgiebig *thoroughly*
die Auskunft (-¨e) *information*
der Ausländer/die -in *foreigner*
aus I machen *to switch/turn off*
die Ausnahme (-n) *exception*
sich aus I schließen~ *to exclude oneself*
aus I sehen~ *to look (like)*
außer (+ dat.) *besides, except (for)*
außerhalb *outside (of a town)*
sich aus I sprechen~ für (+ acc.) *to speak in favour of*
die Ausstellung (-en) *exhibition*
sich aus I tauschen *to exchange views*
aus I treten~ aus (+ dat.) *to leave (a club, a society, etc.)*

der Badeurlaub (-e) *swimming holiday*
die Bahn (-en) *railway*
mit der Bahn *by rail*
der Bahnhof (-¨e) *station*
bald *soon*
der Ballungsraum (-¨e) *conurbation*
die Banklehre (-n) *banking apprenticeship*
die Batterie (-n) *battery*
der Bauingenieur (-e)/die -in *civil engineer*
(das) Bayern *Bavaria*
bedeuten *to mean*
die Bedeutung (-en) *importance*
beeindruckend *impressive*
begegnen (+ dat.) *to encounter*

sich begeistern für (+ acc.) *to be enthusiatic about*
behindert *handicapped*
das Beispiel (-e) (für + acc.) *example (of)*
bekannt *well-known*
der/die Bekannte (-n) (adj. n.) *acquaintance*
bekehren *to convert (someone)*
bekommen~ *to get, to receive*
belasten *to strain, burden*
belegen *to occupy (a room)*
sich bemühen *to make an effort, try*
benutzen *to use*
das Benzin *petrol, gasoline*
bequem *comfortable; convenient(ly)*
bereits *already*
der Berg (-e) *mountain*
berichten *to report*
der Beruf (-e) *job, profession*
  Was sind Sie von Beruf? *What job do you do?*
berufstätig *(gainfully) employed*
beschäftigen *to employ*
sich beschäftigen mit (+ dat.) *to concern oneself with*
Bescheid wissen (über + acc.) *to know (about)*
die Besichtigung (-en) *sightseeing*
die Besorgnis (-se) *concern*
bestätigen *to confirm*
bestehen~ *to exist, to be; to pass (an exam)*
bestellen *to order*
besuchen *to visit*
betreiben~ *to pursue; do; to run (a business, company)*
der Betrieb (-e) *business, factory*
die Bevölkerung (-en) *population*
bevölkerungsreich *densely populated*
sich bewerben~ (um + acc.) *to apply (for)*
der Bewerber (-)/die -in *applicant*
bewusst *conscious*
die Bezahlung *pay*
beziehungsweise *alternatively, or*
bezüglich (+ gen.) *concerning, with regard to*
die Bibliothek (-en) *library*
der Bienenhonig *(bee) honey*
bieten~ *to offer*
das Bild (-er) *picture, image*
bilden *to form, to constitute*
die Bildung *education*
binden *to bind*
die Biologie *biology*
die Biomasse (-n) *biomass*
das Blatt (-¨er) *leaf; sheet, newspaper*
blau *blue*
der Blick (-e) *view, glance*
die Branche (-n) *sector, industry*
die Boulevardzeitung (-en) *tabloid*
brechen~ *to break*
der Brite (wk.n.)/die -in *Briton*

die Brücke (-n) *bridge*
das Buch (-¨er) *book*
die Buche (-n) *beech (tree)*
bummeln *to stroll*
der Bundeskanzler/die -in *Federal Chancellor*
das Bundesland (-¨er) *federal state*
der Bundespräsident (wk.n.) *Federal President*
der Bundestag *Federal Parliament*
der Bürger (-)/die -in *citizen*
das Büro (-s) *office*
die Bushaltestelle (-n) *bus stop*

der Chef (-s)/die -in *boss, head*
die Chemie *chemistry*
das Cholesterin *cholesterol*
der Cholesterinspiegel (-) *cholesterol level*
der Computer (-) *computer*

dabei sein~ *to be there; to be in the process of*
das Dach (-¨er) *roof*
dagegen *against that; on the other hand*
danach (+ dat) *after that, then*
danken (+ dat) *to thank*
dann *then*
auf Dauer *in the long term*
der Deckel (-) *lid; (coll.) driving licence*
denken~ *to think*
deswegen *therefore, for this reason*
deutlich *clear(ly), significant(ly)*
dicht *densely; closely*
der Dienst (-e) *service*
der Dienstleistungssektor (-en) *service sector*
das Ding (-e) *thing*
der Direktor (wk. n.)/die -in *director, head teacher*
diskutieren *to discuss*
der Dokumentarfilm (-e) *documentary (film)*
der Dom (-e) *cathedral*
doppelt so … wie *twice as … as*
das Dorf (¨-er) *village*
da ist 'was dran *there's some truth in that*
durch | führen *to conduct; carry out*
durchgehend *all day, all the time*
der Durchschnitt (-e) *average*
dürfen *to be allowed to*
die Dusche (-n) *shower*
sich unter die Dusche stellen *to take a shower*

die Ecke (-n) *corner*
um die Ecke *around the corner*
egal *all the same*
ehrlich gesagt *quite honestly*
die Eiche (-n) *oak tree*
eigen *own (adj.)*
die Eigenschaft (-en) *characteristic*
eigentlich *actual(ly)*
ein | atmen *to breathe in*
eindeutig *clear(ly), unambiguous(ly)*

ein | führen *to introduce*
einfach *simple, simply*
eingebunden *tied, constrained, bound*
die Einheit (-en) *unity*
ein | kaufen *to shop*
das Einkommen (-) *income*
ein | laden~ *to invite*
die Einladung (-en) *invitation*
ein | richten *to arrange, to furnish*
die Einschätzung (-en) *estimation*
einschließlich (+ gen.) *inclusive of, including*
ein | sehen~ *to recognize, acknowledge*
ein | sparen *to save*
ein | treten~ (in + acc.) *to join*
die Einwirkung (-en) (auf + acc.) *effect (on)*
der Einwohner (-)/die -in *inhabitant*
einzigartig *unique*
empfehlen~ *to recommend*
die Energie (-n) *energy*
die Energiequelle (-n) *source of energy*
die Energiesparlampe (-n) *energy-saving bulb*
die Englischkenntnisse (plur.) *knowledge of English*
entdecken *to discover*
enthalten~ *to contain, to include*
entlassen~ *to dismiss*
entscheiden~ *to decide*
sich entschuldigen *to apologize*
entsorgen *to dispose of (waste)*
sich entspannen *to relax*
entsprechend *corresponding, respective*
die Entwicklung (-en) *development, trend*
meines Erachtens *in my opinion*
erbringen~ *to provide*
das Ereignis (-se) *event*
die Erfahrung (-en) *experience*
erforderlich *necessary*
die Erforschung (-en) *research*
ergänzen *to complete*
das Ergebnis (-se) *result*
sich erinnern an (+ acc.) *to remember*
erklären *to explain*
erledigen *to deal with, attend to*
sich ernähren von (+ dat.) *to feed oneself on, live on*
die Ernährung *nutrition*
ernennen~ *to appoint*
erneuerbar *renewable*
erreichen *to reach*
erscheinen~ *to appear*
erst *first; only, not until*
ersticken *to suffocate*
sich erstrecken auf (+ acc.) *to stretch to, extend to*
der/die Erwachsene (-n) (adj. n.) *adult*
erzeugen *to generate, to produce*
essen~ *to eat*

das Exemplar (-e) *copy*
der EZ-Zuschlag (-¨e) *single room suplement*

fahren~ *to go (in a vehicle), drive*
die Fahrerei *travelling backwards and forwards*
die Fahrerlaubnis (-se) *licence to drive*
die Fahrschule (-n) *driving school*
der Fall (-¨e) *case; fall*
  auf keinen Fall *under no circumstances; lit. in no case*
die Farbe (-n) *colour, paint*
feiern *to celebrate*
Feierabend machen *to finish work*
fern | sehen~ *to watch TV*
fertig *finished, ready*
das Fest (-e) *party, celebration*
die Festspiele *(neut. plur.) festival*
fest | stellen *to ascertain*
finden~ *to find, to consider*
flächenmäßig *in area*
der Flegel (-) *lout*
fleißig *hard-working, industrious*
fließend *fluent(ly)*
der Flughafen (¨) *airport*
das Flugzeug (-e) *plane*
folgen (+ dat.) *to follow*
der Folgeschaden (¨) *harmful effect*
die Forderung (-en) *demand*
der/die Fortgeschrittene (-n) (adj. n.) *advanced learner*
der Fotograf (wk. n.)/die -in *photographer*
der Franzose (wk. n.)/die Französin *Frenchman/ Frenchwoman*
die Fremdsprache (-n) *foreign language*
sich freuen (über + acc.) *to be glad (about)*
sich freuen auf (+ acc.) *to look forward to*
froh *glad*
führen *to lead, to conduct; to run (a business etc.)*
der Führerschein (-e) *driving licence*
die Führung (-en) *guided tour*
der Fuß (-¨e) *foot*
  zu Fuß *on foot*

gar nicht *not at all*
der Gast (-¨e) *guest*
die Gaststätte (-n) *restaurant, inn*
das Gebäude (-) *building*
geben~ *to give*
geboren *born*
  Wann bist du geboren? *When were you born?*
Gebrauch machen von (+ dat.) *to make use of*
der Geburtstag (-e) *birthday*
gefährlich *dangerous*
gefallen~ (+ dat.) *to be pleasing*
  Es gefällt mir. *I like it.*
das Gefühl (-e) *feeling*
gehören *to belong*

die Geisteswissenschaften *Humanities*
geistig *mental(ly)*
der Geldmangel *lack of money*
die Gelegenheit (-en) *opportunity*
gelegentlich *occasionally*
das Gelenk (-e) *joint*
gelingen *to succeed*
Es ist uns nicht gelungen, ... *We didn't succeed in ... We didn't manage to ...*
gelten~ als *to be regarded as*
gemächlich *leisurely*
genau *exact(ly), precise(ly)*
genau(er) hinschauen *to take a close(r) look*
geöffnet *open*
das Gepäck *luggage*
gepflegt *well-kept*
geradeaus *straight on*
geregelt *regulated*
geschädigt *damaged*
die Geschäftsreise (-n) *business trip*
geschehen~ *to happen*
das Geschenk (-e) *present*
die Geschichte (-n) *history; story*
geschieden *divorced*
das Geschirr *crockery, dishes*
der Geschmack (-¨er) *taste*
gesellig *sociable*
die Gesellschaft (-en) *society*
das Gesetz (-e) *law*
gestalten *to arrange, form, shape*
gestresst *stressed*
gesundheitlich *from the health point of view*
gewöhnen *to familiarize*
an etwas gewöhnt sein *to be used to something*
gewöhnlich *usually*
der Glascontainer (-) *glass container*
glauben (+ dat.) *to believe*
die Globalisierung *globalization*
das Glück *(good) fortune*
Glück haben *to be lucky*
glücklicherweise *fortunately*
gratulieren (+ dat.) *to congratulate*
die Grenze (-n) *border, frontier*
großartig *magnificent(ly) splendid(ly)*
der Grund (-¨e) *reason*
gründen *to found*
das Grundgesetz *Basic Law (constitution of the Federal Republic)*
gründlich *thorough*
die Gründlichkeit *thoroughness*
der Grundpfeiler (-) *cornerstone*
der Grüne Punkt *lit. the Green Dot (sign on products to indicate that a wrapping should be recycled)*
der Gymnasiallehrer (-)/die -in *grammar school teacher*
das Gymnasium (Gymnasien) *(German) grammar school*

halten~ von (+ dat.) *to think of*
die Haltestelle (-n) *(bus, train, tram) stop*

die Hand (-¨e) *hand*
der Handel *trade*
handeln *to trade*
die Hauptschule (-n) *secondary school*
der Hauptschulabschluss (-¨e) *secondary-school leaving exam after 9 years of schooling*
heiter *funny; cheerful; bright*
Das kann ja heiter werden! *That will be fun! (ironic)*
die Heizplatte (-n) *hotplate*
die Heizung (-en) *heating*
helfen~ (+ dat.) *to help*
der Herr (-en) (wk. n) *gentleman*
her l stellen *to produce, manufacture*
das Herz (-en) (wk. n.) *heart*
die Hilfe (-n) *help, assistance, aid*
der Hin- und Rückflug (-¨e) *return flight*
hin l schauen *to look (at)*
hinterher *afterwards*
hin l weisen auf (+ acc.) *to point out*
die Hochschule (-n) *institution of Higher Education*
höchstens *at the most*
die Hochzeit (-en) *wedding*
die Hoffnung (-en) *hope*
der Honig *honey*
hören *to hear, to listen to*

immer *always*
immerhin *all the same, nevertheless*
der Industriekaufmann/die -frau *person with three years' business training*
die Industrienation (-en) *industrialised nation*
das Ingenieurwesen *engineering*
insgesamt *in total, in all*
sich interessieren (für + acc.) *to be interested in*
Italienisch *Italian (language)*

das Jahr (-e) *year*
vor zwei Jahren *two years ago*
zweimal im Jahr *twice a year*
das Jahrhundert (-e) *century*
je *in each case*
jeder/-e/-es *each, every*
jedenfalls *in any case*
jeweils *in each instance*
der Journalist (-en) (wk. n.)/ die -in *journalist*
der/die Jugendliche (-n) (wk. n.) *young person*
der Junge (-n) (wk. n.) *boy*
(die) Jura *Law*

der Kaffee (-s) *coffee*
die Kammer (-n) *chamber*
der Kandidat (-en) (wk. n.)/die -in *candidate*
der Kater (coll.) *hangover; tomcat*
kaufen *to buy*
der Kegelclub (-s) *bowling club*
die Kehrseite (-n) *the other side*
der Kellner (-)/die -in *waiter/ waitress*

die Kernenergie *nuclear energy*
die Kiste (-n) *box, old banger (car)*
klappen *to turn out all right*
klar *clear*
das Klischee (-s) *cliché*
der Kloß (-¨e) *dumpling*
kochen *to cook, to make (coffee)*
die Kochnische (-n) *small cooking area; lit. cooking niche*
der Kollege (-n) (wk. n.)/ die -in *colleague*
das Kolpingwerk *Kolping organisation (named after a Catholic priest)*
komisch *funny, strange*
Das hört sich komisch an. *That sounds strange.*
die Konkurrenz *competition*
konkurrenzfähig *competitive, viable*
können *to be able to*
das Körnchen (Wahrheit) *grain (of truth)*
körperlich *physically, bodily*
kosten *to cost*
die Kosten (plur.) *cost(s)*
kostspielig *expensive*
die Kraft (-¨e) *force, power*
die Krankheit (-en) *disease, illness*
der Krebs *cancer*
der Kreislauf (-¨e) *circulatory system*
die Kreuzung (-en) *crossroads*
der Kühlschrank (-¨e) *refrigerator*
kulturinteressiert *interested in the arts*
sich kümmern um (+ acc.) *to take care of, look after, concern oneself with*
der Kunde (-n) (wk. n.)/die Kundin *customer, client*
die Kunst (-¨e) *art*
die Kur (-en) *cure (at a spa)*
kursiv *in italics*

das Labor (-s/-e) *lab*
der Lack (-e) *varnish*
der Laden (-¨) *shop*
das Land (-¨er) *country; federal state*
die Landschaft (-en) *scenery*
der Landwirt (-e) *farmer*
lang *long*
langfristig *long-term, in the long run*
langjährig *of many years*
langsam *slow(ly)*
längst *long since*
langweilig *boring*
Wird Ihnen nicht manchmal langweilig? *Don't you get bored sometimes?*
laufen~ *to run, walk*
auf dem Laufenden sein *to be up to date*
die Laufbahn (-en) *career*
laut *loud, noisy*
lebendig *lively*
die Lebensart (-en) *way of life*
der Lebenslauf (-¨e) *CV*

die Leberzirrhose (-n) *cirrhosis of the liver*
legen *to lay, put*
leiden~ *to suffer*
leid tun~ *to be sorry*
Es tut mir leid *I am sorry*
die Leistung (-en) *performance, achievement; what is included (in a package holiday)*
die Leistungsanforderung (-en) *demands on performance*
der Leistungsdruck *pressure to perform, to work harder*
lieben *to love*
lieber *preferable*
Ich gehe lieber ins Kino. *I prefer to go to the cinema.*
liegen~ (in + dat.) *to lie (in); to be situated (in)*
liegen bleiben~ *to be left over, undone*
links *on the left*
Gehen Sie nach links. *Go left.*
der/das Liter (-) *litre*
sich lohnen *to be worthwhile*
lösen *solve; to obtain (a ticket)*
los | gehen~ *to start, set off*
die Luft (-¨e) *air*
Lust haben *to feel like, to want to*

die Macht (-¨e) *power*
das Mädchen (-) *girl*
die Mahlzeit (-en) *meal*
die Malerei *painting*
manche *some*
manchmal *sometimes*
marktdominierend *dominating the market*
die Marmelade (-n) *jam*
die Maßnahme (-n) *measure*
die Mathematik *mathematics*
die Medaille (-n) *medal*
die Kehrseite der Medaille *on the other side of the coin*
die Medien (plur.) *media*
die Mehrheit (-en) *majority*
die Mehrwegflasche (-n) *reusable bottle*
meinen (zu + dat.) *to think about, to have an opinion on*
die Meinung (-en) *opinion*
meistens *mostly*
die Menge (-n) *quantity*
die Mensa (-en) *refectory, university dining hall*
der Mensch (-en) (wk. n.) *human being, person*
Mensch! *wow!*
merkwürdig *strange, peculiar*
der/das Meter (-) *metre*
der Metzger (-)/die -in *butcher*
die Metzgerei (-en) *butcher's (shop)*
die Minderheit (-en) *minority*
miteinander *with one another*
mit | gehen *to go along with*
das Mitglied (-er) *member*
mit | machen *to take part, to participate*
der Mittag *midday*
zu Mittag essen *to have lunch*
mittags *midday, lunchtime*
die Mitte (-n) *middle, centre*

der Mittelpunkt (-e) *centre*
(die) Mitternacht *midnight*
die mittlere Reife *secondary-school-leaving certificate taken after 10 years of schooling*
der Modellbau *model-building*
mögen *to like*
die Möglichkeit (-en) *possibility*
die Moralpredigt (-en) *(moralizing) lecture*
motiviert *motivated*
der Müll *rubbish, garbage*
der Mülleimer (-) *rubbish bin*
die Mülltrennung *separation of waste*
der Mund (-¨er) *mouth*
die Musik *music*
müssen *to have to, must*
die Muttersprache (-n) *mother tongue*

der Nachbar (-n) (wk. n.)/ die -in *neighbour*
die Nachfrage (-n) *demand*
die Nachrichtensendung (-en) *news broadcast*
das Nachschlagewerk (-e) *reference work*
nach | sehen~ *to have a look*
der Nachteil (-e) *disadvantage*
der Nachweis (-e) *proof, evidence*
einen Nachweis erbingen *to produce evidence*
die Nadel (-n) *needle*
die Nähe *proximity*
in der Nähe (von + dat.) *near*

nämlich *lit. namely; you see*
der Name (wk. n.) *name*
die Nase (-n) *nose*
die Nase voll haben (coll.) *to have had enough*
natürlich *natural(ly), of course*
die Naturwissenschaft (-en) *natural science*
nehmen~ *to take*
nervenaufreibend *nerve-racking*
neulich *recently*
der Nichtraucher die -in (-) *non-smoker*
nie *never*
niedrig *low*
normalerweise *normally*
die Note (-n) *mark, grade*
nötig *necessary*
notwendig *necessary*
nur *only*
nutzen *to use*

die Öffentlichkeit *public*
oft *often*
öfters *fairly often*
ordentlich *tidy*
die Ordnung *order, orderliness, tidiness*
ordnungsliebend *liking to see things neat and tidy*
der Ort (-e) *place*
die Ostseeküste *Baltic Coast*

die Partnerstadt (-¨e) *twin town*
passen *to match*
passieren *to happen*
pendeln *to commute*

die Pension (-en) *guesthouse, pension*
die Personalabteilung (-en) *personnel department*
der Personalberater (-)/die -in *personnel consultant*
die Personalfortbildung (-en) *staff development*
das Pflanzenöl (-e) *vegetable oil*
die Podiumsdiskussion (-en) *panel discussion*
der Politiker (-)/die -in *politician*
der Polizist (-en) (wk. n.)/die -in *police officer*
das Praktikum (die Praktika) *work placement*
der Präsident (-en) (wk. n.)/ die -in *president*
das Problem (-e) *problem*
die Prüfung (-en) *examination*
der Punkt (-e) *point, full stop, dot*

der Quatsch (coll.) *nonsense*

der Rand (-¨er) *edge*
raten~ (+ dat.) *to advise*
die Ratesendung (-en) *panel game, quiz show*
die Realschule (-en) *school geared to the mittlere Reife exam (roughly equivalent to 16+ school-leaving exam)*
das Recht (-e) (auf + acc.) *right to*
das Recht *law*
recht haben *to be right*
rechts *on the right*
nach rechts *to the right*
das Recycling *recycling*
recyceln *to recycle*
die Redaktion (-en) *editorial staff*
reden (über + acc.) *to talk (about)*
der Referent (-en) (wk. n.)/ die -in *expert, adviser*
die Regel (-n) *rule*
regelmäßig *regular(ly)*
regeln *to regulate, to settle*
regional *regional(ly)*
reichen *to suffice*
Das hat mir gereicht. *That was enough for me.*
die Reihe (-n) *series*
rein *pure, clean*
reinigen *to clean*
die Reisebegleitung (-en) *accompanied tour, lit. tour accompaniment*
der Reiseleiter (-) *courier*
reiselustig *keen on travelling*
der Reiseverlauf (-¨e) *tour plan; lit.: tour course*
das Reiseziel (-e) *destination*
der Renner (-) *hit*
renovieren *to renovate*
der Rentner (-)/die -in *pensioner*
der Richter (-)/die -in *judge*
richtig *right, correct*
die Richtung (-en) *direction*
der Rohstoff (-e) *raw material*
die Rolle (-n) *role*
die Ruhe *peace, quiet*
rund *around*

die Sache (-n) *thing, matter*
der Saft (-¨e) *juice*
die Sammelstelle (-n) *collecting point*
sauber *clean*
sauber machen *to clean*
das Sauerkraut *sauerkraut, pickled cabbage*
schädigen *to harm, damage*
schaffen (coll.) *to manage*
schaffen~ *to create*
der Schalter (-) *ticket window*
schätzen *to appreciate, estimate*
schauen (auf + acc.) *to look (at)*
die Scheibe (-n) *slice*
schlafen~ *to sleep*
schlecht *bad*
schließen~ *to shut, close*
schließlich *after all, finally*
der Schluss (-¨e) *end*
zum Schluss *finally*
der Schnitt (-e) *average*
schon *already*
schrecklich *terrible*
der Schreibtisch (-e) *desk*
der Schreiner (-)/die -in *carpenter*
die Schreinerlehre (-n) *carpentry apprenticeship*
der Schutz *protection*
der Schweinebraten (-) *roast pork*
die Schwiegereltern (plur.) *parents-in-law*
schwierig *difficult*
die Schwierigkeit (-en) *difficulty*
der Schwimmunterricht *swimming lessons*
das Schwindelgefühl (-e) *feeling of dizziness*
der See (-n) *lake*
die See (-n) *sea*
die Seehöhe *sea level*
die Sehenswürdigkeit (-en) *sight (worth seeing)*
die Seite (-n) *side; page*
selbstständig *self-employed; independent*
selten *rare(ly)*
das Semester (-) *semester*
das Seminar (-e) *seminar*
senden *to broadcast*
der Sender (-) *(radio/TV) station*
setzen *to put, place*
sicher *safe, secure; sure(ly), certain(ly)*
sicherlich *certainly, undoubtedly*
der Sinn (-e) *sense*
Ski fahren~ *to go skiing*
sofort *immediately*
sogar *even*
die Solarenergie (-n) *solar energy*
die Solarzelle (-n) *solar cell*
der Soldat (-en) (wk. n.)/die -in *soldier*
sollen *ought, should*
der Sondermüll *hazardous waste*
sonnabends *on Saturdays*
die Sonne (-n) *sun*
die Sonnenenergie (-n) *solar energy*

sonst *otherwise*
die Sorge (-n) *worry*
Machst du dir keine Sorgen? *Don't you worry?*
sowieso *anyway, in any case*
der Sozialarbeiter (-)/die -in *social worker*
der Sozialpädagoge (-n) (wk. n.)/die -pädagogin *person with a degree in Social Education*
der Spaß (-¨e) *fun*
Es macht mir Spaß *I enjoy it*
speziell *special(ly)*
spielen *to play*
der Spitzenreiter (-) *leader, front runner*
Sport treiben *to do sports*
sprechen *to speak*
der Sprit *(coll.) petrol*
das Staatsexamen (-) *state exam; similar to a degree*
ständig *constant(ly)*
die Stange (-n) *stick*
eine schöne Stange Geld *a small fortune*
stark *strong(ly)*
der Starnberger See *large lake near Munich*
statt | finden~ *to take place*
staunen (über + acc.) *to be amazed (at)*
stehen~ *to stand*
steigen~ *to rise*
sich steigern *to increase*
stellen *to put, place*
die Stellung (-en) *position, job*
stellvertretend *deputy*
sterben~ *to die*
stimmen *to be correct*
der Stoff (-e) *substance*
die Störung (-en) *disturbance*
die Straßenbahn (-en) *tram*
streng *strict(ly)*
stressfrei *free of stress*
stricken *to knit*
der Strom *electricity*
der Student (-en) (wk. n.)/ die -in *student*
der Studienabschluss (-¨e) *roughly equivalent to a degree; lit. end of studies*
der Studienplatz (-¨e) *university place*
die Studienzeit (-en) *period of study*
die Stunde (-n) *hour, lesson*
suchen *to search, to look for*
die Süßigkeiten (plur.) *sweet things, confectionery*
der Supermarkt (-¨e) *supermarket*

die Tabellenkalkulation (-en) *spreadsheets*
der Tagesablauf (-¨e) *daily routine*
die Tageszeitung (-en) *daily paper*
der Tanzclub (-s) *dance club*
tanzen *to dance*
der Tanzkurs (-e) *dancing classes*
sich täuschen (-e) *to be wrong, to be mistaken*

der Teelöffel (-) *teaspoon*
der Teil (-e) *part*
teilen *to share*
teuer *dear, expensive*
die Textverarbeitung *word processing*
das Theaterstück (-e) *play, drama*
das Thema (Themen) *subject, topic*
(das) Thüringen *Thuringia – one of the sixteen German 'Länder'*
toll (coll.) *fantastic, great*
der Tourist (-en) (wk. n.)/ die -in *tourist*
der Traum (-¨e) *dream*
treffen~ *to meet*
trennen *to separate*
der Trost *consolation, comfort*
tun~ *to do*
das Turnier (-e) *tournament*
typisch *typical(ly)*

die U-Bahn (-en) (= Untergrundbahn) *tube, subway*
über | einstimmen (mit + dat.) *to agree (with)*
überfüllt *overcrowded*
überhaupt nicht *not at all*
übermorgen *the day after tomorrow*
die Übernachtung (-en) *overnight stay*
übernehmen~ *to take on*
überprüfen *to check (over)*
überregional *national, nationwide*
übersetzen *to translate*
übertreiben~ *to exaggerate*
übrigens *by the way*
umfassend *comprehensive*
die Umfrage (-n) *survey, opinion poll*
die Umgebung (-en) *surrounding area*
um | gehen~ mit (+ dat.) *to deal with*
umsonst *free of charge*
umweltbewusst *conscious of the environment*
der Umweltflegel (-) *lout (in environmental matters)*
das Umweltministerium *Ministry of the Environment*
der Umweltschutz *environmental protection*
unbedingt *definitely, at all costs*
unbemerkt *unnoticed*
ungeheuer *huge(ly), immense(ly)*
unheimlich viel *a huge amount*
das Unrecht (-e) *injustice*
sich unterhalten~ (über + acc.) *to talk (about)*
die Unterhaltung *entertainment*
die Unterhaltungsserie (-n) *serial*
der Untermieter (-) *lodger*
unternehmen~ *to do, undertake*
der Unterricht *instruction, lessons*
unterrichten *to teach, instruct*
unterschiedlich *different(ly), varying*
der Untertitel (-) *subtitle*

unterwegs sein *to be away, to be on a trip*
unvergleichlich *incomparably*
der Urenkel (-)/die -in *great-grandchild*
der Urlaub (-e) *holiday, vacation*
der Urlauber (-) *holidaymaker*

die Veranstaltung (-en) *event*
die Verantwortung *responsibility*
verbessern *to improve*
verbieten~ *to prohibit, to ban*
verbinden *to join, combine*
das Verbot (-e) *ban*
verbringen~ *to spend (time)*
verdienen *to earn*
die Verfassung (-en) *constitution*
verfassungsgemäß *constitutional*
zur Verfügung stehen *to be available, at one's disposal*
vergangen *past*
die Vergangenheit (-en) *past*
vergessen~ *to forget*
der Vergleich (-e) *comparison*
im Vergleich (zu/mit + dat.) *compared (to/with)*
vergleichen *to compare*
die Verhandlung (-en) *negotiation*
verhängen *to impose (a ban)*
verheiratet *married*
der Verkehr *traffic*
das Verkehrsamt (-¨er) *tourist information office*
verkennen~ *to fail to appreciate, recognize*
der Verlag (-e) *publishing company*
verlangen *to demand*
Das ist zu viel verlangt. *That is asking too much.*
verlassen~ *to leave*
verlieren~ *to lose*
vermeiden *to avoid*
vermitteln *to give, provide; to arrange, mediate*
die Verpackung (-en) *wrapping, packaging*
verpesten *to pollute*
verpflichten *to oblige, commit*
verplanen *to book up completely, to plan every minute*
verregnet *rainy, wet, spoilt by rain*
verrückt *mad, insane*
verschieden *various, different*
die Versicherungsfirma (-firmen) *insurance company*
das Verständnis *understanding*
verstärken *to reinforce, to increase*
der Versuch (-e) *experiment, attempt*
versuchen *to try*
vertauschen *to exchange; to mix up*
vertraut sein (mit + dat.) *to be familiar (with)*
der/die Verwandte (-n) (adj. n.) *relative*
verwenden *to use*

verzichten auf (+ acc.) *to do without*
vierzehntägig *fortnightly*
das Volk (-¨er) *people, nation*
voll *full*
vollkommen *complete(ly)*
vor allem *above all*
vor | behalten~ *to reserve (the right)*
vor | bereiten *to prepare*
die Vorbereitung (-en) *preparation*
vorher *in advance, beforehand*
vor | kommen~ *to occur*
die Vorlesung (-en) *lecture*
der Vorlesungsaal (-säle) *lecture theatre*
die Vorliebe (-n) *preference*
vor | nehmen~ *to carry out; to mean*
der Vorsatz (-¨e) *intention, resolution*
vor | schlagen~ *to suggest, propose*
die Vorschrift (-en) *regulation*
vor | stellen *to introduce*
sich (etwas) vor | stellen *to imagine (something)*
die Vorstellung (-en) *idea, concept*
der Vorteil (-e) *advantage*
das Vorurteil (-e) *prejudice*
vor | ziehen~ *to prefer*

wachsen~ *to grow*
die Wahrheit (-en) *truth*
wahrscheinlich *probably*
der Wald (-¨er) *forests*
das Waldsterben *death of forests*
wandern *to ramble, hike*
warnen (vor + dat.) *to warn (against)*
was für ...? *what kind of ...?*
die Wäsche *laundry, washing*
waschen~ *to wash*
der Waschsalon (-s) *launderette*
im Wechsel *alternating*
weder ... noch *neither ... nor*
weg | kommen~ (von + dat.) *to get away from*
(das) Weihnachten *Christmas*
weiter *further*
weitaus *by far, much*
weitgehend *largely, to a large extent*
die Welt (-en) *world*
weltbekannt *famous throughout the world*
der Weltmeister (-) *world champion*
werden~ *to become*
die Werkstatt (-¨en) *workshop*
die Werkzeugmaschine (-n) *machine tool*
der Wert (-e) *value*
wert *worth*
wichtig *important*
widersprechen~ *to contradict*
wiedervereinigt *re-united*
wieder | verwerten *to recycle*
wie viel? *how much, how many*

willkommen *welcome*
wirtschaftlich *economic/ally*
das Wirtschaftsklima *economic climate*
das Wirtschaftswunder (-) *economic miracle*
wissen~ *to know (a fact)*
der Wissenschaftler (-)/die -in *scientist, scholar, academic*
die Witwe (-n) *widow*
der Witz (-e) *joke*
die Woche (-n) *week*
wohin? *where … to?*
sich wohl | fühlen *to feel at home*
wollen *to want to, intend to*
womöglich *where possible*
das Wörterbuch (-¨er) *dictionary*
wunderschön *really beautiful*

die Zahl (-en) *number*
der Zähler (-) *meter*
zeigen *to show*
zeitaufwendig *time-consuming*
eine Zeit lang *for a while*
der Zeitmangel *lack of time*
zeitraubend *time-consuming*
die Zeitschrift (-en) *journal, magazine*
ziehen~ *to move, pull*
ziemlich *fairly*
zirka *about, approximately*
der Zivildienst *community service (instead of military service)*
zuerst *at first*
zufrieden *satisfied*
der Zug (-¨e) *train*
im Zuge von (+ dat.) *in the wake of*
zu | hören (+ dat.) *to listen to*
die Zukunft *future*
zu | machen *to close*
die Zumutung (-en) *imposition*
zunächst *first, initially*
der Zustand (-¨e) *state*
die Zusteigemöglichkeit (-en) *pick-up point; lit. getting-on possibilities*
zwar *admittedly*
die Zweigstelle (-n) *branch, subsidiary*
in der Zwischenzeit *in the meantime*

English–German glossary

This glossary is not intended to be comprehensive. It does not contain many of the more basic words generally learned at the beginner's level.

~ indicates that this verb or its root form can be found in the List of common irregular verbs.

| indicates that a verb is separable (e.g. **an | kommen**).

With job titles, nationalities, etc., the female version is usually given in an abbreviated form, e.g. **der Akademiker** (-)/**die -in.** In the plural, feminine nouns ending in **-in** add **-nen**, e.g. **die Akademikerin, die Akademikerinnen.**

Abkürzungen (abbreviations)

acc. – accusative, adj. n. – adjectival noun, coll. – colloquial, dat. – dative, neut. – neuter, gen. – genitive, plur. – plural, wk. n. – weak noun.

to abolish **ab | schaffen**
about **zirka, ungefähr**
achievement **die Leistung (-en)**
acquaintance **der/die Bekannte (-n) (adj.n.)**
actual(ly) **eigentlich**
admittedly **zwar**
adult **der/die Erwachsene (-n) (adj.n.)**
advantage **der Vorteil (-e)**
to advise **raten~ (+ dat.)**
afterwards **nachher, hinterher**
age **das Alter**
ago – two years ago **vor – vor zwei Jahren**
to agree (with) **überein | stimmen (mit + dat.)**
aid **die Hilfe (-n)**
air **die Luft (-¨e)**
airport **der Flughafen (¨)**
already **schon, bereits**
always **immer**

apart from **abgesehen von (+ dat.)**
to apologize **sich entschuldigen**
to appear **erscheinen~; aus | sehen**
applicant **der Bewerber (-)/ die -in**
to apply for **sich bewerben~ (um + acc.)**
approximately **zirka, ungefähr**
architect **der Architekt (-en) (wk. n.)/die -in**
arm **der Arm (-e)**
arrival **die Ankunft (-¨e)**
to arrive **an | kommen~**
art **die Kunst (-¨e)**
to ascertain **fest | stellen**
assistance **die Hilfe (-n)**
to assume **an | nehmen~**
attempt **der Versuch (-e)**
autumn **der Herbst**
average **der Durchschnitt (-e)**
to avoid **vermeiden~**

bad **schlimm, schlecht**
ban **das Verbot (-e)**
bank **die Bank (-en)**
battery **die Batterie (-n)**
to be able **to können**
to be amazed (at) **staunen (über + acc.)**
to be interested in **sich interessieren (für + acc.)**
to be right **recht haben**
beach **der Strand (-¨e)**
to become **werden~**
beginning **der Anfang (-¨e)**
to believe **glauben (+ dat.)**
to believe in **glauben an (+ acc)**
to belong **gehören (+ dat.)**
birthday **der Geburtstag (-e)**
black **schwarz**
blue **blau**
body **der Körper (-)**
to book **reservieren, buchen**
border **die Grenze (-n)**
boring **langweilig**
born – When were you born? **geboren – Wann bist du geboren?**
boss **der Chef (-s)/die -in**
boy **der Junge (-n) (wk. n.)**
boyfriend **der Freund (-e)**
to break **brechen~**
to breathe **atmen**
bridge **die Brücke (-n)**
to bring **bringen~**
to broadcast **senden**
building **das Gebäude (-)**
to burn **brennen~**
bus stop **die Bushaltestelle (-n)**
business trip **die Geschäftsreise (-n)**
butcher's (shop) **die Metzgerei (-en)**
to buy a ticket **eine Fahrkarte lösen**
by the way **übrigens**

to call **rufen~;** *(phone)* **an | rufen~**
can (to be able to) **können**
cancer **der Krebs**
capital **die Hauptstadt (-¨e)**

career **die Laufbahn (-en)**
carpenter **der Schreiner (-)/ die -in**
carpet **der Teppich (-e)**
to carry **tragen~**
case; in any case **der Fall (-¨e); jedenfalls**
cathedral **der Dom (-e)**
cause **die Ursache (-n)**
to cause **verursachen**
cautious **vorsichtig**
to celebrate **feiern**
centre **die Mitte (-n); der Mittelpunkt (-e)**
century **das Jahrhundert (-e)**
certain(ly) **sicher**
characteristic **die Eigenschaft (-en)**
Christmas **(das) Weihnachten**
cinema – to go to the cinema **das Kino (-s); ins Kino gehen**
citizen **der Bürger (-)/die -in**
to clean **reinigen, putzen, sauber machen**
clean **sauber, rein**
to clear up **auf | räumen**
clear(ly) **klar, deutlich**
client **der Kunde (-n) (wk. n.)/ die Kundin**
climate **das Klima (-s)**
to close **schließen~, zu | machen**
cloud **die Wolke (-n)**
cold **kalt**
colleague **der Kollege (-n) (wk. n.)/die -in**
colour **die Farbe (-n)**
to combine **verbinden~**
comfortable **bequem**
to commute **pendeln**
company **die Gesellschaft (-en), die Firma (Firmen)**
to compare **vergleichen~**
comparison **der Vergleich (-e)**
to compel **zwingen~**
competition **die Konkurrenz**
competitive **konkurrenzfähig**
to complete **ergänzen**
complete(ly) **vollkommen**
computer **der Computer (-)**
to conduct **führen, leiten**
to confirm **bestätigen**
to congratulate **gratulieren (+ dat.)**
conscious(ly) **bewusst**
constant(ly) **ständig**
constitution **die Verfassung (-en)**
contain **enthalten~**
to contradict **widersprechen~**
to cook **kochen**
copy **das Exemplar (-e)**
corner **die Ecke (-n)**
correct **richtig**
to cost **kosten**
cost(s) **die Kosten (plur.)**
country **das Land (-¨er)**
to create **schaffen~**
crockery **das Geschirr**
crossroads **die Kreuzung (-en)**
current **der Strom (-¨e)**
customer **der Kunde (-n) (wk. n.)/die -in**
to cut **schneiden~**
CV **der Lebenslauf (-¨e)**

to damage **schädigen**
damaged **geschädigt**
to dance **tanzen**
dangerous **gefährlich**
dear **teuer; lieb**
to decide **entscheiden~**
demand **die Nachfrage (-n)**
to demand **verlangen**
to depart **ab | fahren~**
department **die Abteilung (-en)**
department store **das Kaufhaus (-¨er), das Warenhaus (-¨er)**
departure **die Abfahrt (-en)**
to depend on **ab | hängen von (+ dat.)**
dependent on **abhängig von (+ dat.)**
desk **der Schreibtisch (-e)**
development **die Entwicklung (-en)**
dictionary **das Wörterbuch (-¨er)**
to die **sterben~**
different **verschieden**
different from **anders als**
difficult **schwierig**
difficulty **die Schwierigkeit (-en)**
direction **die Richtung (-en)**
director **der Direktor (-en) (wk. n.)/die -in**
disadvantage **der Nachteil (-e)**
to discover **entdecken**
to discuss **diskutieren**
disease **die Krankheit (-en)**
dishes **das Geschirr**
to dismiss (sack) **entlassen**
to disturb **stören**
disturbance **die Störung (-en)**
divorced **geschieden**
to do **machen, tun~**
dream **der Traum (-¨e)**
to dream **träumen**
to drive **fahren~**

each **jeder/-e/-es**
ear **das Ohr (-en)**
to earn **verdienen**
economic/ally **wirtschaftlich**
economy **die Wirtschaft**
edge **der Rand (-¨er)**
edition **die Ausgabe (-n)**
education **die Bildung**
egg **das Ei (-er)**
electricity **der Strom**
to employ **beschäftigen**
employed **berufstätig**
employee **der/die Angestellte (-n) (adj. n.)**
to encounter **begegnen (+ dat.)**
end **der Schluss (-¨e); das Ende (-n)**
energy **die Energie (-n)**
to enter **eintreten~ (in + acc.)**
entertainment **die Unterhaltung**
entrance **der Eingang (-¨e); der Eintritt (-e)**
environment **die Umwelt**
environmental **protection der Umweltschutz**
to estimate **schätzen**
even **sogar**
every **jeder/-e/-es**
exact(ly) **genau**

to exaggerate **übertreiben~**
examination **die Prüfung (-en); das Examen (-)**
example (of) **das Beispiel (-e) (für + acc.)**
excellent **ausgezeichnet, hervorragend**
except (for) **außer (+ dat.)**
exception **die Ausnahme (-n)**
excursion **der Ausflug (-¨e)**
exhibition **die Ausstellung (-en)**
to exist **existieren**
exit **der Ausgang (-¨e)**
expensive **teuer; kostspielig**
experience **die Erfahrung (-en)**
experiment **der Versuch (-e)**
to explain **erklären**
to export **aus | führen**
eye **das Auge (-n)**

factory **der Betrieb (-e), die Fabrik (-en)**
fairly **ziemlich**
familiar **vertraut**
famous **berühmt**
fear **die Angst (-¨e)**
feeling **das Gefühl (-e)**
to fetch **ab | holen**
finally **schließlich, zum Schluss**
to finish **beenden**
to finish (one's studies) **ab | schließen~**
to finish work **Feierabend machen**
flight **der Flug (-¨e)**
fluent(ly) **fließend**
to fly **fliegen~**
fog **der Nebel**
to follow **folgen (+ dat.)**
foot; on foot **der Fuß (-¨e); zu Fuß**
to forbid **verbieten~**
foreign language **die Fremdsprache (-n)**
foreigner **der Ausländer/die -in**
forest **der Wald (-¨er)**
to forget **vergessen~**
fork **die Gabel (-n)**
to form **bilden**
fortunately **glücklicherweise**
to found **gründen**
full **voll**
full stop **der Punkt (-e)**
fun **der Spaß (-¨e)**
funny **komisch**
further **weiter**
future **die Zukunft**

game **das Spiel (-e)**
garbage **der Müll**
garbage can **der Mülleimer (-)**
garlic **der Knoblauch**
gasoline **das Benzin**
general(ly); in general **allgemein; im Allgemeinen**
gentleman **der Herr (-en) (wk.n)**
to get **bekommen~**
to get up **auf | stehen~**
gift **das Geschenk (-e)**
girl **das Mädchen (-)**
girlfriend **die Freundin (-nen)**
to give **geben~**
glad **froh**
glance **der Blick (-e)**
to go **gehen~**

to go (in a vehicle) **fahren~**
to go away **weg I gehen~; weg I fahren~**
to go out **aus I gehen~**
globalization **die Globalisierung**
goal **das Ziel (-e);** *(in sport)* **das Tor (-e)**
grade (at school or college) **die Note (-n)**
green **grün**
to grow **wachsen~**
guest **der Gast (-¨e)**
guesthouse **die Pension (-en)**

hand **die Hand (-¨e)**
handicapped **behindert**
to happen **geschehen~, passieren**
hard-working **fleißig, arbeitsam**
to have **to müssen**
head teacher **der (Schul-) Direktor (-en) (wk. n.)/die -in**
health **die Gesundheit**
to hear **hören**
heart **das Herz (-en) (wk. n.)**
heating **die Heizung (-en)**
help **die Hilfe (-n)**
to help **helfen~ (+ dat.)**
to hide **verstecken; verbergen~**
history **die Geschichte (-n)**
holiday **der Urlaub (-e)**
honest(ly) **ehrlich**
honey **der Honig**
to hope **hoffen**
hope **die Hoffnung (-en)**
host **(-ess) der Gastgeber (-)/ die -in**
hot **heiß**
hour **die Stunde (-n)**
human being **der Mensch (-en) (wk. n.)**

illness **die Krankheit (-en)**
image **das Bild (-er)**
to imagine **sich vor I stellen**
immediately **sofort**
importance **die Wichtigkeit, die Bedeutung**
important **wichtig, bedeutend**
impressive **beeindruckend**
to improve **verbessern**
income **das Einkommen (-)**
independent **selbstständig; unabhängig**
rare(ly) **selten**
industrious **fleißig**
information **die Auskunft (-¨e)**
inhabitant **der Einwohner (-)**
inn **die Gaststätte (-n)**
instead of **anstatt (+ gen.)**
insurance **die Versicherung (-en)**
to introduce (a person) **vor I stellen**
to introduce (a subject/object) **ein I führen**
invitation **die Einladung (-en)**
to invite **ein I laden~**

jam **die Marmelade (-n);** *(traffic)* **der Stau (-s)**

job **der Beruf (-e); der Arbeitsplatz (-¨e); die Stellung (-en)**
joint **das Gelenk (-e)**
joke **der Witz (-e)**
journal **die Zeitschrift (-en)**
journalist **der Journalist (-en) (wk. n.)/die -in**
to judge **beurteilen**
judge **der Richter (-)/die -in**
juice **der Saft (-¨e)**
to jump **springen~**

knife **das Messer (-)**
to know (a fact) **wissen~**
to know (be acquainted with) **kennen~**
knowledge **die Kenntnis (-se)**

laboratory **das Labor (-s/-e)**
lack **der Mangel (¨)**
lady **die Dame (-n)**
lake **der See (-n)**
law **das Gesetz (-e)**
Law **Jura; das Recht**
to lay **legen**
to lead **führen, leiten**
leader **der Führer (-), der Leiter (-)**
leaf **das Blatt (-¨er)**
to leave **lassen~; verlassen~**
lecture **die Vorlesung (-en)**
left **links**
lesson **die Stunde (-n)**
library **die Bibliothek (-en)**
lid **der Deckel (-)**
to lie **liegen~**
to like **mögen, gern haben**
limit **die Grenze (-n)**
to listen to **zuhören (+ dat.)**
litre **der/das Liter (-)**
lively **lebendig**
long **lang**
to look at something **sich etwas an | schauen**
to look for **suchen**
to look forward **to sich freuen auf (+ acc.)**
to lose **verlieren~**
loud **laut**
to love **lieben**
low **niedrig**
luck; to be lucky **das Glück; Glück haben**
luggage **das Gepäck**
to lunch **zu Mittag essen**
lunch **das Mittagessen (-)**

mad **verrückt**
magazine **die Zeitschrift (-en)**
to manufacture **her | stellen**
majority **die Mehrheit (-en)**
married **verheiratet**
to match **passen**
match **das Spiel (-e); der/das Match (-e/-s)**
material **der Stoff (-e)**
matter **die Sache (-n)**
meal **die Mahlzeit (-en)**
to mean **bedeuten**
measure; take measures **die Maßnahme (-n); Maßnahmen treffen~**
to meet **treffen~, begegnen (+ dat.)**
member **das Mitglied (-er)**

mental(ly) **geistig**
metre **der/das Meter (-)**
midday **der Mittag**
middle **die Mitte (-n)**
midnight **die Mitternacht**
minority **die Minderheit (-en)**
month **der Monat (-e)**
moon **der Mond (-e)**
mostly **meistens**
mother tongue **die Muttersprache (-n)**
motorway **die Autobahn (-en)**
mountain **der Berg (-e)**
mouth **der Mund (-¨er)**
to move (house) **um | ziehen~**
movie – go to the movies **der Film (-e) – ins Kino gehen**
music **die Musik**
must (to have to) **müssen**

name **der Name (-n) (wk. n.)**
nation **das Volk(-¨er); die Nation (-en)**
near **in der Nähe (von + dat.)**
necessary **nötig, notwendig, erforderlich**
needle **die Nadel (-n)**
negotiation **die Verhandlung (-en)**
neighbour **der Nachbar (-n) (wk. n.)/die -in**
neither ... nor... **weder... noch ...**
never **nie**
nevertheless **immerhin, dennoch, trotzdem**
news **die Nachrichten**
news broadcast **die Nachrichtensendung (-en)**
noisy **laut**
nonsense **der Quatsch**
normally **normalerweise**
nose **die Nase (-n)**
now and again **ab und zu**
nuclear power **die Kernkraft, die Atomkraft**
number **die Zahl (-en), die Anzahl (-en)**
nutrition **die Ernährung**

occasionally **gelegentlich**
to occur **vor | kommen~**
of course **natürlich**
to offer **bieten~, an | bieten~**
often **oft**
only **nur**
to open **öffnen, auf | machen**
open **offen; geöffnet**
opinion **die Meinung (-en)**
opportunity **die Gelegenheit (-en)**
to order **bestellen**
other **ander -er/-e/-es**
otherwise **sonst, ansonsten**
ought to **sollen**
to own **besitzen~**
own **eigen -er/-e/-es**

page **die Seite (-n)**
paint **die Farbe (-n)**
to paint **malen**
painting **die Malerei**
parking place **der Parkplatz (-¨e)**
part **der Teil (-e)**
part (role) **die Rolle (-n)**
to pass (an exam) **(eine Prüfung) bestehen**

past **die Vergangenheit**
payment **die Bezahlung (-en)**
peculiar **merkwürdig; eigenartig**
pension **die Rente (-n)**
pensioner **der Rentner (-)/ die -in**
people **die Leute; das Volk (-¨e)**
performance **die Leistung (-en)**
petrol **das Benzin**
to phone **an | rufen; telefonieren (mit + dat.)**
photographer **der Fotograf (-en) (wk. n.)/die -in**
physically **körperlich**
picture **das Bild (-er)**
place **der Ort (-e)**
to place **setzen, stellen**
plane **das Flugzeug (-e)**
to play **spielen**
to please, be pleasing **gefallen~ (+ dat.)**
police officer **der Polizist (-en) (wk. n.)/die -in**
population **die Bevölkerung (-en)**
position **die Stellung (-en)**
possibility **die Möglichkeit (-en)**
power **die Kraft (-¨e); die Macht (-¨e)**
precise(ly) **genau**
to prefer **vor | ziehen~**
prejudice **das Vorurteil (-e)**
preparation **die Vorbereitung (-en)**
to prepare **vor | bereiten**
present **das Geschenk (-e)**
present (time) **die Gegenwart**
probably **wahrscheinlich**
to produce **her | stellen, produzieren, erzeugen**
profession **der Beruf (-e)**
to prohibit **verbieten~**
proof **der Nachweis (-e)**
protection **der Schutz**
public **öffentlich**
public **die Öffentlichkeit; das Publikum**
to pull **ziehen~**
pure **rein**
to put **legen, stellen, setzen**

quantity **die Menge (-n)**
queen **die Königin (-nen)**
quiet(ly) **ruhig; still**

rail – by rail **die Bahn – mit der Bahn**
railway **die Bahn (-en), die Eisenbahn (-en)**
rain **der Regen**
to ramble **wandern**
to reach **erreichen**
ready **fertig**
reason **der Grund (-¨e)**
to receive **erhalten~**
recently **neulich**
to recommend **empfehlen~**
red **rot**
refrigerator **der Kühlschrank (-¨e)**
regular(ly) **regelmäßig**
to regulate **regeln**
relative **der/die Verwandte (-n) (adj. n.)**
to relax **sich entspannen**

to remember **sich erinnern an (+ acc.)**
to report **berichten**
report **der Bericht (-e)**
research **die Forschung (-en)**
to rest **sich ausruhen**
result **das Ergebnis (-se)**
reunification **die Wiedervereinigung**
to ride **reiten~**
right **rechts**
right (correct) **richtig**
right (to) **das Recht (-e) (auf + acc.)**
to rise **steigen~;** *(get up)* **auf | stehen~**
role **die Rolle (-n)**
roof **das Dach (-¨er)**
row **die Reihe (-n)**
rubbish **der Müll**
rubbish bin **der Mülleimer (-)**
rule **die Regel (-n)**
to run **laufen~**

safe(ly) **sicher**
satisfied **zufrieden**
scenery **die Landschaft (-en)**
scientist **der Wissenschaftler (-)/die -in**
sea **die See (-n); das Meer (-e)**
to search **suchen**
secure(ly) **sicher**
sense **der Sinn (-e)**
to separate **trennen**
series **die Reihe (-n)**
to serve **dienen (+ dat.)**
to set off **los | gehen~**
to share **teilen**
shop **der Laden (¨); das Geschäft (-e)**
to show **zeigen**
shower; take a shower **die Dusche (-n); sich duschen**
to shut **schließen~**
side **die Seite (-n)**
similar(ly) **ähnlich**
simple, simply **einfach**
to sit **sitzen~**
to sit an exam **eine Prüfung ab | legen**
to skate **Schlittschuh laufen~**
to ski **Ski fahren~, Ski laufen~**
to sleep **schlafen~**
slice – a slice of bread **die Scheibe (-n) – eine Scheibe Brot**
slow(ly) **langsam**
to smell (of) **riechen~ (nach + dat.)**
snow **der Schnee**
sociable **gesellig**
society **die Gesellschaft (-en)**
solar energy **die Solarenergie (-n)**
soldier **der Soldat (-en) (wk. n.)/die -in**
sometimes **manchmal**
soon **bald**
speed **die Geschwindigkeit (-en)**
to spend (money) **aus | geben~**
to spend (time) **verbringen**
splendid(ly) **großartig**
spoon **der Löffel (-)**
spring **der Frühling**
to stand **stehen~**

state **der Staat (-en)**
state (condition) **der Zustand (-¨e)**
station **der Bahnhof (-¨e)**
to stay **bleiben~**
to stop **auf | hören; halten~**
story **die Geschichte (-n)**
straight on **geradeaus**
strict(ly) **streng**
to stroll **bummeln**
strong(ly) **stark**
subject **das Thema (Themen)**
subway **die U-Bahn (-en) (= Untergrundbahn)**
succeed; We didn't succeed in … **gelingen~; Es ist uns nicht gelungen, …**
to suffer **leiden~**
to suffice (be enough) **reichen, genügen**
to suggest **vor | schlagen~**
summer **der Sommer**
sun **die Sonne (-n)**
sunshine **der Sonnenschein**
supermarket **der Supermarkt (-¨e)**
survey **die Umfrage (-n)**
to swim **schwimmen~**

to take **nehmen~**
to take place **statt | finden~**
to talk (about) **reden (über + acc.)**
taste **der Geschmack (-¨e)**
to teach **unterrichten**
team **die Mannschaft (-en)**
terrible **schrecklich**
to thank **danken (+ dat.)**
then **dann**
thing **das Ding (-e); die Sache (-n)**
to think **denken~, glauben, meinen**
thorough(ly) **gründlich**
to throw **werfen~**
tidy **ordentlich**
time **die Zeit (-en)**
tired **müde**
topic **das Thema (Themen)**
trade **der Handel**
to trade **handeln**
traffic **der Verkehr**
traffic lights (set of) **die Ampel (-n)**
train **der Zug (-¨e)**
training **die Ausbildung**
tram **die Straßenbahn (-en)**
to translate **übersetzen**
trend **die Entwicklung (-en); der Trend (-s)**
truth **die Wahrheit (-en)**
to try **versuchen**
tube **die U-Bahn (-en) (= Untergrundbahn)**
typical(ly) **typisch**

umbrella **der Regenschirm (-e)**
to understand **verstehen~**
unemployment **die Arbeitslosigkeit**
unity **die Einheit**
to use **nutzen, benutzen, gebrauchen, verwenden**
usually **gewöhnlich**

vacation **der Urlaub (-e)**
value **der Wert (-e)**
various **verschieden**
view **der Blick (-e)**
village **das Dorf (-¨er)**
to visit **besuchen**
voice **die Stimme (-n)**

wage **der Lohn (-¨e)**
waiter/waitress **der Kellner (-)/ die -in**
to want **wollen**
to wash **waschen~**
to watch TV **fern | sehen~**
way out **der Ausgang (-¨e)**
weak **schwach**
to wear **tragen~**
weather **das Wetter**
wedding **die Hochzeit (-en)**
week **die Woche (-n)**
Welcome! **Willkommen!**
well-known **bekannt**
white **weiß**
widow **die Witwe (-n)**
widower **der Witwer (-)**
winter **der Winter**
world **die Welt (-en)**
worry – Don't worry! **die Sorge (-n) – Mach dir keine Sorgen!**
to write **schreiben~**

yard **der Hof (-¨e)**
to yawn **gähnen**
year **das Jahr (-e)**
yellow **gelb**

zero **die Null (-en)**

Grammar index

References are to units.

Credits

Front Cover: © Beyond Fotomedia GmbH/Alamy

Back cover and pack: © Jakub Semeniuk/iStockphoto.com, © Royalty-Free/Corbis, © agencyby/iStockphoto.com, © Andy Cook/iStockphoto.com, © Christopher Ewing/iStockphoto.com, © zebicho – Fotolia.com, © Geoffrey Holman/iStockphoto.com, © Photodisc/Getty Images, © James C. Pruitt/iStockphoto.com, © Mohamed Saber – Fotolia.com

Pack: © Stockbyte/Getty Images